Working Papers

Working Papers

Selected Essays and Reviews
by Hayden Carruth

Edited by Judith Weissman

The University of Georgia Press Athens

Copyright © 1982 by the University of Georgia Press
Athens, Georgia 30602

All rights reserved

Set in 10 on 13 Palatino
Design by Sandra Strother
PRINTED IN THE UNITED STATES OF AMERICA

Library of Congress Cataloging in Publication Data

Carruth, Hayden, 1921–
  Working papers.

    1. Literature, Modern—20th century—History
and criticism—Collected works.   2. Poetry, Modern—
20th century—History and criticism—Collected
works.   I. Weissman, Judith.   II. Title.
PN771.C336   809'.04   81-4404
ISBN 0-8203-0583-9   AACR2

FOR MABEL AND GEORGE DENNISON

Contents

Contents

Contents

Contents

Acknowledgments

Permission to reprint the essays and reviews listed below was kindly granted by the editors of the periodicals where they first appeared:

"The Phenotype," in the *Carleton Miscellany*, reprinted from the *Carleton Miscellany*, © Carleton College, October 24, 1960.

"Sartre on Genet," in the *Chicago Daily News*, now the *Chicago Sun-Times*, © Field Enterprises, Inc., 1963. Review by Hayden Carruth.

"Wasting His Talent on Finks and Funks," in the *Chicago Daily News*, now the *Chicago Sun-Times*, © Field Enterprises, Inc., 1965. Review by Hayden Carruth.

"Natural Elegance," in the *Chicago Daily News*, now the *Chicago Sun-Times*, © Field Enterprises, Inc., 1966. Review by Hayden Carruth.

"Two Notes on Experiment," in *Genesis West*, © Genesis West and The Chrysalis West Foundation, 1963.

"Poets on the Fringe," in *Harper's Magazine*, copyright © 1979 by Harper's Magazine. All rights reserved. Reprinted from the January 1980 issue by special permission.

"Multiple Disguises," in *The Hudson Review*, copyright © The Hudson Review, Inc., 1963. Reprinted by permission of the author.

"Pursy Windhum Lucigen," in *The Hudson Review*, copyright © The Hudson Review, Inc., 1964. Reprinted by permission of the author.

"People in a Myth," in *The Hudson Review*, copyright © The Hudson Review, Inc., 1966. Reprinted by permission of the author.

"Materials from Life," in *The Hudson Review*, copyright © The Hudson Review, Inc., 1967. Reprinted by permission of the author.

"A Meaning of Robert Lowell," in *The Hudson Review*, copyright © The Hudson Review, Inc., 1967. Reprinted by permission of the author.

"Fallacies of Silence," in *The Hudson Review*, copyright © The Hudson Review, Inc., 1973. Reprinted by permission of the author.

"Levertov," in *The Hudson Review*, copyright © The Hudson Review, Inc., 1974. Reprinted by permission of the author.

"The Question of Poetic Form," in *The Hudson Review*, copyright © The Hudson Review, Inc., 1976. Reprinted by permission of the author.

"Dr. Williams's *Paterson*," in *The Nation*, © The Nation, 1951.

"The Run to the Sea," in *The Nation*, © The Nation, 1951.

"Understanding Auden," in *The Nation*, © The Nation, 1951.

"Stevens as Essayist," in *The Nation*, © The Nation, 1952.

"MacLeish's Poetry," in *The Nation*, © The Nation, 1953.

"Poets without Prophecy," in *The Nation*, © The Nation, 1963.

"A Kind of Revolt," in *The Nation*, © The Nation, 1963.

"Scales of the Marvelous," in *The Nation*, © The Nation, 1964.

"Melancholy Monument," in *The Nation*, © The Nation, 1969.

"Love, Art, and Money," in *The Nation*, © The Nation, 1970.

"The Writer's Situation," in the *New American Review*, later *The American Review*, © Bantam Books, Inc., 1970. Reprinted by permission of the author.

"Seriousness and the Inner Poem," in the *New York Quarterly*, © The New York Quarterly, 1971.

"In Defense of Karl Shapiro," by Hayden Carruth, in *The New Republic*, reprinted by permission of *The New Republic*, © The New Republic, Inc., 1960.

"William Carlos Williams as One of Us," by Hayden Carruth, in *The New Republic*, reprinted by permission of *The New Republic*, © The New Republic, Inc., 1963.

"A Focus, a Crown," in the *New York Times Book Review*, © 1970 by The New York Times Company. Reprinted by permission.

"The Anti-poet All Told," in *Poetry*, © 1949 by The Modern Poetry Association. Reprinted by permission of the editor of *Poetry*.

"'Without the Inventions of Sorrow,'" in *Poetry*, © 1955 by The Modern Poetry Association. Reprinted by permission of the editor of *Poetry*.

"'To Fashion the Transitory,'" in *Poetry*, © 1956 by The Modern Poetry Association. Reprinted by permission of the editor of *Poetry*.

"Two Books," in *Poetry*, © 1958 by The Modern Poetry Association. Reprinted by permission of the editor of *Poetry*.

"What Shall We Do, What Shall We Think, What Shall We Say?," in *Poetry*, © 1962 by The Modern Poetry Association. Reprinted by permission of the editor of *Poetry*.

"The Closest Permissible Approximation," in *Poetry*, © 1963 by The Modern Poetry Association. Reprinted by permission of the editor of *Poetry*.

"Poetic Mythology," in *Poetry*, © 1964 by The Modern Poetry Association. Reprinted by permission of the editor of *Poetry*.

"Upon Which to Rejoice," in *Poetry*, © 1965 by The Modern Poetry Association. Reprinted by permission of the editor of *Poetry*.

"Poetry of Abstraction," in *Poetry*, © 1967 by The Modern Poetry Association. Reprinted by permission of the editor of *Poetry*.

"Ezra Pound and the Great Style," in *The Saturday Review*, copyright © 1966 by *The Saturday Review*. All rights reserved. Reprinted by permission.

"The Act of Love: Poetry and Personality," was first published in the *Sewanee Review* 84: 2 (Spring 1976). © 1976 by the University of the South. Reprinted with the permission of the editor.

"Poet of Civility," in *The Southern Review*, © 1970 The Southern Review. Reprinted by permission of the author.

"Delmore, 1913–1966," in *The Texas Quarterly*, © 1967 by The University of Texas at Austin. Reprinted by permission of the author and the copyright holder.

"Not Too Late for Words," in the *Village Voice*, reprinted by permission of the *Village Voice*. Copyright © The Village Voice, Inc., 1971.

"The Dry Heart of Modesty," in *The Virginia Quarterly Review*, © The Virginia Quarterly Review, 1963.

Introduction

IT IS DIFFICULT to write an introduction to the works of any living author, and it is particularly difficult to write about this selection of Hayden Carruth's essays and reviews. His work seems awesomely rich, full, complete—thirty years of essays that begin with Pound and end with numerous younger poets in mid-flight. But the appearance of completeness is illusory, for these essays are no more than a tenth of those Carruth has written. I am particularly sorry not to include a review of a group of critical books on Spenser and three notes on Pope, to whom Carruth brings the same sense of joyful discovery that he brings to poets whom he is actually reading for the first time. But some principles of selection were necessary, and one was that I would try to present, through these essays, a history of the last thirty years of literature. (Occasional departures from even this principle were made, as in the inclusion of the review of Casanova's memoirs. I included that review because it was thematically so well connected with others on love and aristocracy.) This selection concludes with a review that points toward the future, on what poets may do in the 1980s, because this volume should not appear to be nicely and neatly *finished*. Plenty of people are still writing, and Carruth is still reviewing them.

The title, *Working Papers*, modest as it is, was chosen by Carruth years ago, when he first planned to publish a collection of his essays. It is still appropriate now: it is modesty that characterizes these essays, and Carruth's poems, and Carruth himself. In addition, the subtle pun of the title, the several meanings of the phrase, are too important to abandon. It is true that this book is sketchy, a draft, in a way, of the polished book of literary criticism that Carruth might have written in another life. Most of these essays and reviews were written as real *work*—which, in our society, means labor performed in exchange for money. The reviews, particularly, were the work Carruth did instead of being part of a university—they got him out of school, like the working papers of sixteen-year-old boys in the 1930s.

In need of money, Carruth has taken review assignments as they came, on books which he did not choose. The few long, fully developed essays here—like those on Robert Lowell and on "Poetry and Personality"—make me wish that he had been able to write more of them, rather than being driven by necessity into doing so many brief reviews. But there is no reason to mourn over what he has done, or to treat this volume as one of promise rather than fulfillment, of frustration rather than realization. How many people in the privileged world of academia have written anything as good as this collection of reviews? Their genesis as work, as daily labor, has given them life. Carruth wrote them, not for the audience of scholarly journals, but often for newspapers or political magazines like *The Nation* or the *New Republic*. (Some, of course, were for more literary journals, though not academic ones, like *Poetry* and the *Hudson Review*.)

Some of the humanity of these essays and reviews also springs from Carruth's knowledge that he could help to determine the success of other people's books and affect how much money they made. The importance of reviewing, and of Carruth's reviewing in particular, became strikingly clear to me one evening when we attended a reading by a middle-aged poet who will never be rich or famous. He was amazed and delighted that Hayden Carruth had driven thirty miles to hear him, and after the reading, in private talk, recalled Carruth's review, many years earlier, of one of his books. "My marriage was falling apart, I was cracking up. I had written what I knew was my best book, and no one would review it. Except you. You knew it was good. Man, you saved my life." The man was not joking.

A well-known reviewer has a lot of power. He can give outrageously high praise to his friends, who will then of course return the favor; he can put down rivals and newcomers who are potential rivals, and anyone who has dared to insult him; above all, he can advertise himself. Carruth never does any of this. The unspoken values of these essays and reviews—humility, modesty, generosity, self-effacement—are the most important values of all. Carruth occasionally acknowledges the flawed, human self which, like everyone else, he certainly has—as in the essay on Robert Lowell, when he says that he envies Lowell's wealth and privilege, and easy success and fame as a poet—but how miraculously free from the bitterness of self these essays and reviews are! How encouraging to the young, how respectful to the old and out of fashion, how sincerely interested in the work of other writers.

Everyone who has read Carruth's poems knows some of the troubles of his life and can figure out that he wrote these lucid and kind reviews under some of the most difficult of human circumstances. The tone and texture are so even, strong, almost imperturbable, that it is an effort to remember that Carruth's daily intercourse with the human world has been unusually painful and difficult, and that he lived most of the last twenty years in northern Vermont, an especially poor man in a place where nearly everyone was poor. These reviews do not have the feeling of loneliness, which always does harm, though it sometimes also does good. They are so friendly, social, communicative. They could not be more different from the cranky soliloquies that we might expect from someone who has lived Carruth's life.

That life is not entirely absent here, however. The changes in the essays reflect Carruth's own life as well as his participation in a general cultural life. Most important is a change in his language. At the beginning, he sounds like what he was, an ambitious young editor of a prestigious urban magazine, *Poetry*, located in a big city, Chicago. By the end, we can hear Vermont in his voice. He is looser, more colloquial, more concerned with everyday life, nature, agriculture. One sentence, from the last review, will be sufficient illustration: "Dullness sprang up in the fertile soil of American poetry during the seventies like colorless saprophytes in a damp pine forest." This is not the talk of a Vermont farmer. It is the talk of an extraordinarily intelligent and observant man who knows both the world of poetry and culture, and the plants of the Vermont woods, and understands both well enough to make use of one as an exceedingly precise metaphor for the other. A cultural tragedy is implied in this, a tragedy that informs Carruth's sense of the world. No one would bother to remark that Shakespeare or Milton or Wordsworth knew both culture and nature, but in our country the division has been growing deeper and deeper between the country and the city, agriculture and learning, the small community and the larger world. Carruth's life is extraordinary because he has known all of these possibilities so fully, and it has also been extraordinarily sad because he has known the pain of losing each of them.

Carruth's personal history is of less importance here than the other histories he writes about. The events of the world, as excluded from the New Criticism as the personalities of the poet and critic, are very much in evidence here. World War II, the Holocaust (before it became a fashionable topic), atomic weapons, racism in the United States (do other critics remember George Jackson?), and always, the suffering of the poor under the innumerable oppressions of government and bureaucracy. We hear occasionally about the problems of artists, too; but thank God we never hear that their sufferings are greater than those of the rest of the world. Justice and injustice, happiness and suffering, good and evil—yes, good and evil—and their consequences for the human race as a whole—those are always the final terms by which Carruth tests literature. These essays are not crudely utilitarian in any way; Carruth never says that some piece of writing is good simply because it contains some particular social idea or value. The utilitarianism (an unjustly disparaged philosophy in any case) is subtle and indirect. It lies in Carruth's refusal to let us forget that the ultimate context for art is the world—and that the world has been a very ugly place in the last thirty years. He has seen horror as clearly as anyone can, but has resisted the temptation to believe that an artist has the right to isolate and protect himself. He has held onto his vision of the sufferings of the world tenaciously, grimly, and above all, without cynicism.

The book, however, is primarily about neither Carruth nor the fall of the West. It is about literature and literary criticism. Carruth's interest in the literary criticism of the last thirty years has been more limited than his interest in poetry. He has not bothered with the bizarre explosion of academic criticism in the last few years, and we do not yet know what he has to say about the likes of Lacan and Derrida. Here he has written mainly about the New Criticism and some reactions to it, in his reviews of Karl Shapiro, Northrop Frye, Paul Elmer More, Joseph Frank, Martin Price, Eliseo Vivas, John Hall Wheelock, Edmund Wilson, George Steiner. Carruth shows the same respect and generosity toward other critics as he does to other poets; he admires intelligence, learning, scholarship, and love for the tradition of literature, in others. He deplores readings that include no glance at the outside world or that rest on esthetic values alone.

Carruth's own criticism is always on the verge of becoming philosophy. And he writes comfortably, surely more comfortably than most poets would, about philosophical and historical prose. Camus, Sartre (on Genet), Genet, de Rougemont, Eliot, Eliot on Bradley, Casanova, Yevtushenko, Irving Singer, Gottfried Benn, Wyndham Lewis—a rather odd collection here, which, we must remember, Carruth did not choose. Such a disparate group does, oddly, belong together, for

Carruth has unified them with two recurrent themes, the difficulties of human love, and the relation of art to the world. The European existentialists are among the heroes of this book, and surely its villains (I do not choose the word lightly) are Benn and Lewis. They are the primary examples of the evil to which men can come when they decide that they have the right to choose art over life. Carruth does not simply label them fascists and let them go, as a less conscientious critic might have done. He gives them the same intelligent care in reading that he gives to the others, and even praises them when they deserve praise. But he never allows their virtues—intelligence, skill, style—to obliterate his knowledge of the wickedness of what they believe. He cannot pardon them for writing well when what they say is evil.

Poetry is the subject of most of these essays, which constitute a perpetual reproach to the joylessness of academic criticism. There is joy in them. Read them—and remember what it was like to read for the first time Pound, Williams, Auden, Stevens, Muir, Ferlinghetti, Levertov, Aiken, Rukeyser, Duncan, Eliot, Perse, Lowell, Schwartz, Jarrell, Berryman, Zukofsky, Berry. Carruth is a graceful master of the myriad techniques of literary criticism, using them with ease to range widely, in lucid analysis of individual poems or poets, or the psychological development of a poet's work, or the poet's connection with a tradition which Carruth knows and reveres (a tradition which includes John Clare and William Barnes along with Shakespeare and Wordsworth). Though Carruth calls only a few human failings evil—cruelty, selfishness, fakery—he finds goodness in many places.

> *Paterson* . . . is a poem intense, complicated, and absorbing, one of the best examples of concision of poetry that I know.

> The love poems [of MacLeish], and there are many, written during every phase of the poet's career and under every aspect of feeling, are often splendid, composed with a restraint and exactness of language that is songlike, reproducing the sensuousness of ideas very evocatively, the basic eroticism of human thought.

> Opulence—it is the quality most of us would ascribe to the poetry of Wallace Stevens before all others; profusion, exotic luxuriance.

This is hard substance, and the poems [of Muir] have about them, beyond their verbal utilitarianism, a kind of obduracy of spirit that we associate with the Scotch Presbyterian sensibility.

Force, directness, affection for the separate word and the various parts of speech (especially participles), knowledge of cadence and syntax, as components of meaning rather than vicissitudes of fabrication—there can be no doubt that Miss Rukeyser can write good poetry.

Perse writes a kind of pure poem of sensibility, an analytic of the heart, a conceptualizing poem. Without meter, without any rhythm except the self-sustaining verbal flow, his poetic principle, as one would expect in so abstract a composition, is pure grammar.

He has resolved to accept reality, all reality, and to take its fragments indiscriminately as they come, forging from them this indissoluble locus of metaphorical connections that is known as Robert Lowell.

In his war poems Randall Jarrell did rise, as if in spite of himself and at the command of a classical force outside himself, to his moment of tragic vision.

They all derive from his [Wendell Berry's] experience as a subsistence farmer, and they celebrate the earth and the strength a man gains from contact with soil, water, stone, and seed. Make no mistake, these are poems in praise of Aphrodite of the Hot Furrow, full of generative force, even though their manner is seldom rhapsodic.

What word can describe Carruth's way of reading? *Pleasure* and *joy* have become debased—perhaps the word I am searching for is *celebration*.

Finally, Carruth has written a few, late, precious essays on the general subject of poetry—"The Writer's Situation," "Seriousness and the Inner Poem," "The Question of Poetic Form," "The Act of Love: Poetry and Personality"—which I would not attempt to summarize. They are rich and graceful and lucid, and unashamedly intelligent. And so I return to Carruth's history—not, this time, the change from the city to the country or from privilege to chosen poverty—but the history of growth into simultaneous modesty and confidence, seriousness and humor, humanity and wisdom. Again, I look for a word: can *adult* or *mature* still mean anything good when they have come to mean "pornographic"? I cannot think of one word with which to express my recognition that all these qualities could not belong to a young man. The complementary qualities of these late essays are highlighted in two sentences in "The Question of Poetic Form":

> Well, it seems to me that Plato made a very shrewd observation of human psychology when he conceived his ideals—if he was the one who actually conceived them (I am ignorant of pre-Socratic philosophy). . . .
>
> . . . I believe the closed pentameter couplet was natural to Pope, "organic," if you like, and if his poems are not as well unified *poetically* as any others of a similar kind and scope, if the best of them are not *poems* in exactly the same sense we mean today, then I don't know how to read poetry. (But I do.)

He feels free to offer an interpretation of Plato and also admits the limitations of his knowledge—an admission which itself establishes a breadth of knowledge which exceeds that of most current critics, who do not mention the fact that pre-Socratic philosophy exists. A younger and more anxious critic might have written a pompous little aside on where the interested reader might check up on pre-Socratic philosophy. Carruth can let it go. And he can also assert himself as a younger person could not, and say, in a biting parenthetical clause, that of course he knows how to read poetry. How good it is to read the work of someone whose knowledge and experience are so deep that he can make judgments without arrogance and without defensiveness.

But it would be wrong to make Carruth sound too much like the wise, good-hearted elder sage. There is always a more mysterious power in his writing, a power generated by the simultaneous existence of another pair of paradoxical qualities. I will use his own words, first on Lowell, second on Leroi Jones, to define those qualities: "this is tough, this is homely, this is American" and "our Shelley." Most of what I have praised in the essays belongs to the homely, American side of Carruth, to his affinity with Twain and Whitman, who never call people stupid or ugly, but only cruel or hypocritical or self-righteous, who value sanity and love, the natural world and the common man. Shelley is here too, in the combination of rage and spirituality, visions of horror and visions of ethereal beauty, and fury at the sight of wrong that can only be felt by someone who wants perfection. Parts of the first essay in the book, Carruth's defense of Pound, sound almost as if they were copied from Shelley's "Defense of Poetry."

> Poetry is the reason for all things humanly true and beautiful, and the product of them—wisdom, scholarship, love, teaching, celebration. Love of poetry is the habit and need of wise men wherever they are, and when for some reason of social or personal disadjustment they are deprived of it, they will be taxed in spirit and will do unaccountable things. Great men will turn instinctively to the poetic labor of their time, because it is the most honorable and useful, as it is the most difficult, human endeavor. Every spiritual faculty of man is a poetic one, and in poetry is that working of the spirit which engages man and his world in an intelligible existence. Only in poetry is man knowable to himself.

In the late essays the language is compressed, the tone, sober—but Shelley is still here, for example, in "The Act of Love: Poetry and Personality":

> It follows that poetry is social, though not in any sense of the term used by sociologists. It follows that poetry is political, leaving the political scientists far behind. Maybe it even follows that if the substance of a poem, or part of it, is expressly though broadly social or political, this fact will reinforce the subjective communalism of the poet's intention in his transcendent act; but that is a question—the interrelationship of substance and the vision of form, or of moral and aesthetic feeling—to which twenty-five years of attention have given me no answer. Yet many, a great many, of our finest poems, especially as we read backward toward the evolutionary roots of poetry, seem to suggest such a hypothesis, and in any event we know that political substance is not, and in itself cannot be, inimical to poetry. Finally it follows that the politics of the poet, in his spirituality, will be a politics of love. For me this means nonviolent anarchism, at least as a means; I know no end.

Carruth has none of the qualities that alienate some people from Shelley—frothy poetic excess, squeamish disdain for earthly life—but the two are alike in their deep, pessimistic, undying spirituality. Despite his personal suffering, Carruth's spirituality has endured, as Shelley's might not have. Carruth never writes with the weary ease that often comes with self-confident skill and assured success. The late essays are less joyful than the early ones but just as loving; they are less hopeful but more dogged in their vitality. Carruth has endured without settling into stoicism because he has refused to cease either suffering or hoping. His progress has taken him continuously deeper into the knowledge of his own humanity, and of the humanity of literature.

JUDITH WEISSMAN

The Anti-Poet All Told

Part of an editorial in *Poetry*, 1949, at the time of the attacks on the Fellows in American Literature of the Library of Congress for their award of the Bollingen Prize to Ezra Pound, with particular reference to two scurrilous articles by Robert Hillyer in the *Saturday Review of Literature*.

WHATEVER IS THE OUTCOME of the Ezra Pound case, the enemies of poetry must not be allowed to damage the process of our art through their untoward anger. No one can tell what the progress of poetry will be, though editors in their small shrewdness may try to guess. But certainly the poets of the future will take into account the poetic achievement of our time. Many generations will pass before a young poet can overlook the work of Ezra Pound; only by understanding it and using it—or perhaps by designedly, knowingly discarding it— will the poet of the future be able to acknowledge his vocation intelligently and properly.

The serious poet today, although he can scarcely escape the annoyance of meeting the enemies of poetry, must disregard them. Only when, as in the present instance, they convene in threatening proportions, should he honor them with a determined protest. But they must never interfere.

For the strength of poetry is its eternal human truth. I am embarrassed, in an age which has resolved to be pragmatic, to repeat a statement so bare and unsophisticated. The truth of poetry is compounded of the trained and sensitive emotions and the penetrating insights of great men, squabble as we may over the means by which these elements come to be, and it acts with a force that can create new forms and charge them with the most intense meaning of experience. Every experience uncovers a new aspect of truth, and truth is the only agent which can shape and give meaning to an experience. In poetry truth and experience come together, there to be intermixed, formalized, expressed. Only in the meeting of truth and experience can poetic form be created, and any beforehanded imposition of rules will distort the process (except as habit itself, in the full sense of earned discipline, can be an experiential factor). Insofar as any poet is corrupted in either element, truth or experience, his poem will be imperfect, although it may be valuable for other reasons.

It seems to me that one of the most confusing words in the entire controversy is the word *modern*. I do not know, offhand, whether it has in the past been so strenuously applied to the new poetry of any age, but I suppose that it has—we recall the quarrel of the Ancients and the Moderns 250 years ago in England, satirized by Swift in *The Battle of the Books*. Nor do I know that the blame for its establishment and continued application to the poetry of the first half of the twentieth century can be put to any particular quarter. But I do know that the word inherently represents a shortness of insight, and it should not be used any longer. In the first place, "modern poetry" is a historical fallacy. Pound, Eliot, Stevens, Williams, and many others who are conventionally attacked by the contemporary enemies of poetry, began writing in the early years of this century. Several generations of poets have grown up since then, all more or less influenced by these innovators. Why, but for the obduracy of the enemies of poetry, should it be necessary to defend so well established a body of literature? Second, and more important, the obvious dissimilarities of our poetry to the great poetry of any other age are essentially proofs of sameness. The qualities of "modern poetry" that distinguish it have been achieved by the same experimental process, the same exercise in poetic faith, that made distinguishable the poetry of the age of Donne, or Pope, or Keats. A failure to understand "modern poetry" and its processes (I except an honest disliking of it; one need not justify the temperamental aspects of taste in any time) is a failure to understand any poetry, since the reading of poetry is not an antiquarian study, but an immersion in eternal contemporaneousness. The antiquarian is a modern who studies the Middle Ages; the reader of Chaucer is a person temporarily living in them. The early poems of our period are already unintelligible to young antiquarians, but to readers of poetry, who are equipped with a concept of poetic process and with a sensitiveness to total poetic structure, they are part of all living literature. It is just such a series of "revolutions," however each one may inflame the rebellious feelings of its adherents at the time, that makes a continuous and "living" literature; the word *modern* is a misnomer that obscures, if it does not contradict, the word *poetry*.

The strength of poetry is the strength of life; only poetry can give to life an active, purposive commitment to truth and experience. The enemies of poetry, who are also the enemies of life, would destroy both.

Now, when death has conquered so much of the world, spreading its destruction and futility, its unreason and untruth, its immorality which is the final ugliness, when so many people have been deprived by monstrous systems and corrupt philosophies of the inherent privilege of esthetic performance, now poetry is needed more than ever. Poetry is the only antidote, the type of good action and unsullied thought. Poetry is the reason for all things humanly true and beautiful, and the product of them—wisdom, scholarship, love, teaching, celebration. Love of poetry is the habit and need of wise men wherever they are, and when for some reason of social or personal disadjustment they are deprived of it, they will be taxed in spirit and will do unaccountable things. Great men will turn instinctively to the poetic labor of their time, because it is the most honorable and useful, as it is the most difficult, human endeavor. Every spiritual faculty of man is a poetic one, and in poetry is that working of the spirit which engages man and his world in an intelligible existence. Only in poetry is man knowable to himself.

Such are the values of poetry, independent of local or temporary events; they cannot die. But they can be restricted, neglected, distorted. This is the danger confronting us in the present attack by the enemies of poetry. The poet today, who perhaps bears a greater responsibility to his office than poets ever have before, must exert all his powers to magnify poetry and maintain its purity. This is his proper work and his certain defense.

Dr. Williams's Paterson

A review of *Paterson* (Book Three), from *The Nation*, April 8, 1950.

THIS THIRD BOOK in Dr. Williams's projected long poem (the fourth and final book is promised "by 1951") is at first reading the most difficult of the three we now have, and at the eighth reading some details of structure and aspects of meaning remain unclear. Nevertheless we can begin to perceive what will be the shape, scope, and texture of the finished work; this book helps to expand and clarify a number of themes, heretofore obscure, in the first two books. When the three are read in sequence they reveal, through interlacing symbols and thematic references, a close and compact development. More than ever it becomes apparent that Dr. Williams has in mind a whole, inseverable poem, not a discrete tetralogy, as many of those who reviewed the first two books were led to assume.

The meaning of the poem so far can best be elucidated through a compressed examination of its symbols. Paterson, then, is a city and also a man, a giant who lies asleep, whose dreams are the people of the city, whose history is roughly coterminous with and equal to the history of America. He is diseased with slums and factories and the spiritlessness of industrial society; his character—usually as observer—walks about, sometimes as a plain citizen, sometimes as a hero, often as "Dr. Paterson," the poet himself. Beside Paterson lies a mountain, which is a woman, upon whose body grow trees and flowers, with the city park at her head. The city-man and mountain-woman are the two basic facts of the poem; they are activated by the four elements. A river, broken by a falls, flows between them and has, beyond its obvious sexual meaning, the further significances of flowing time and of language, usually the fundamental or premental language of nature. Earth is the speaker that knows this language, the "chatterer." Fire is the creative act, in love or art. Wind is, if my reading is correct, inspiration, the integrator, the carrier of sounds and smells. Though generally benign, these forces may be malevolent too, for fire, flood, cyclone, and earthquake all occur in this poem.

Another duality, which is enforced on these basic symbols, is that of marriage-divorce. As divorce is a principal symptom of social disorder, so it is also of historical disorder: man has been divorced from his beginnings, his sources. The city is, in one sense, divorced from the mountain by the river of time and language. Dr. Williams also uses the word *blockage*: man has been blocked from an understanding of his real self in nature by the modern institutions of church, university, commerce, and so forth. Dr. Williams seems to be saying that the only way to escape these blocks is to ignore them, to sidestep them and experience marriage directly. Thus, in the river, it is the falls which is important, the present act and present moment which unite the man and the woman, the city and the mountain, in a "plunge" that "roars" now with the language which lies hidden in the past above and the future below.

This third book has been described by Dr. Williams as a search for a language. Yet much of it is spent in inveighing against what we ordinarily call language. The abstractions of scholarship are the poet's primary anathema, but he extends his disgust to include almost all human speech. "No ideas but in things," he says repeatedly—the objectivist doctrine carried to its extreme. Abstract "meaning" is the enemy, "an offense to love, the mind's worm eating out the core." The dead authors in the library are "men in hell, their reign over the living ended," their thoughts trapped in inflexible, dead rhetoric. Even the poet's own work is suspect; at one point he admonishes himself: "Give up the poem. Give up the shilly-shally of art."

This seems to put the poet in a difficult situation, since there honestly isn't much reason to be writing a poem (much less to publish it) if one must write in a bad language. Dr. Williams's conclusions on this head are not as clear as one might wish, but he appears to be saying that the poet can resolve his predicament through a doctrine of invention. The good language is the language of the river, articulated by the falls. The poet cannot hope to imitate the falls, but he can learn from it. By forgetting the past, by writing spontaneously, even carelessly, by grounding all speech firmly in natural objects, the poet can *create* a language in nature that is essentially an act, not a meaning—an act of love and union. By working constantly at a peak of inventiveness, he can elevate this language to a level of independence which is its own justification.

Paterson, when it is finished, will make a great hunting ground for the explicators. There are virtually hundreds of symbols—Dr. Williams would protest my continued application of this word to the *things* of his poem, which he calls, elsewhere, objects; but although one happily and admiringly grants the objectiveness of his objects, their purity and wholeness in his poems, the pristine quality of their existence as other identities, one still must insist on the profound meanings and feelings that attach to them, and this is all I wish to suggest by my choice of terms—there are hundreds of symbols and allusions to be tracked down, related, explained, and if he sticks to his text this will annoy Dr. Williams considerably. Essays will be written, for instance, on the many uncomplimentary allusions, often disguised, to T. S. Eliot and his works. There will likewise be essays on the other writers mentioned (Pound, Stevens, a few younger poets), on the various flowers (extremely important through all Dr. Williams's works), on the dog. Yet I would like to recommend one prior question to the critics before they begin.

Perhaps I can put it best this way. Twenty-five years ago Eliot felt that he should explain some of the sources and meanings of *The Waste Land* in accompanying notes; for Dr. Williams this is unnecessary. We are better readers now. Furthermore Dr. Williams's symbols are made from objects we all know in our own experience, rather than from cultural devices, and the meanings given to them are drawn from a common fund of ideas and feelings. But I think we should call on Dr. Williams for another kind of note—a definite note on prosody. He himself sees the trouble, and at one point he says to the reader, rather sharply: "Use a metronome if your ear is deficient, one made in Hungary if you prefer." But I think he misses the mark. Any reader with an ear for poetry will easily respond to Dr. Williams's astonishingly pure feeling for the rhythms of the American language. It is not meter or cadence that bothers me, but the line. These lines are not run over, in the Elizabethan sense; they are not rove over, in the Hopkinsian sense; nor are they carefully turned over, as in the poetry of H.D., where breath and sense as well as cadence determine the line-length; they are hung over, like a Dali watch. They break in the most extraordinary places—at least often they do—with no textual, metrical, or syntactical tension to help us feel the movement, or even the presence, of the line-units. If this is done for typographical effect, as sometimes appears, it is ineffectual, for it interferes with our reading. If it is done to indicate a certain way of reading the poem, then we should be told what it is.

Dr. Williams has explained in the past that he uses this device of the short, oddly broken line to obtain the effect of speed in a lyric poem. But *Paterson*, by rough estimate, will be five thousand lines long when it is finished. In such a large dose the effect is, instead, limpidity, constantly bolstered by interjections and typographical novelties; sustained verbal power is seldom achieved.

Perhaps I am a dull reader; if so, these matters can be explained. And in fairness to me they ought to be explained, if not by Dr. Williams then by some prosodist sympathetic to his method. The question of *Paterson's* value as poetry should put the critics face to face with questions they have been dodging for years. What kinds of lines and sentences does one put next to each other to create a long free-form poem? Is it an arguable prosodic hypothesis that the metrical beat, to the exclusion of the line, is the basic unit of poetry? How is aural structure to be sustained in a long poem in which line-values are suppressed?

"The Run to the Sea"

A review of *Paterson* (Book Four), by William Carlos Williams, from *The Nation*, August 25, 1951.

THE PUBLICATION of book 4, entitled "The Run to the Sea," completes Dr. Williams's long poem. It is an event of primary importance in American literature. *Paterson*, in the first place, is a poem intense, complicated, and absorbing, one of the best examples of the concision of poetry that I know; a prose paraphrase of its ideas and attitudes would occupy many hundreds of pages. And in the second place, *Paterson* is the major work—it has been so announced—of a poet who has already achieved great distinction as an American author. In the years ahead it will receive close attention from the critics. Here in this first short notice of the poem my most useful service will be a limited one—a statement of the superficial responses that occur on a first reading, and a forecast of some of the questions that will attract the critics later on.

The first thing that strikes a reader who has read through the four books of *Paterson* is the ease and naturalness on one hand and the compactness and completeness on the other that Dr. Williams has given to the symbols or, as he would prefer to call them, the *objects* of his poem. In this respect it is instructive, though risky, to compare *Paterson* with other long poems of our time—*The Bridge*, say, and *The Waste Land*. One sees immediately that whereas those two poems were written by young men, *Paterson* is the work of a poet who has lived with his material for many years; his thoughts and feelings, complex though they are, are altogether familiar to him, almost instinctive. With a minimum of juggling, fixing, and contriving—such as show through here and there in both the other poems—Dr. Williams fits his materials together naturally and gets the maximum of work from them. They have many values, many extensions, yet his objects are precisely related at all levels. In spite of his assertion several times that a "whole poem" is impossible, he has obviously had the whole poem in mind all along, and he has constructed it around objects which are as complex and powerful and consistent at the beginning as at the end.

The interpretation of these objects—the city, the park, the falls, the elements, the man with a dog, the flower, the crow, and so on and so on—will be one of the critics' jobs; it won't be easy. Yet the main theme is clear. Modern society has been divorced from its healthy and natural sources by the corruptions of church, state, commerce, and education; we can be saved only through language, a new language, a newly *invented* language, which will be free from the traditions of intellectual society and will constitute an act of marriage with nature as it appears in the earth, in men and women, and in ourselves. In other words the poet can save us if we will listen. Two objections can be raised to such a theme: first, that it is "untrue"; second, that it is worn out. To the former I should reply that this idea may be untrue and even dangerous, but like any genuine emotional response it is a valid motivating force for a work of art, and is proved to be so by the existence of the work of art itself. And in response to the second objection, I should simply point out that themes in poems appear worn out if they present themselves in worn-out language or worn-out forms. *Paterson* is as fresh and vigorous as any critic could ask.

The great questions raised by *Paterson* are technical ones, which in itself should have an invigorating effect on criticism, our science of nebulosities—if the critics will meet the challenge. The question of prosody, for instance. Can a poet, as Dr. Williams contends, invent a new poetic language, free from traditional meters, free even from traditional syntax, based solely on modern American speech? This is not an easy question, it is not to be decided offhand, as many people apparently think, and we need essays, good ones, to investigate it. Then the question of structure. Dr. Williams compiles his poem—the right term—by the method of associative juxtaposition that has become familiar to us in modern poetry, but he deviates from prior practice by including a good many prose passages. These are documentary—letters, newspaper clippings, medical records, and the like—and they are well chosen and interesting. But one does not want to read them twice. Do they derive literary value from their juxtaposition to verse? Or is this perhaps carrying the catalogue-of-ships device too far?

A word should be said about book 4 itself. Unfortunately it seems to me less satisfactory than the preceding books. It is less well integrated and the writing is more discursive, as if it had been done hurriedly. It begins with a mock pastoral, satiric and sardonic in intent. The middle section concerns the paradox of science that both heals and destroys, and it contains also a digression on the similar effects of money and credit. The final part is a long lyric of recollection; Paterson, the man-city, remembers the many murders that have occurred and thinks of the sea of blood toward which his people are flowing. All these elements refer to aspects of the previous books. The poem ends with a last picture of the poet who bathes harmlessly and carelessly in the sea.

Among the lines of an episode about his son, the poet gives us this parenthetical sentence: "(What I miss, said your mother, is the poetry, the pure poem of the first parts.)" This happens to be a true statement, for the final parts of *Paterson* do not have the lyric intensity of the two first books. But my reason for quoting it here is to give an example of something Dr. Williams does over and over again, and to point out another problem for the critics. Dr. Williams utterly destroys the convenient fiction that the poet and the man are separable. What are we to say about this sentence except that the poet is giving us a criticism of his own poem, made by his wife? Such intimacies occur often, some of them much more pointed than this. Nothing could be more contrary to the common practice of poets who think they are more important than themselves—that they are spokesmen, prophets—and who therefore give themselves, even when they are dealing with obviously personal experience, a larger character and more public decorum than the individual person can claim in reality. Dr. Williams is more unassuming and more difficult. His candor is refreshing. He lays his life on the line for everyone to look at. But how is the critic to deal with these passages without turning his eye from the poem to the private person? Ethical and esthetic considerations are compounded, with results that may turn out to be both confusing and salutary.

Yet in the end one sees that what emerges from *Paterson* is, after all, a sensibility larger than life, a prophetic sensibility. The poem has been called a "personal epic." That seems to be a contradiction in terms, and I should prefer to call it a long lyrical meditation. But though it is personal, even private, it is public too, it is in some ways cosmic, and it operates on all levels at once. Certainly the poet is motivated by a concern and awareness that far transcend his private circumstances, and certainly his poem is tied very closely to the state of American society. It is a beautiful poem, a convincing poem, and a poem of manifold cultural and social uses.

Understanding Auden

A review of *Auden: An Introductory Essay*, by Richard Hoggart, from *The Nation*, December 22, 1951.

IF, AS I HAVE JUST DONE, you read most of W. H. Auden's writings at one stretch, you are likely to come away bewildered by the number and diversity of your impressions. There is, most apparently, the writer's astonishing virtuosity. In prose and verse he is equally at home. The forms he has chosen extend from the loosest and most discursive to the tightest and most epigrammatic, and he has often adapted to his purposes the archaic or *outré* contrivances of other literary eras. In the individual word his abilities are most appreciable; no one knows more words or uses them more precisely, no one is better at manipulating their colors, sounds, and meanings. Auden's sudden shifts of temperament are baffling and sometimes annoying, for he can be both brilliant and dull, clownish and pedantic, persuasive and disagreeable, all in a single short poem. You feel sometimes that there is a mutiny in his vocabulary, words like squadrons fighting for possession of the page.

The easiest way to attack this amplitude is to discard the failures, and under the severest measure, which one can easily afford to apply to Auden, my own liking falls exclusively on the short poems—the songs, some of the sonnets, ballads, nursery rhymes, meditative and dramatic lyrics—a medium-sized bookful of fine poems. I was pleased to see that they come from every phase of Auden's career, including several from his recent collection, *Nones*. Yet in some ways the choice is disquieting, for Auden has devoted a great deal of his attention to longer works. His plays all seem to me imperfect; *The Quest* is almost aggressively elliptical; *The Sea and the Mirror* is pretentious and badly integrated; *The Age of Anxiety*, in spite of passages in which the alliterative verse, based on the old English model, comes really alive in contemporary idiom, remains by turns unfathomable and boring. Auden's best long poem, I think, is *New Year Letter*, and his best play is *For the Time Being*.

In one of his published letters to Christopher Isherwood, Auden wrote: "We are all too deeply involved with Europe to be able, or even to wish, to escape. The truth is, we are both only really happy living among lunatics." If you substitute for *living* the word *journeying*, you have a pretty good description of Auden's situation as a poet, for one of his consistent themes is the journey, the search, the questing traveler in an insane and desperate society. Who is to say that this is a romantic vision, or anything but an exact statement of contemporary reality? Yet the notion has its dangers, especially for the poet-as-traveler. How does one cope with, and at the same time please, the insane? What help do the insane offer to the search? How do crazy people deal with memory, tradition, and value? The traveler's hope becomes his virtuosity, precisely Auden's forte; he is an entertainer, a sleight-of-hand artist. Thus he may please his crazy hosts, but if he does not he has a good chance of escaping to the next town. His danger is that his skill may get out of hand. In Auden's long poems, the very public poems in which he pursues large issues of social, moral, and metaphysical concern, his virtuosity does get out of hand. He is too much the entertainer, and when he gets to the troublesome part of the argument he resorts too often to the entertainer's bag of rhetorical tricks—the capitalized Abstraction, the generalized notion from politics or psychiatry, the scrap of a foreign language. On the formal level bizarre and difficult verse forms tumble after one another kaleidoscopically, and sections of prose intrude against the ear. We find the shocking instead of the genuinely pertinent metaphor. These long works tend to be programs of brilliant fragments—vaudeville—not poetic units. Some short poems too suffer from these defects, but others are about ideas so particular or experiences so personal that the evasions and corroborations of virtuosity become unnecessary. And it is worth noting that the most successful long poem, *New Year Letter*, in terms of prosody and structure is the least "clever" of them all.

This is only a suggestion of the problems that face the critic of Auden's work; difficult problems, for Auden has insisted on being difficult. Yet Mr. Hoggart, in this first long study of Auden's writing, has made a good beginning. Wisely he has limited himself to an introduction to Auden's poetry: his book is primarily neither exegesis nor criticism. He distinguishes the periods of Auden's development, the main characteristics of his style, the principal elements of his thought. He speculates briefly on such matters as sources, influences, and motivations. He is helpful, in other words, and I do not mean to suggest that his book is merely a stereotyped guide for students who are producing term papers. On the contrary it is an intelligent essay that recognizes the limits of what can be said about a poet who has written a great deal but who is still in mid-career.

Auden has said that art is a game. OK, the idea has obvious affinity with his talents and with his whole cultural situation; for him it is a principle to be taken seriously, I gather, and to be elaborated in many areas of contemporary response—an issue too complex to be discussed in a brief review. But as a plain statement the game-theory is crude and dangerous, for one of the essential requirements of a game is that it be unproductive, while art is not art at all unless it makes something. It is true that Auden has spent a great deal of time in play; but his best poems, as Mr. Hoggart shows, are scarcely the result of a game.

Stevens as Essayist

A review of *The Necessary Angel*, by Wallace Stevens, from *The Nation*, June 14, 1952.

AMONG READERS OF POETRY one sometimes hears: "Ah, yes, Wallace Stevens—a very fine poet no doubt, but how can you account for a man who persists in writing about such silly subjects?" On the one hand, this. On the other, the injustices the man has suffered from those who do take him seriously, critics who have written admirably about Keats or Hart Crane but who have nothing but twaddle to say

about Stevens. In this predicament, between the devilishly uninformed and the deep blue connoisseurs, it has been up to Mr. Stevens
to save himself, and this he has done by collecting in one volume
seven of his important essays in prose.

Stevens is a poet who believes in the supremacy of poetry. Unlike
many of his colleagues, who turn to traditional dogmas or outside
disciplines for their support, he refuses the opinion that art is a game,
a propaganda, or a ceremony. For him poetry is a means toward truth,
and he says it unabashedly. It is man's best means, for its implement is
man's greatest faculty, the imagination, superior to the philosopher's
reason or the scientist's repetitive experimentalism. And poetry, if it
succeeds, possesses also the power to bestow upon its participants an
automatic by-product—ennoblement.

Thus Stevens gets down to fundamentals immediately, to the level
of the artist. And his main point is that the poet's imagination is useless unless he brings it to bear squarely upon reality. For him reality is
the vastly differentiated, often discouraging presence of this actual
world, untinctured by intimations of any farther intelligence. It is a
reality of almost unlimited beauty for those who can deal with it imaginatively and in its own terms. The poet who can order and make
comprehensible an aspect of this reality, through the imaginative con-
junction of resemblances, participates in the discovery of a truth. He
ennobles himself and his readers, and to him belong the moral and
intellectual rewards of nobility. Reality is for the poet, as for all men,
the "necessary angel," whose protection saves him among word-
workers from becoming only another radio announcer howling across
the wind.

As a poet Stevens's duty has been to write poetry, to explore reality.
He has written many poems, many admirable poems, some truly
great poems. But as a poet who feels the insecurity of the poet's position in the modern commercial, pragmatic, positivist world, Stevens
has given himself the secondary duty to write about poetry. He has
made a definition of poetry; he has studied the way poetry works. He
has given us several theories of the processes of imagination, theories
about metaphor, analogy, and resemblance, theories about epistemol-
ogy and human personality. He has been especially concerned with
the way poets look at reality, the way each man sees a tree differently,
for these various views comprise what we can apprehend of existence, and they are our *raison d'être* as sensible beings.

But what do we usually hear about Stevens? Among his admirers he is a high romantic, a direct descendent of impressionism, a mage of the poetic ritual. Among his critics he is a funambulist, a hedonist, a decadent. Both parties have been too much impressed by the externalities of his style, his eccentric rhetoric and his occasionally rococo vocabulary. They have failed to see the kind of precision he has obtained through these means. They have seized upon and exaggerated those poems which present an exotic view of the world, poems of Florida and Tehuantepec, and they have neglected the poems which extol the august beauty of mundane things.

The fact is that the ideas Stevens expresses in these essays, and that he has always expressed in his poems, bear a much closer affinity to Wordsworth, to Sidney, or to certain poets of the pagan world than they do to the decadents of the late nineteenth century. Insofar as our world is decadent in comparison with some other, I suppose Stevens is too, though I should prefer to use some such word as *refined* or *elaborate*. The nobility that Stevens has sought is obviously not Homer's; it is modern, intellectual, and subtle; it is heroic only in its spiritual or esthetic staunchness. Perhaps it is not nobility at all, but a kind of very good intelligence or very intelligent goodness that we in our moral sedentariness can still aspire to. But whatever it is, it is not foolishness or frippery. It is earnest, though not deadly earnest, and its products—Stevens's poems—are serious works, constructed to a measure which allows no extraneous or supercilious ornament. It is inconceivable that a poet whose concept of poetry is the one enunciated in these essays could be vulnerable to affectation or preciosity, though he has his disguises. Stevens has created a theory of the value of poetry which is as austere as any ever conceived, and his poems are hard grapplings with reality, out in the open, away from the cul-de-sacs of spiritual remoteness that have trapped so many of the rest.

The development of Stevens's thought has been, if one hesitates to say logical, at least consistent and in a line with its own objectives. Most of his ideas are not original—his affinity to Wordsworth has already been pointed out by J. V. Cunningham—but they have been rigorously tested by the poetic conditions of modernity. Nor has Stevens tried to write criticism. His essays are more nearly an operating program for poets, for one poet particularly, Stevens himself. Hence they are an important adjunct to, or defense of, his poetry; and in this sense at least, though I think also in others, they are indispensable.

I do not want to turn from these essays without noticing their extraordinary qualities as literature. Like his poems, Stevens's prose contains many prodigious remarks: "The centuries have a way of being male"; "The supreme example of analogy in English is *Pilgrim's Progress*"; "When we look back at the period of French classicism . . . , we have no difficulty in seeing it as a whole." These will scare the scholars half out of their wits. So much the better; a little area must be reserved. But we know that Stevens likes to shock us, and we laugh and look for the most outrageous and exotic surmises, until all at once they are no longer outrageous and exotic but the astute and respectable thoughts of a man who lives in Hartford, Connecticut. These are rich essays, simply constructed but richly and elegantly written. They contain many examples, an anthology-full of quotations from the most various and delightful authors, all very much to Stevens's purpose, but all exciting to come across for their own sake. All told *The Necessary Angel* is as pleasant, instructive, and inspiring a book as I have read in a long, long time.

MacLeish's Poetry

A review of *Collected Poems, 1917–1952*, by Archibald MacLeish, from *The Nation*, January 31, 1953.

READING FOR THE FIRST TIME the collected poems of any poet, the span of his achievement with all its false starts and wrong directions, is often an awakening and rather humbling experience, and I think it is especially so in the case of Mr. MacLeish's *Collected Poems*. There is in the first place the volume itself, compact, fat with poetry—a real accomplishment, to write so much. Poets who last long enough to publish their collected poems are professionals, writers who have stuck to their job over the years, and like all professionals they are not ashamed to offer their work in impressive quantities. Yet they have, too, the professional's critical sense; they pare their volumes clean of surplusage. Mr. MacLeish has done these things admirably. His book contains 407 pages of poetry and not a verse that shouldn't be there.

Which is not to say that all the poetry in this book is first-rate poetry. One can scarcely ask Mr. MacLeish to erase great chunks of himself. That is for us, the readers—remorseless surgeons—to do. And we have hacked away at him pretty successfully during the last ten or fifteen years, amputating poems with unembarrassed abandon. Mr. MacLeish has made this easy for us, in fact, by failing in his attempts to write affirmatively public poems, patriotic poems, poems inspired by liberal political enthusiasm. He succeeded, it is true, much better than many others who were trying, during the depression years, to do the same thing, but still he failed. It is easy for us to cut away these poems. They are good sense, but they aren't good poetry; they are propagandistic, frothy, bombastic, forcedly folkish, uncontrolled. Indeed, by turns they are almost everything that poems ought not to be. I mean such poems as "America Was Promises," "Colloquy for the States," some of the radio dramas and shorter pieces. Mr. MacLeish himself has left many poems from this period out of his book, but he has left enough in to give us unmistakable souvenirs—a little collection from the closet shelf, dated, tarnished, strangely remote.

As for his longer works, "The Pot of Earth," "The Hamlet of A. MacLeish," "Actfive," and others, Mr. MacLeish seems to have a penchant for hanging them on structures outside themselves, usually well-known works of literature. They have no narrative or dramatic content themselves, but are essentially long meditations and literary flourishes held together by constant reference to the exterior source; and though they contain brilliant passages, one's interest flags from this constant sense of derivativeness or purely cultural hybridization. "Conquistador" is his most original long poem and his best; it remains good reading, in spite of the tricks, the unnecessary ellipses, broken phrases, curious punctuation.

I said that reading these collected poems is a humbling experience, and it is true. For in spite of all our amputations, our rusty scalpels and contrary diagnoses, the patient lives. We are left with little to say. Maybe there wasn't anything wrong with him in the first place.

Mr. MacLeish's short lyrics remain his best poems. "You, Andrew Marvell" is famous, but the other lyrics on time and death, with the recurrent image of the turning planet, seem to me—many of them—just as good, including such poems as "Bahamas" and "The Old Man to the Lizard" that are printed in the section of his most recent work.

The love poems, and there are many, written during every phase of the poet's career and under every aspect of feeling, are often splendid, composed with a restraint and exactness of language that are songlike, reproducing the sensuousness of ideas very evocatively, the basic eroticism of human thought. Among the latest poems are several that challenge, very explicitly, the cheapness and stupidity of commercial society, and one, a reply to T. S. Eliot, which makes the replies we have had from younger poets seem like childish tantrums by comparison.

Finally at the end of the book is Mr. MacLeish's latest long work, a verse drama for radio entitled *The Trojan Horse*. I think it may be his best work of the kind. It has been broadcast by the BBC, but not in this country.

The Bollingen Prize in Poetry, which has become in a few years the closest thing we have to a respectable honorific in the art, has just been awarded to Mr. MacLeish, thereby enrolling him more or less officially in the company of which his *Collected Poems* shows him to have been a member all along.

"Without the Inventions of Sorrow"

A review of *The Collected Poems of Wallace Stevens*, from *Poetry*, February 1955.

OPULENCE—it is the quality most of us would ascribe to the poetry of Wallace Stevens before all others; profusion, exotic luxuriance. We have a permanent impression of poems which teem with rich, strange, somehow forbidden delights. Just to read again the titles of his poems is to awaken this sense of the extraordinary abundance: "Tea at the Palaz of Hoon," "The Bird with the Coppery, Keen Claws," "Sea Surface Full of Clouds," "The Man with the Blue Guitar," "Mrs. Alfred Uraguay," "The Owl in the Sarcophagus," "Angel Surrounded by Paysans," "The Irish Cliffs of Moher"—and hundreds more, of course. They surround us, as it were, like an incomparable gallery.

Nor is the idea of a gallery out of place in speaking of the collected edition of Mr. Stevens's poems. I was continually impressed, as I sauntered among the hundreds of poems in this volume, by the way in which they present to us the whole movement of this century in art; no exhibition of paintings could be more expressive of the modern artist's aims and methods. Of course the poet's very graphic way with imagery reminds one naturally of painting; the bright, Mediterranean colors and the arranged interiors, as in the opening lines of "Sunday Morning," recall to me most clearly, I think, Matisse, though there are many other connections and associations. The chief point, however, is that in these poems the many influences on the art of our time can be seen plainly: French, pastoral, metaphysical, Homeric, and so on; and the many aims: to originate, to shock, to reexamine, to analyze, and above all to deal uncompromisingly with the realities of the contemporary world.

In point of time Stevens's career as a writer has been coextensive with the development of modern art, at least as it has occurred in this country, and the career itself, as recorded in these poems, reveals the stages through which we have come to believe the masters must always pass. The chronology is not definite, but the main lines are clear. There are the early masterpieces of conventional technique— "Sunday Morning" and a few shorter poems in regular blank verse. There are the poems in which this technique begins to shift under an experimental impetus; of many examples, "The Comedian as the Letter C." There are the sheer experiments, often fragmentary and uncharacteristic, and there are the excesses—poems in which a manner that has pleased the poet for a time is pushed too far, into conscious or unconscious self-caricature. There are the variations on a constant theme—many of them apparently impromptu—of the middle period, when the poet was working toward a strong and individual style with which he could master any material no matter how complex or "unpoetic." And there are the later poems which sometimes revert to an old simplicity, though with the resonance gained from the years. The progression has been accompanied—quickened, pervaded, impelled—by a relentless amendment and elaboration of the poet's theme, and the lavishness of his invention has never diminished.

But why do we always come back to our impression of opulence? One thinks immediately of the abounding images from the natural world:

The rocks of the cliffs are the heads of dogs
That turn into fishes and leap
Into the sea.

It is true that the rivers went nosing like swine,
Tugging at banks, until they seemed
Bland belly-sounds in somnolent troughs.

On an old shore, the vulgar ocean rolls
Noiselessly, noiselessly, resembling a thin bird,
That thinks of settling, yet never settles, on a nest.

The cricket in the telephone is still.
A geranium withers on the window-sill.

But do they really abound? It has been much more difficult than I expected it would be to find these four detachable examples, and even they are not truly representative. The fact is, most of the poems are single metaphors, short, whole, compact, even spare; the images are used frugally and pointedly; they are integral and functional, never merely decorative. Even the long poems are generally composed of short sections, separated and numbered, which each conform to this pattern of lyric rigor, and the few long poems which do comprise sustained passages of narrative or exposition are surprisingly unadorned—not counting "The Comedian as the Letter C," which we can now regard as an early experiment. In other words the poems themselves, when we examine them without our preconceptions, contain neither denser nor more ornate imagery than we should expect to find in 534 pages of poetry by anyone else, and in many cases the comparison, especially if it were with the work of his contemporaries, would show Stevens's poems to be the simpler in design, structure, and figuration.

Perhaps then it is a question of the poet's subject, his *materia*. Many of the poems, true enough, and especially the earlier ones, do convey an exotic scene, a Caribbean radiance of sun-drenched seas and forests. "Hibiscus on the Sleeping Shores," "The Idea of Order at Key West," "O Florida, Venereal Soil"—these and many others, most of them from *Harmonium*, the poet's first book, are clearly visions of splendor. But the first poem in the second book is called "Farewell to

Florida," and thereafter Stevens's characteristic scene is not tropical
but northern, and there are as many celebrations of drab and wintry
occasions as of summer. Again I was surprised to find how few of the
poems are in fact given to outright flourishes of earthly glitter.

The poems from *Harmonium* are doubtless the best known. They
have been republished many times in anthologies and repeatedly discussed by the critics. They have become a regular part of university
courses in modern literature. And many of them are brilliant; it isn't
surprising that they are used as displays. But they are not as good as
the later poems, and emphatically they do not reveal the qualities of
Stevens's whole accomplishment. The advantage of this collected edition is the prominence it gives to the main body of poems.

I think we conclude finally that in the texts themselves the language is the only constant ratification of our sense of the poet's opu-
lent invention. There is nothing new in the idea of Stevens as a master
of language. But to explore the pages of this collection is to be aston-
ished, literally, by the range and intensity of his rhetorical genius. It is
not virtuosity, for the virtuoso's performance is theoretically attain-
able by anyone who works hard enough, whereas Stevens excels at
what only he can do. It is a perfection, a pressing extension within the
formulations of his own strict style and prosody, of the aptitude for
naming which lies at the base of any writer's talent. Someday perhaps
an industrious scholar will count the number of different words Stevens has used; certainly it would be interesting to see that magnitude
measured. Stevens delights in odd words, archaic words, foreign
words that he can wrest to an English meaning. In this respect he is
like Whitman, but to my ear better than Whitman, for I am never embarrassed by Stevens's importations: he dominates and controls the
foreign words with an authority Whitman never achieved. More exactly, Stevens is Elizabethan in his attitude toward language, high-
handed in the extreme. When all else fails he derives words anew,
gambling with the recognizable roots and associations:

> *The grackles sing avant the spring*
> *Most spiss—oh! Yes, most spissantly.*

Such delight in language is infectious, and we are convinced, as we
should be, when Stevens says to us,

> *Natives of poverty, children of malheur,*
> *The gaiety of language is our seigneur.*

Stevens is the delighted craftsman whose delight is, in part, the access of gratification which comes upon the exercise of mastery. His pleasure is endless because it is part of his work, past and present; it is transmissible because we too, in reading his poems, share that mastery.

True poetry is instinct with this delight—and with much more, of course. With meaning which transcends its verbal properties. With a passion which makes whole the verbal elements. As it happens, Stevens's delight in language is concomitant to his entire vision, his argument. If there is space in this short tribute for only a glance at one or two technical aspects of his poetry, I think we can be sure that for many readers in years to come the meaning and the passion of Stevens's poetry will be its dominant rewards. Certainly as readers and critics become more familiar with the whole body of work, we shall see more and more clearly how *humane* has been the impulse behind this delight that is interpretive of our actual world. Make no mistake, these poems have been written as solace for intellectual and moral hardship, not simply as verbal indulgences. Even now, in this book of beautiful, impeccable, famous poems, we have something so intimately a part of our time and scene that we are almost persuaded to say, appropriatively: "This is what we have been able to do; by these poems we are willing to be known."

"To Fashion the Transitory"

From *Poetry*, September 1956.

THE PROBLEM OF TIME in Edwin Muir's poetry dominates all others, and I suppose this allies him to the so-called metaphysical tradition in modern literature. But it is a loose and problematical alliance. If the metaphysical tradition is characterized in part by certain habits of significant ambiguity in thought and substance, or by a certain mental posture of irony which infiltrated the liturgical sensibility of medieval writers and which has endured as a creative mode in the erotic and political imaginations of Renaissance times and our own, then by contrast Muir's poetry is straightforward, singleminded, and virtually Wordsworthian in manner and tone. Muir is a fabulist, a poet of dreams and visions; he relies for his effects upon a high degree of poetic realism. By poetic realism I mean not a naturalistic technique but a deeper realism that makes matter-of-fact use of the poetic conventions for what they are—the easiest, clearest, and most economical means of coming to terms with the substance of one's feelings and imaginings. Muir lived for a number of years in central Europe and devoted a good deal of time to translating modern German literature, especially the novels and stories of Kafka, and it is not surprising that he should have learned something from the writer who, more than any other, has demonstrated the use of a conventional medium for the realistic embodiment of a fantastic substance. But at the same time it is important to recognize that the essential ingredients of Muir's poetic manner, as well as the main elements of his thought and feeling, took form before he began translating Kafka, and that few other poets have equalled the skill with which he has used the conventions of English prosody—his verse-making, song-making genius. Some of Muir's poems are among the best that have come from Great Britain during the first half of this century.

Time, for Muir, appears under its ancient aspect of the thief, a doubly invidious figure because it steals away in "deadly days" and "melting hours" the objects and values that it alone has been able to create. Eternity, especially in the earlier poems, is simply time's extent, with the awful blanknesses of prehistory and posthistory at either end:

> So, back or forward, still we strike
>   Through time and touch its dreaded goal.
> Eternity's the fatal flaw
>   Through which run out world, life, and soul.

But at least one other kind of eternity, the eternity of mind, in which human beings escape from the flow of time into the permanence of conceptual or symbolic actions, appears in many poems, and in the later poems a third kind of eternity, akin to that of traditional Christian belief, offers something like a resolution to the time problem. The progression from an amorphous materialism through the eternity of the mind to something "more than half Platonic" is evident in the poems.

Because men and women are able to exist both in and out of time, they possess, against time's depredations, an existential advantage that is unique (discounting angels): the abilities to remember and to dream. By these means they create their own time. In the eternity of mind, dreams and memories—together with fables, their universalized counterpart—furnish the very substance of meaning; life is fabulous, and in the individual experiences of it the great events are enacted again and again, so that its meaning is perpetually reinforced. The individual's dreams and profoundest memories are prefigured in humanity's fables. Muir would admit, I think, that these concepts are more than faintly Jungian. But this does not imply a direct connection; the ideas were "in the air" thirty years ago, and in any case it is clear that Muir worked them out in terms useful for him solely in his poems. Perhaps this concern for meaningful archetypal figurations aligns Muir after all with the metaphysical and postsymbolist tradition considered in its functional aspect, but with this difference: Muir disdains the search for objectifications among the intellectual conventions of the age and instead confines himself to the task of constructing a modern typology from the pristine sources of experience—myth and dream. This is perfectly evident in the poems. Each of them is an assault against time, a failing assault, of course, as all such assaults must be, written out of the eternity of mind to recreate and reinterpret the perpetual fable of man's dreams and memories. This is hard substance, and the poems have about them, beyond their verbal utilitarianism, a kind of obduracy of spirit that we associate with the Scotch Presbyterian sensibility. How many of the poems derive from actual dreams we cannot tell; yet certainly many of them, especially such Kafka-like poems as "The Escape" and "The Interrogation," have the quality of dreams—terror and absurdity reduced to the commonplace occurrences of the mind. Images of anxiety recur throughout the poems, and several poems are superb reenactments of anxiety itself:

> *But when you reach the Bridge of Dread*
> *Your flesh will huddle into its nest*

> For refuge and your naked head
> Creep in the casement of your breast,
>
> And your great bulk grow thin and small
> And cower within its cage of bone,
> While dazed you watch your footsteps crawl
> Toadlike across the leagues of stone.

That exactness of subjective detail, cast in the ordinariness of conventional verse, is what tells us that Muir himself has crossed such a bridge more than once. And even more prominent in the poems than anxiety is its aftermath, melancholy, the irreducible sadness of the person who cannot complete the gesture of acceptance and resignation:

> I do not want it so,
> But since things so are made,
> Sorrow, sorrow,
> Be you my second trade.

The central fable to which Muir returns again and again is, of course, that of fallen man, for the Fall is the universal fable of man's entrance into time, into history, the moment when he begins to dream and remember. "What shape had I before the Fall?" he asks. What "dragon brood" roamed the earth then? His dim memories of a splendidly heraldic age haunt his poems, and he speaks of "the journey back," back beyond our ancestries to the fabulous origins. Little by little the primal place grows clearer, and the journey itself, back through the eternity of the mind, lightens new corners of dreamed and fabulous experience. The patterns of value consolidate. Of the search for Eden, Muir writes:

> If I should reach that place, how could I come
> To where I am but by that deafening road,
> Life-wide, world-wide, by which all come to all,
> The strong with the weak, the swift with the stationary,
> For mountain and man, hunter and quarry there
> In tarrying do not tarry, nor hastening hasten,
> But all with no division strongly come
> For ever to their steady mark, the moment,

> *And the tumultuous world slips softly home*
> *To its perpetual end and flawless bourne.*

And in dreams and memories the "deafening road" is traveled cease-lessly, the road that opens out from Eden and carries us to our only compensations—the transitory values of our mutual arts and the per-manent values of our shared and inherited experience. Our experi-ence is legendary, embodied in dreams and fables that are known to all of us. And in its largest aspects it transcends our arts:

> *Old gods and goddesses who have lived so long*
> *Through time and never found eternity,*
> *Fettered by wasting wood and hollowing hill,*
>
> *You should have fled our ever-dying song,*
> *The mound, the well, and the green trysting tree,*
> *They are forgotten, yet you linger still.*

In his *Autobiography* Muir says that he did not begin to write poetry until he was thirty-five. One regrets the loss of the youthful poems he might have written. In many ways Muir brought to his poetry the ideal verbal equipment, for like a number of other modern writers whose work is important to us Muir came from a linguistic backwater of the British Isles, in his case Orkney; his native speech, a dynamic, still logopoeic dialect, has been a noticeable factor in his poems, as have the remnants of Nordic myth that survived among the island folk during his childhood. On the other hand Muir has not allied him-self with the nationalistic poets of Scotland; perhaps as an Orkney man he was too much out of the mainstream of even Scottish provin-cial life to identify himself with it. Instead he has chosen the hard lot of literacy in the contemporary world—wisely, I think—and has de-voted himself to the available audience and the usable resources of the mind. The result is a poetry of the modern sensibility at its broad-est self-consciousness, a poetry which, in its use of dreams and mem-ories and in its strong idiom, objectifies an enduring, undermost reality, beneath appearances of time or place. Like the surrealists, Muir deals with our perpetually incipient apprehensions of what is; but unlike them he is concerned with the basic human ingredients, not with the individual ego. Elsewhere I have called him a subrealist.

The term is somewhat misleading, but perhaps it conveys the distinction I have in mind.

Muir's preference is for what John Crowe Ransom has called the light line, the folk measure of ballad and hymn. Some of his poems on legendary or heraldic themes are in fact ballads transmuted or refined, and thus belong to an old tradition of English literature. They are lyrical ballads of a new order. But Muir has often used the pentameter too, and one of his commonest stylistic devices is the play of long, intricate syntactical units against the simple regularity of standard English meter. The opening sentence of "The Labyrinth," for instance, extends for thirty-five lines without effort, surely an enviable feat. Some of his shorter lyrics consist of a single sentence. These qualities are a part of Muir's poetic realism, a style that does not shun inversions or other unnatural or "literary" constructions provided they derive from the force of reality in thought, feeling, and dream, and it is this real substance that one comes back to repeatedly in writing about his work. The closest he himself has come to a discussion of technique is his poem "All We":

> *All we who make*
> *Things transitory and good*
> *Cannot but take*
> *When walking in a wood*
> *Pleasure in everything*
> *And the maker's solicitude,*
> *Knowing the delicacy*
> *Of bringing shape to birth.*
> *To fashion the transitory*
> *We gave and took the ring*
> *And pledged ourselves to earth.*

And yet one is not aware of the "delicacy"; it lies in the poetic act, in the discriminations and perceptions, not in the poem. The object, the poem itself, is instead shaped of earth, not perdurable, in fact transitory, but nevertheless ingrained with the maker's love and the most lasting elements of human nature and experience; and such poems as "The Annunciation," "The Journey Back," "Variations on a Time Theme," "The Island," and "The Horses" will last for a good many seasons in the eternity of the mind.

Two Books

Excerpts from a review of several books, including *Overland to the Islands*, by Denise Levertov; and *A Coney Island of the Mind*, by Lawrence Ferlinghetti; from *Poetry*, November 1958.

. . . DENISE LEVERTOV OFFERS US something quite different, a free and supple poetry, personal, unaffected, mature. She is a wise and gifted poet. Last year, when she published a small pamphlet called *Here and Now*, Kenneth Rexroth praised her work highly and claimed her as a natural leader for his avant garde, the coterie he has mustered to wage battle against the academic elements in American verse. Whatever Miss Levertov's personal affiliations may be, I think this was a disservice to her. She is not an experimentalist, she does not write in a context of revolt. True, her verse is unmetered; but this is 1958, the controversy Mr. Rexroth insists on pursuing today died painlessly some decades ago. Miss Levertov is not a leader, if one can judge her by her poems. Not power politics but the problem of language in her own work is what interests her. Once we see this, we can already assign her, I think, a clearly defined place among the feminine poets, mostly American, who have done so much for poetry in this century, and we can recognize that her work is very much worth our attention.

In the substance of her poems, as in their language, Miss Levertov gives us nothing particularly experimental. Her theme is the primacy of things, her approach is by way of invocation. This is the kind of reism we have heard of before from Dr. Williams and the objectivists. In fact it would be easy to put Miss Levertov down as a follower of Dr. Williams and let it go at that, but this would be an error. I wish I knew enough recent French poetry to speak authoritatively about the affinity I think I see between her work and what little French verse has reached me. I apologize for my ignorance. But isn't there something of Char and Ponge and a few of the younger French poets in this virtually nuptial transcendence sought in the unities of objectification? At any rate the free but purposeful directness of her writing and her care for the values of language bring Miss Levertov much closer to the French than to the San Francisco school. What distinguishes her is acuteness of perception, what we would like to call taste if that word didn't suggest something too frivolous; it is an acuteness in seeing and in hearing, in judging the qualities of things and in discriminating the qualities of language. Her management of rhythmic pause and stress sets her apart from any other young poet I know who is working in unmetered forms. I should say she pays as close attention to the small—and of course the large—motions of accent and sound in her verse as any poet writing in the "classical" tradition. Indeed it would be a mistake to call her a romantic. Instead it is as if she had been transposed, with a thoroughly contemporary consciousness, to some preclassical, pastoral scene. Her work is skillful, unlabored, close to nature, seemingly indifferent to the codifications and orthodoxies yet to come.

Miss Levertov's new book, *Overland to the Islands*, contains a number of fine things. Some of them are "The Instant," "Action," "The Absence," "A Supermarket in Guadalajara, Mexico." At the same time I feel bound, in this brief tribute, to say that none of these new poems impresses me quite as much as the one called "Beyond the End" from her previous collection. . . .

The last poet in our mixed catch, Lawrence Ferlinghetti, quite properly and recognizably is to be identified with the San Francisco group. He is the proprietor of City Lights Bookshop, a center of the group's activities, and as such has had a good deal to do with organizing the fraternated arts program which has been so much admired during the past couple of years in the Bay area; and he has published much of the group's output in his series of City Lights pamphlets. Moreover his own work as a poet has been conspicuously acclaimed by members of the coterie and others. His new book, *A Coney Island of the Mind*, contains both old and new work, and presumably represents Mr. Ferlinghetti's own selection of the poems he considers his best.

His intention is clearly announced on the cover of his book. "I have been working," he writes, "toward a kind of *street poetry* . . . to get poetry out of the inner esthetic sanctum and out of the classroom into the street. The poet has been contemplating his navel too long, while the world walks by. And the printing press has made poetry so silent that we've forgotten the power of poetry as 'oral messages'. The sound of the streetsinger and the Salvation Army speaker is not to be scorned." The voice of Vachel Lindsay sounds through these words, and many others' as well. Once I read an excellent paper on the same subject by John Masefield.

One means by which Mr. Ferlinghetti has attempted to ingratiate his "oral messages" with a popular audience is to write them for accompaniment by a jazz group, and a section of his book has been devoted to poems produced in this way. Here are a few excerpts from one of them, "Junkman's Obbligato":

Let us arise and go now
to where dogs do it
Over the Hill
where they keep the earthquakes
behind the city dumps
lost among gasmains and garbage.
Let us see the City Dumps
for what they are.
My country tears of thee.
Let us disappear
in automobile graveyards
and reappear years later
picking rags and newspapers
drying our drawers
on garbage fires
patches on our ass.
Do not bother
to say goodbye
to anyone.

. . . .

Let us arise and go now
under the city
where ashcans roll
and reappear in putrid clothes
as the uncrowned underground kings
of subway men's rooms.
Let us feed the pigeons
at the City Hall
urging them to do their duty
in the Mayor's office.
Hurry up please it's time.
The end is coming.

> *Flash floods*
> *Disasters in the sun*
> *Dogs unleashed*
> *Sister in the street*
> *her brassiere backwards.*
>
> . . . .
>
> *Let's cut out let's go*
> *into the real interior of the country*
> *where hockshops reign*
> *mere unblind anarchy upon us.*
> *The end is here*
> *but golf goes on at Burning Tree.*
> *It's raining it's pouring*
> *The Ole Man is snoring.*
> *Another flood is coming*
> *though not the kind you think.*
> *There is still time to sink*
> *and think.*
> *I wish to descend in society.*
> *I wish to make like free.*
> *Sing low sweet chariot*
> *Let us not wait for the cadillacs . . .*

and on and on for six pages. It must be wonderful to be able to be satisfied with such easy stuff.

First, what is this as poetry? Mr. Ferlinghetti may not like printing presses, but he has consigned his work to the printed page, to be read in silence, and I suppose we may judge it as we would any other verse. The temptation is to let these excerpts—fairly quoted, I swear—damn themselves and to say no more about it. But so much has already been said by the avid and uninformed that probably something explicit from a contrary view is needed here. I want to introduce one more quotation by way of comparison, the opening lines of Miss Levertov's "Beyond the End." This is a poem which Mr. Ferlinghetti presumably tolerates since he himself was its publisher.

> *In 'nature' there's no choice—*
> *flowers*

swing their heads in the wind, sun & moon
are as they are. But we seem
almost to have it (not just
available death)

It's energy: a spider's thread: not to
'go on living' but to quicken, to activate: extend . . .

It's a pity to chop off such a fine poem, but perhaps my point is made. Granting these are two very different poems—and very different poets—does this comparison of works which have been composed in the same general tradition of unmetered verse show that Mr. Ferlinghetti has any awareness at all of English as a medium of sounds, motions, accents? Or does it simply show what can happen to a great formal impulse, whether Pound's, Eliot's, or Williams's—or from all together—when it has percolated through forty years of mediocre sensibilities? Mr. Ferlinghetti claims to write for the street, in the language of the street, yet you can hear on any street in this country language more beautifully and meaningfully and vigorously cadenced than this, even taking into account the porcine discontinuity of most American discourse. "Junkman's Obbligato" is as flaccid and nerveless as putty. The first requirement of any poetry is a respect for the capacities of language, the negative or "tough" capacities as well as the others, and a sensitivity to its sounds and speeds. I detect no trace of these in Mr. Ferlinghetti's verse. And what shall we say about this unformed cynicism, this blatant, squashy irony? Or about this look-what-I'm-doing-now degradation of works and emblems which, in spite of it all, remain untouched? It is puerile. What about this easy glorification of depravity? Mr. Ferlinghetti mentions anarchism in his poem. Only place the poem next to Kropotkin's *Memoirs*; which is genuine will be apparent at once. The point is that the proof of glory must be in the poem, in the wresting of it from word and image, and that goes for the glory of depravity as much as for any other. You don't get it from slovenly verse. And besides, we have been through Mr. Ferlinghetti's world already, long, long ago, or so it now seems. Sentimentality, fakery, prop cardboard slums on a Hollywood lot. It was chicanery then, and it is now too. I don't say much of our reality isn't there for the writer who can deal with it truly. . . .

Second, what about street poetry, what about poetry and jazz? I have listened to some of the recordings made by Mr. Ferlinghetti and Mr. Rexroth with jazz groups, and I find them no better than previous experiments with poetry and music. Edith Sitwell's, for instance. William Walton's music for *Façade* at least supported the verse; still one could not follow the reading without a text, and Dame Edith's performances minus music were at least equally effective. In the case of the San Francisco experiments there are clearly two autonomous activities going on at the same time, so that the hearer's attention is jerked from one to the other in a perplexity of indecision: when the poetry is good the music interferes with it; when the music is good the poetry, though it can be partly shut out, remains a nuisance. The arts are separate. And if they weren't it would be desirable to separate them. Which is not to say that words and music cannot be combined in song. Song is another case altogether, involving special, now largely forgotten rules of procedure. (But it is worth noting that the most successful popular poet in America in recent times has been Joe Hill.)

As for street poetry it seems to me that a few truisms may clear the air. (1) Popular poetry must be lively, musical, rhythmical, iterative, the broadside ballad and today's advertising jingle being two obviously successful types. Mr. Ferlinghetti's poetry, on the contrary, is mostly tuneless, mostly arhythmic, and mostly, I imagine, hard to remember. (2) Popular poetry, except for some kinds of erotic verse, should possess a strong narrative content. Mr. Ferlinghetti's has none at all. (3) Popular poetry must be as short as is consistent with the active development of the theme. Mr. Ferlinghetti is often rather long-winded. (4) Popular poetry must be concrete. Mr. Ferlinghetti, though not abstruse by any means, is usually abstract; here he is far from his objectivist associates. And (5) popular poetry must contribute, at least supportively, to the national, racial, or at any rate undifferentiatedly social myth. Mr. Ferlinghetti might argue with me about the value of his poetry in this connection, but I find his attitudes so generally negative, in spite of interspersed affirmations of poverty, sex, freedom, and so on, that I don't see how they could attract anything but an essentially frivolous audience.

Finally, has "street poetry" ever been created by self-conscious poets? Has it ever had anything at all to do with literature or the literary world, as we use these terms? Aren't its locus and frame of reference always exclusively in the popular culture, if not in the subculture? (Another great popular poet, W. C. Handy, stole everything he wrote from folk sources.) What conditions must be satisfied before the educated poet can *honestly* write for an illiterate or semiliterate audience?

Probably I have said too much on this topic. Let me end by agreeing wholly with those who deplore the hardening of our literary tastes, the institutionalization of our literary life. We do indeed need new things in our poetry, we need them desperately. But I wonder if we can be helped appreciably by poets whose idea of the new is merely a resuscitation of squabbles that died thirty years ago. The issue is a continuing one, they will say, the battle against academicism is never won. True, but the avant garde must wage its fight in terms that are currently moving and significant. It must offer us a coherently revised image of ourselves in forms that derive rationally from the immediate complex of art and experience. Above all it must propose a renewal of our contact with the permanent verities, not a further estrangement. The ultimate weapon of the avant garde, aside from talent, is common sense. And it seems to me that in esthetic terms the direction indicated by Miss Levertov is more sensible, and thus likely to be more useful, than the one indicated by Mr. Ferlinghetti.

In Defense of Karl Shapiro

A review of *In Defense of Ignorance*, by Karl Shapiro, from the *New Republic*, June 20, 1960.

KARL SHAPIRO HAS WRITTEN an animated, corrupt, repetitious, illogical, necessary, and dangerous book. He has written it in defense of the indefensible—ignorance—and he has given it a shrill and ranting tone which will affront a good many readers. But perhaps this is necessary, because what Shapiro has also done, very courageously, is to throw into the open the whole plight of American poetry at the present time; and although there has been a good deal of sniping and bitching among coterie poets in recent years, he is the first prominent poet to have attempted it. The plight, of course, is just what all poets and critics, even those whom Shapiro attacks most sharply, are worried about. But most of them have shied away from serious public discussion of it because they have felt that such a discussion might jeopardize their own entrenched positions in the literary world or, more commonly, because they have had no real answers to the problems raised by the snipers and bitchers and have feared that discussion could lead only to confusion and pessimism.

Shapiro for years has been chipping away at the critics. His antipathy goes back at least to the awarding of the Bollingen Prize to Ezra Pound in 1949. Usually heretofore his remarks have been rather sedate, in the style of polite academic dialogue, but his general position has been clear. Now he abandons politeness, and in the heat of his argument (perhaps generated in part by the silence which has greeted him until now) he says many foolish things and often says them badly. But he at least does not disguise his animus or try to sugarcoat his convictions. The roots of his feeling are exposed clearly in the early pages of the introductory essay. "Criticism," he writes, "is an attitude of mind, not simply a method of elucidation. It is what remains when literature itself has begun to expire. Criticism flourishes when literature has failed." And he goes on to say that modern criticism has substituted ideology for judgment, has elevated didactic poetry to a supreme position, has concentrated attention on meaning rather than on poetic value, and finally has itself supplanted poetry as the fashionable genre for young writers. I am not sure that criticism in itself is a sign of a failing literature; on historical grounds one could argue the opposite. But as for the rest of Shapiro's charges, I do not see how anyone can deny them: they are demonstrably true, as anyone with the least acquaintance of life in our primary literary centers, which are mostly attached to university graduate schools, will acknowledge.

Shapiro sums up by proclaiming himself an unabashed antiintellectual, and this is the nub of the matter. "The intellectual," he writes disparagingly, "cannot experience anything without *thinking* about it." The italics are his own and indicate plainly to which camp he belongs; that is, to the peculiarly modern camp which believes that by mere force of feeling you can split asunder thought and experience, and then choose which of the two you prefer.

The split simply isn't possible. Thought and experience are bound together. Being bound together, neither can exist by itself, at least not if we agree as practical men and women—that is, leaving aside the lucubrations of epistemologists, behaviorists, and other such—that we mean by experience something more than an instantaneously forgotten sensation. Consequently every poet since the beginning of time has been of necessity an intellectual according to Shapiro's definition: he has thought about his experience. Take the American poets of the twentieth century whom Shapiro condemns as intellectuals and whom other poetry-readers applaud as the authors of our most important poems. Even in their old age these men are sensualists; at least so I have observed; and however much inevitable thinking they may do about their experience, they are always eager for the experience itself, sometimes to the point of disgrace. Indeed, isn't this the burden of their work, the thing that typifies "modern poetry"? Over and over, in a thousand ways, we have celebrated the genuineness of what is felt, heard, seen.

Not long ago I got a letter from a young woman who is a splendid poet. I mean that her work is full of what we look for in splendid poems, freshness of imagery and metaphor, clearly perceived objects, and so forth. Yet her poems remain slight. She told me in her letter that she was concerned to expunge from her poetry the last vestige of abstraction, and by abstraction she meant ideas. She wanted no thoughts in her poems at all, just things. She wanted her poems to be as concrete as apples or pears. Archibald MacLeish said it too—remember? "A poem should not mean but be." Well, thirty years ago, or whenever MacLeish wrote that line, I'm sure his statement was a necessary antidote to the moralizing tendencies of much previous verse; but I'm equally sure that MacLeish himself would have agreed to call his statement an antidote, something contrived partially and exaggeratedly, even dangerously, in order to effect a cure. The truth is that if a poem is to live it must both mean and be. The further truth is that it can't be one without the other, since thought and experience are symbiotically connected. As for abstraction, if we grant that a work of art is made of parts and that these parts must move—that is, that a work of art cannot be static, which is the beginning of any esthetic system—then we must agree that these parts are in dynamic relationship to one another. And since all relationships are abstractions, one's poem is grounded in abstraction whether one likes it or not. A poem *is* an idea.

From his base in antiintellectualism Shapiro continues, in the succeeding essays of his book, to an attack on virtually all modern poetry and criticism, and especially on the Pound-Eliot-Yeats triumvirate, which he holds responsible for the present literary predicament. He says many absurd things, as when he implies that Eliot consciously conspired to seize literary power by means of dishonest criticism, and he makes some outright misstatements, as when he says that Pound could not have found a publisher for *Mauberley* without Eliot's help. But the main point is that in his attack, based on certain claims of justice, Shapiro sweeps away, very unjustly, poems and ideas that all of us, including Shapiro, must agree are valuable. In his analysis of poems by Yeats and Eliot, for instance, he himself uses techniques of close reading that developed in modern criticism after the publication of Richards's *Principles of Literary Criticism*; shall we throw out those very useful techniques? Shapiro himself could not get along without them. Shall we throw out the good poems, however few or many, that have been written by Yeats, Pound, Eliot, H.D., Stevens, Cummings, Williams, Tate, Auden, and so on, and so on, the chief figures of the twentieth-century revolution in poetry, simply because these poets have also been guilty of excesses? For that matter has any lively period of literature ever avoided excess? This is the heart of the problem, I think. What Shapiro really deplores is the excess, not the base from which it springs. But he fails to make this clear in his book.

I have said that the book is both necessary and dangerous. It is necessary because somebody had to say that the school of Eliot has, roughly speaking, become our orthodoxy, an informal academy entrenched in our teaching and publishing apparatus. Much recent verse is dry, God knows, and anyone who has circulated among our academic establishments is aware that many of the people who produce it are dry people. Honest, dull verse-grinders, they turn out their stanzas formulaicly and sustain their places of power and prestige by just these means. The dryness comes from the orthodoxy— that much seems inescapable—and Shapiro has said this very well. But his book is dangerous too because on the basis of this truth it appeals to the ignorant on behalf of a destructive, narrow program. By the ignorant I don't mean those who have done poorly in school; that doesn't have much to do with poetry. I mean those who through laziness or impatience have not examined the workings of human consciousness; which is to say, the young. These are the ones who will fail to understand that what we need is not poetry circumscribed by a stipulated kind of experience and a determined kind of response, nor poetry written according to anyone's prescriptions, but poetry reconstituted on the permanent foundations. Let us reassert an old principle. As far as art is concerned—and probably as far as life is concerned—the only and always valid thought will be that which arises from and refers to genuine felt experience, whatever that experience may be. No remove from experience, no dilution of it, will do. If once this is pounded into the heads of our young people, I guarantee the production of dry verse will fall off sharply. And perhaps at the same time we will be able to take, at last, a dispassionate view of the poetry and criticism of our own so recently bygone era.

The Phenotype

A review of *Primal Vision: Selected Writings of Gottfried Benn*, edited by E. B. Ashton, from the *Carleton Miscellany*, Autumn 1960.

PAYOLA AND CONFLICT OF INTEREST being what they are these days, I had better admit right at the beginning that I was hired to perform minor editorial services in connection with the manuscript of *Primal Vision*. Aside from other considerations, loyalty to my sometime employer might lead me to hope for the book's success. Anyone who wishes for this reason to discount what I have to say is invited to do so. The fact is, however, that I am in no way whatever responsible for the contents of the book, and am besides such a poor student of German that I cannot judge the details of the translations. But I saw the manuscript with Mr. Ashton's corrections entered by hand, and from this I conceived the greatest respect for his judgment and editorial skill; his selection from Benn's poems, essays, and longer pieces is just and illuminating, his supervision of the work of the translators has been touched, I think, with genius, and the translations he has done himself are remarkably good representations of Benn's style, both verse and prose, as nearly as I can tell it. Benn's style is by no means an easy one to reproduce. Benn himself, perhaps a little proudly, noted its "acuity." It is a tough style, clipped, witty, also fluid, very professional; at the same time ornate, metaphorical, crammed with exotic reference. The closest thing we have to it is the poetry of Wallace Stevens, but so many other matters set the two writers apart that we can't speak of an actual resemblance. Here is a page from Benn's *Novel of the Phenotype*:

A world of contradictions—but, after all, the world has seen a lot: the coronation of boy-favorites, divine honors paid to a white horse, a mausoleum built to the memory of a goblet, a beautiful tree tricked out with jewelry—and now this dismemberment! However, our situation is not favorable. All one hears about life, about the mind, about art, from Plato to Leonardo to Nietzsche, is not crystal-clear, contains dodges—are we not publicly discussing non-objectiveness? Yes, indeed, we doubt the very substance that has given rise to these words, we doubt its experiences and forms of happiness, we doubt its method of presenting itself, we doubt its images. We have scarcely more than a few paces ahead of us on earth and little of what is earthly; everything is a tight fit now, everything must be very carefully weighed, we gaze pensively at the veined chalices of big flowers into which the butterflies of night sink in their rapture. Our realm is never larger than a page, no wider than a painted hat with a feather in it, or a fugue—and beyond is billowing chaos. It is March, there is a touch of the insalubrious about this park; even in this plain, in this depression, the irises look tense, open too suddenly, yesterday mere buds, they burst out in a sort of self-defloration, in a blue leaping towards the light, young and hard like sword-blades—and beside them more weapons: bell-buds, catkins swollen to bursting-point, certain and smooth-formed right to their purple or bee-brown rim—weapons of a hostile power, a superior force shattering all resistance—Nature herself. Faced with this, one has to summon up all one's strength.

Gottfried Benn was born in 1886 and died in 1956. He was a physician who spent much of his professional life in the medical corps of the German army. In his own country his reputation as a writer, in degree and in quality, somewhat resembled Eliot's or Valéry's in theirs. I don't mean that he was fully as prominent as either, though before his death he was certainly regarded as the grand figure of the modern literary revolution in Germany, dean of the expressionists. The reasons for his neglect so far in the United States—before *Primal Vision* translations had appeared here in only two or three out-of-the-way magazines, and American critics had paid him virtually no attention—are twofold: first, much of his best poetry is untranslatable; second, his association with the Nazi movement in Germany alienated him from readers on the Allied side.

I am going to skip over the question of Benn's Nazism, but not because it is in any sense unimportant. On the contrary it is close to the whole problem of Benn's place in modern art and thought. But it is also an exceedingly complex question which cannot be discussed properly in a review. Let it suffice to say simply that Benn was not a party member, that he was in the party's favor for only a few months at the beginning of the Nazi regime, that he and his works were suppressed for years as he was shunted among minor military posts, that it is very difficult to tell from his published expressions to what extent he committed himself personally to the particulars of the party dogma, but that, on the other hand, he did definitely acquiesce in and publicly support the party program in 1933. And of course he never went into exile or made a clear denunciation of the party, as did a number of other prominent German writers later on in the 1930s. Benn's early support of the party program seems to have been less a function of any political rationale than of a profound nihilism, his "doubt [of] the very substance that gives rise to these words," and this then becomes the crux of the matter.

When I sat down to reread *Primal Vision* before writing this review, I had just finished reading *Also Sprach Zarathustra* in the translation by Walter Kaufmann. The bearing of the one upon the other would have been obvious even if for Benn the prime example of the culture hero were not Nietzsche, whose final dementia is brought forward in nearly every work as the exemplary specimen of modern despair. (According to Dr. Kaufmann it was merely paresis.) Benn is the echo that rings—a little distantly—through the collapsed ruin of Nietzsche. The philosopher's antitheistic braggadocio becomes in the poet a defiantly morose refusal to believe in anything. With all metaphysics shot to pieces, nothing objectifiable remained, the universe evaporated, mentality was reduced to the refuge of expression. "Singing," Benn wrote,

—that means forming sentences, finding expressions, being an artist, doing cold, solitary work, turning to no one, apostrophizing no congregation, but before every abyss simply testing the echoing quality of the rock-faces, their resonances, their tone, their coloratura effects. This was a decisive finale. After all: artistics! It could no longer be concealed from the public that here was a deep degeneration of substance. On the other hand, this lent great weight to the new art: what was here undertaken in artistic terms was the transference of things into a new reality proved by the laws of proportion, to be experienced as the expression of a new spiritual way of coming to terms with existence, exciting in the creative tension of its pursuit of a style derived from awareness of inner destiny. Art as a means of producing reality: this was the productive principle of the new art.

Frankly I have to exert myself forcibly to remember that there was a time when such statements seemed fresh and clear and exciting, clean blades with which to strike down the pussyfoots and sanctimonious punks. Now I am more likely to be filled with nausea. On the one hand, a "deep degeneration of substance"; on the other, Ethiopia, Spain, the gas chambers, the torture rooms. Suffering went on in spite of the "new reality." Went on and on, in fact, terror and rapine and destruction in onslaughts as unending as newsprint—until the very last one of us, beyond all play-acting and romanticizing, recognizes his own truly damaged soul. What is left but to be sensible? We begin to confess at last that we have gone backward, not forward; into the old reality, not the new; backward to an existential origin in the lowliest domain of experienced fact—substance itself. Poetry's misfortune is that it has not gone with us.

For what has happened to the art itself, aside from everything else? The force that was for a moment the great liberator of poetry, the formal revolution, became in two decades, three at the most, merely the atomizer, the etherealizer, and poetry evaporated in a mist of unimportance. Even the novel has been emptied, and stands now, if it stands at all, like the hollow trunk of a once green tree. Benn's "world of expression," in which he tried so brilliantly to live, is in plain terms the cult of form after all. We have seen it in action elsewhere, under prettier and perhaps less accurate names—Eliot's classicism, Pound's professionalism, Jolas's revolution of the word, and so on. Even Dr. Williams and the objectivists, by reacting violently in the opposite— or is it the same?—direction and trying to disinfect poetry of ideas, that is, to dehumanize it, have arrived at somewhat the same predicament. In short I am impressed by the way in which Benn seems to embody the logical extension of our whole movement from Baudelaire through the symbolistes to the great post-Nietzschean figures: into the conflagration which Nietzsche kindled from the splinters of Western thought the artist cast too the last fragments of his human semblance, and though it made a brilliant and many-formed blaze for a while—the blaze of style—in the end the artist emerged with his art burned out and with his profound distrust of meaning turned into the ultimate failure of life—nihilism.

Benn is the epitome, the paragon; he is the type of the innovative artist *entre deux guerres*, the symbolical-cubistical-expressionistical-modernical flower brought to its finest blush. For this reason every writer in America should read his book (not to speak of the pleasure of encountering a great stylist). But what I want to show above all is how this book, *Primal Vision*, exists and of course must exist in time, thus defeating itself: the old reality, the "abyss" of experience, has kept opening itself out while the testament of form has receded in its brittle splendor. We are beyond Benn now, and perhaps we must go behind him too, seeking the origins afresh; and incidentally we must decide quite soon whether or not Benn is a classic, to say nothing of the other grand figures. Perhaps it is a small kind of revolution I am suggesting, very modest, quiet, shy, a little businesslike, without manifestoes—the revolution of experience; for this is the only means by which poetry may be revitalized now. Substance is all—at least for us, at least for the time being. And to whom shall I address myself? Not to the young; they are too dazzled by Benn's achievement, that brilliant architecture of denial and despair. Instead I speak to the middle-aged poets of my own generation, those who have got fifteen or twenty years of word-wrestling under their belts. What fitter champion in the revolution of experience? And the crucial question we must ask ourselves, fellow revolutionaries, is this: just how much of our own reality, our adult experience of the world, unconfined by the stereotypes of another era, have we actually put down on paper?

What Shall We Do, What Shall We Think, What Shall We Say?

A review of *Selected Poems*, by Conrad Aiken, from *Poetry*, February 1962.

Permit me to offer homage to the ghost of Conrad Aiken. Is it an unkindness to address the ghost while the man himself still lives? I think so; yet the unkindness is not my doing. The poet has died, and has become a ghost, and the manner in which I learned of the event I shall now describe, pausing only to say my personal greeting to Mr. Aiken: live long and prosperously.

A few months ago I reviewed Aiken's new book of criticism. I said that it was a good enough book of its kind, but not particularly important, and this is still my opinion. In the course of the review, however, I also said that Aiken is one of the two or three purest and most accomplished poets alive; and shortly afterward a young woman, herself a good poet, took occasion to reprove me for my "sentimental generosity." "How could you praise that old windbag?" she said, or words to that effect. And then a day or two later she gave me a book of her own poems, and when I read them, as I did with pleasure, there in almost every line was the ghost of Conrad Aiken. I picked up three or four magazines lying close to hand, and when I looked at the poems in them, there too was Aiken's ghost. And when I went back to my desk and looked at my own scribbly worksheet lying where I had left it, the ghost of Aiken winked at me unmistakably. By now I was smiling, perhaps a bit craftily, and lines from "Gerontion," *The*

Waste Land, "The Rock" came into my head: the ghost again. Lines from Tate, Warren, Eberhart, Roethke, Lowell—the ghost spoke in them. "Life is an old casino in the park"—Stevens wrote that, one of my favorite lines; and does the ghost speak there too? I don't know, I can't tell; the ghost is, like all proper ghosts, indefinite of outline. But there and there and there; everywhere, in all of us, so deeply ingrained that we have forgotten it, the very breath on which we launch our words.

> *What shall we do—what shall we think—what shall we say—?*
> *Why, as the crocus does, on a March morning,*
> *With just such shape and brightness; such fragility;*
> *Such white and gold, and out of just such earth.*
> *Or as the cloud does on the northeast wind—*
> *Fluent and formless; or as the tree that withers.*
> *What are we made of, strumpet, but of these?*
> *Nothing. We are the sum of all these accidents—*
> *Compounded all our days of idiot trifles,—*
> *The this, the that, the other, and the next;*
> *What x or y said, or old uncle thought;*
> *Whether it rained or not, and at what hour;*
> *Whether the pudding had two eggs or three,*
> *And those we loved were ladies. . . . Were they ladies?*
> *And did they read the proper books, and simper*
> *With proper persons, at the proper teas?*
> *O Christ and God and all deciduous things—*
> *Let us void out this nonsense and be healed.*

> *There is no doubt that we shall do, as always,*
> *Just what the crocus does. There is no doubt*
> *Your Helen of Troy is all that she has seen,—*
> *All filth, all beauty, all honor and deceit.*
> *The spider's web will hang in her bright mind,—*
> *The dead fly die there doubly; and the rat*
> *Find sewers to his liking. She will walk*
> *In such a world as this alone could give—*
> *This of the moment, this mad world of mirrors*
> *And of corrosive memory. She will know*
> *The lecheries of the cockroach and the worm,*
> *The chemistry of the sunset, the foul seeds*

Laid by the intellect in the simple heart . . .
And knowing all these things, she will be she.

She will be also the sunrise on the grassblade—
But pay no heed to that. She will be also
The infinite tenderness of the voice of morning—
But pay no heed to that. She will be also
The grain of elmwood, and the ply of water,
Whirlings in sand and smoke, wind in the ferns,
The fixed bright eyes of dolls. . . . And this is all.

People who are older than I and who had an opportunity to read Aiken's poems as they first were published have paid homage to him—the living poet—already. The dust jacket of *Selected Poems* contains excerpts from comments by Dudley Fitts, R. P. Blackmur, and Allen Tate. But I am the first, as far as I know, to pay homage to Aiken's ghost; and the necessity is forced on me by the almost complete neglect and even discredit into which his poetry has fallen among those who were born after 1920. At some point these younger readers have encountered Aiken's faults, frequently, I think, at second hand. Yes, he is very long-winded sometimes, and sometimes too soft or easy in maneuvering his habitual attitudes and images. The poems occasionally go runny, like a sunbaked city lot after a brief rain. After all, the curse of facility hangs over every poet who possesses Aiken's natural eloquence; neither Stevens, Williams, nor Cummings has avoided it. But can these flaws cover over the great virtues of the lines I have quoted from the *Preludes*?

I am paying homage to Aiken's ghost not because I wish to be solicitous about the past and not primarily because I wish to help in resurrecting Aiken's poetry, though either of these would be reason enough, but rather because I believe in a simple but fundamental principle of poetry. Good verse cannot be written by anyone who does not love words. With love comes intimacy, and with intimacy comes the lover's tough tenderness which will permit no distortion, no uncleanness, no obesity. Disorderly syntax and the fattening metaphor—these are prohibited. Something more than this love, of course, must go into the good poem, but without this love there is no beginning. And precisely this love is what has gone from the main line of development in American poetry today. Whatever the cause, whatever the process, it has gone. This is why the rebel poets, who give themselves so many different identifications but who assemble generally in one group, have broken with the main line. They sense this desuetude of the needful affection, they seek to revive it, and a number of them, including especially Denise Levertov and Robert Creeley, are writing the least awkward good verse we have today. I happen to think that these rebel poets are injuring their work in its aspects of substance, and thus preventing it from growing as strong as it might, by their too-literal reliance on Dr. Williams's proscription of ideas in poetry; because ideas, the organic intellectual product tilled from perception and bred up in imagination and feeling to ever higher forms, are in all good poetry—yes, even in the poetry of Williams himself. But notice the suppleness, strength, flow, assuredness, and lack of pretension in Aiken's lines. Not a single trick, not one affectation; yet there is no loss of power or distinctness. This is the purity I had in mind when I wrote my earlier review; it is the product of a stupendous natural talent. And am I wrong in finding the ghost of Aiken's poetry almost everywhere? I should need pages and pages to investigate the qualities of diction, rhythm, syntax, color, and characteristic imagery that compose this style. But this is not necessary; anyone will recognize this personality animating thousands and thousands of poems written during the past forty years. In fact it is no longer a personality, no longer a style, as these terms are ordinarily used; it is the innate poetic attitude of an era. It may appear in language that is sweet or wry, ironic or solemn, but the basic impulse is undeniable. Those who wish to verify it at first hand may find an adequate representation of Aiken's work in these *Selected Poems*, but I think the *Collected Poems*, which was published five or six years ago and contains many short poems omitted from the new book, is a better buy.

Bear in mind that Aiken's first book was published in 1914, his second in 1916. Among the elders only Pound and Frost preceded him. These early books contained imitative work, since in casting about for an idiom of his own Aiken turned to many sources, even to Masters, even to Masefield, incurring the displeasure of the critics on this account. But in looking back we see that the closest imitations were still well and lovingly written. In most of them Aiken's individuality is discernible, and very quickly this reached a point of maturity at which the imitative process was reversed: others adopted Aiken's stronger line. Today the early welter of crisscrossing influences cannot be disentangled, and probably never will be, at least not completely—even in the case of Aiken and Eliot as students, which has already attracted much attention. But I am interested in the general rather than the particular influence. What credit Aiken will be given in the long run for his performance as a poet of the twentieth century I do not know and do not care to guess. I think his best work is very good, and that is as much as one reviewer can venture. But I hope that, even if his own work turns out to be minor, he will always be well remembered for the way in which his influence—less than Eliot's in matters of taste, less than Pound's in matters of artistic conscience, probably less than Wallace Stevens's or Marianne Moore's in matters of the procedural imagination—has nevertheless exceeded all of these in determining, almost while no one was aware of it, the look and sound of the poetry written in our age.

The Closest Permissible Approximation

A review of *Waterlily Fire: Poems 1935–1962*, by Muriel Rukeyser, from *Poetry*, February 1963.

THESE ARE THE OPENING STANZAS of an early poem by Miss Rukeyser:

> *The drowning young man lifted his face from the river*
> *to me, exhausted from calling for help and weeping;*
> *"My love!" I said; but he kissed me once for ever*
> *and returned to his privacy and secret keeping.*

> *His close face dripped with the attractive water,*
> *I stared in his eyes and saw there penalty,*
> *for the city moved in its struggle, loud about us,*
> *and the salt air blew down; but he would face the sea.*

And one of her recent poems begins:

> *Great Alexander sailing was from his true course turned*
> *By a young wind from a cloud in Asia moving*

Like a most recognizable most silvery woman;
Tall Alexander to the island came.
The small breeze blew behind his turning head.
He walked from the foam of ripples into this scene.

Force, directness, affection for the separate word and the various parts of speech (especially participles), knowledge of cadence and syntax as components of meaning rather than vicissitudes of fabrication—there can be no doubt that Miss Rukeyser can write good poetry. Painters speak of the "painterly" qualities of certain work, meaning the way in which the medium itself becomes important to the esthetic experience, the paint on the canvas an embodiment of thought and feeling (as opposed to the schools which regard the medium as ideally a transparency). There is an analogous quality in Miss Rukeyser's poems. We are always aware of their language, of the way she has worked it into shapes and movements that are basically idiosyncratic. Often this is extremely effective. Sometimes, on the other hand, it leads to the kind of excess that we call mannerism, as in the long passages where she writes without verbs:

Eyes on the road at night, sides of a road like rhyme;
the floor of the illumined shadow sea
and shallows with their assembling flash and show
of sight, root, holdfast, eyes of the brittle stars.
And your eyes in the shadowy red room,
scent of the forest entering, various time
calling and the light of wood along the ceiling
and over us birds calling and their circuit eyes.
And in our bodies the eyes of the dead and the living
giving us gifts at hand, the glitter of all their eyes.

One can see how this might happen; a search for immediacy, a hunger for language genuinely experienced—it was what impelled the imagists. But Miss Rukeyser's characteristic poem is rather long, complex, full of allusion and other intellectual and cultural machinery. I miss the motion-making words that would lend quickness. Instead the effect resembles an impasto, colors heaped on one another until the surface is thick and lightless.

But Miss Rukeyser's best poems are very good indeed, and aside from their virtues of language they possess many virtues of substance. I admire especially the breadth of her response. Personal anxiety and desire are powerfully represented in her work, but so are the exterior aspects of experience, and not just in lyrical or ironic meditations on nature. Her world is essentially urban, her poems occur in a context that is implicitly—sometimes explicitly—technological and political. She seems to know something about architecture and machinery and what happens at political caucuses, the whole texture of actuality right now, and she is very successful in giving us a sense of the combined attraction and repulsion all of us feel in such an environment. It is refreshing. But more than that it is evidence of artistic responsibility, which in itself is meaningful, adding to the emotive power of a work's objective particulars.

Analogous to this is another aspect of her work that is somewhat more difficult to speak about. I mean her vigorous, brave, and I think nearly absolute honesty; this being—honesty—the nearest permissible approximation, in most of our lives, to an absolute of faith. Let us agree on what seems obvious to me: that a large part of lyric poetry is essentially prayer. Where does this leave the poet who cannot acknowledge a supernatural existence? You may go backward and forward through the anthologies of modern poetry and find this problem, a terrible problem, on almost every page. Ninety per cent of the poets are too lazy to deal with it, using such terms as "Lord" and "my God" with the implied reservation that they are fictions. Or they impute a fake divinity to great men, mountains, dead rodents, and such. But suppose you are absolutely honest; suppose, in the straits of reason and experience, you must deny the supernatural but assert the ultranatural, those extreme susceptivities of consciousness which govern our spiritual and moral lives; and suppose you even raise ultranatural experience to a superpersonal level, the racial or the pan-human; do you then agree to call it by the name of God, do you stand up in church and say the Credo with your fingers crossed (as was lately recommended by that noted British "humanist," Basil Willey)? Miss Rukeyser does not. This is the quality of her honesty. She recognizes that there is a point at which symbolism as a poetic technique turns into a substantial instrument of mendacity. I don't say she is an objectivist; far from it. She is no doctrinairian of any kind. And I don't say she has solved the problem. Consider it solely as a tactic of vocabulary: what terms shall the poet invent which can assume the richness and versatility of terms refined in centuries of religious usage?

Remember that even the most determined anti-Christians from de Sade to Sartre have argued in basically Christian terms, because there are no other. It would be mere obstinacy to ask Miss Rukeyser, or any single poet, to do a job which requires a sustained community of genius. Yet I know no other body of work in which the problem has been met more squarely than in hers; nor, generally speaking, any poetry which has brought more imagination and lyrical firmness to the task. Make no mistake, these poems are deeply felt—prayers, I should say, quite desperate prayers for the things that the poet needs but cannot command in the political-technological nightmare of the modern state: peace and justice. For this reason her poems are intrinsically, connately a part of our ethical crisis, which begins to show at least some signs of turning into a genuine social crisis, and as such they ought to win the prior respect and endorsement of us all, especially since the substantial honesty of the poems is inseparable from their superiority as works of art.

William Carlos Williams as One of Us

From the *New Republic*, April 13, 1963.

THE DEATH OF WILLIAM CARLOS WILLIAMS on March 4 was expected and even longed for—in the pitiable way of human beings when they are touched and concerned—by those who knew him. He had been ill for a long, long time. We can be grateful on his account and our own that even during the last tortured years he was able to write some of the time. The work of his final decade contains some of his most beautiful writing, as full of life as ever. And that—his undeviating fidelity to life and all it implies—was the key to everything he wrote, everything he did. It gave him, one fervently hopes, the satisfaction he deserved. Certainly it will continue to satisfy us and those who come after us, if there are any, as we turn to it again and again in his poems.

In paying tribute to Williams I should like to quote a poem of his which has never appeared in any of his books. It was found last summer by Mrs. Williams when she was rummaging among family papers; somehow it had got mislaid. It is called "Child and Vegetables" and was published in the magazine *This Quarter* (vol. 2, no. 4, dated April–May–June 1930); probably it had been written about a year earlier. Here it is.

The fire of the seed is in her pose
upon the clipped lawn, alone

before the old white house
framed in by great elms planted there

symmetrically. Exactly in the center
of this gently sloping scene,

behind her table of squash and green
corn in a pile, facing the road

she sits with feet one by the other
straight and closely pressed

and knees held close, her hands
decorously folded in her lap. Precise

and mild before the vegetables,
the mouth poised in an even smile

of invitation—to come and buy,
the eyes alone appear—half wakened.

These are the lines of a flower-bud's
tight petals, thoughtfully

designed, the vegetables, offerings
in a rite. Mutely the smooth globes

of the squash, the cornucopias
of the corn, fresh green, so still

so aptly made, the whole so full
of peace and symmetry . . .

resting contours of eagerness
and unrest—

No doubt the most famous pronouncement Dr. Williams ever uttered is the one recurrent in his poems, especially *Paterson*, to the effect that there are "no ideas but in things." And no doubt it is also the least understood by his disciples and admirers (who today are many), even though Williams took trouble to amplify his meaning. When they set aside everything in *Paterson* beyond the statement that there are "no ideas but in things," when they say that the statement is literally true, when they claim it as a sanction for their antiintellectual attitudes, and finally when they use it as a warrant for attempting to write poems without ideas, poems which (in their terms) will have the "purity" of "self-existent objects," then they are doing Williams, themselves, and all poetry a grave disservice.

On the face of it the statement is literally not true. Williams, who was a physician as well as a poet and by all accounts a good one, did not believe it to be literally true; without sophistry, he couldn't do so. Take an idea of the order of "a stitch in time saves nine." It is simplistic, coated with layers of sanctimony and unction. Nevertheless it can be stripped of its offensive qualities and revealed at the center as a true idea, what is called a "self-evident" idea. But it is not self-evident because it occurs objectively, in print or in speech; on the contrary, no objects combined in nature could ever express it; it did not exist until a mind made it, and it could not exist now if there were no mind to recover it.

For a long time people have been trying to invent a truth of art which could supersede the truth of objective reality. At some indeterminate point in the history of culture it was seen that the work of art is a dynamic structure, and that like all dynamic structures it possesses a certain self-existent quality, or what we call autonomy. Then about a hundred years ago the concept was seized upon as a means of turning art into an antireality which would have its own laws and its own existence, and which would be more interesting, beautiful, and durable than the objective world. At first the effort issued merely in art-for-art's-sake dilettantism, soon discredited. But through the refinements of the symbolists, expressionists, futurists, surrealists, neo-metaphysicals, etc., the notion gained wide currency among artists and intellectuals, and even among certain branches of philosophy. In essence it holds that language, through the "revolution of the word," has constituted itself a new reality with its own self-revealing authority, different from and fundamentally opposed to the old-fashioned reality, whatever that may have been. At the same time, however, the poem, being a structure of language, possesses its own solely objective being and validity.

Meanwhile other people, including some artists and intellectuals, were being consumed in furnaces, intoxicated in gas chambers, afflicted by rapists and torturers, disinfected by brainwashers—all of reality's old merry pranks.

Clearly neither things nor ideas (nor poems, of course) have the kind of irrelative self-completeness which the autonomists desire, and such self-completeness is only the dream-product of a deeply divisive mania. The truth is that things and ideas and poems are realities among many realities, conformable to the general laws, not opposable in any useful sense. But reality (whatever it is) is intractable, and usually ugly and boring as well, with the result that some people will always try to escape it by one means or another. You can't blame the poets more than the rest. Beyond this, reality consists of Right and Wrong; and since Wrong is by nature always immanent if not ascendant, Right is continually tempted into sanctimony and unction (to say nothing of bigotry), and the effort to resist these temptations is difficult and tedious—another reason for escaping. It is all a misfortune, the whole business, so great a misfortune that people lately have taken to calling it an absurdity. God knows it is absurd. But putting a name on it cannot extricate man from reality, or relieve him, as long as he is alive, from the necessity of thinking about it, of having ideas about it.

What did Williams say? "When a man makes a poem, makes it, mind you, he takes words as he finds them interrelated about him and composes them—without distortion which would mar their exact significance—into an intense expression of his perceptions and ardors that they may constitute a revelation in the speech that he uses." I was tempted to cut this statement or reorder it, to make it more readable. I didn't. Here it is in all its ambiguity and vague inclusiveness. Williams's fine instinct for style nearly always deserted him when he came face-to-face with an ultimate question of principle, especially if it entailed his own feelings about writing. Here his emphasis on words, speech, expression, and so on seems to put him squarely in the antirealist camp, alongside Valéry and Gottfried Benn—the European stylists whom he otherwise deplored. But we know from his whole work that Williams devoted himself, perhaps more sincerely than any other modern poet, to life as it is lived, to reality. He was drawn two ways at once. It is a deep ambivalence, I feel, and it runs through all his writing.

He speaks also of a revelation, without saying what is revealed, though elsewhere he seems to imply that it is beauty in the Keatsian sense. Is it equal to truth, to morality? One can't possibly tell, because like other poetic radicals of his generation Williams distrusted these terms and seldom used them except in disparagement. Nor can we learn much from observing that Williams connected revelation to perceptions and ardors, two imprecise terms which are interesting chiefly because they denote the subjectivity of poetic materials. But if we go back to the verb in Williams's statement—*composes*—I think we can get at the active part of his view of poetry, and we can see how it works by looking once more at the rediscovered "Child and Vegetables."

It isn't a great poem, but it is good enough and quite characteristic. Here are a number of objects—a child, a house, trees, a table, some vegetables, a road. With the great skill which was always his, Williams presented them in all their immediacy and self-proclaiming presence. Very good. But did these objects occur this way in reality? The answer is no. Can things collected in objectivity possess symmetry or any other mode of arrangement? Again no. The arrangement was made by the poet. If you like, it was *seen* by the poet; to me the distinction is academic. The point is that another poet might have seen these objects quite differently: haphazardly or even brutally.

The arrangement, the composition, the disposition: it is everything and it is an idea. It is an idea in the mind, not in things. And can anyone doubt that it is also an idea which entails an act of judgment, *an act of morality*? Even if the whole force and tone of the poem did not assure this, Williams himself made it explicit by his use of such loaded words as *peace* and *symmetry*. This is as close as he ever came to sanctimony, but it is close enough; the poem might be better if these words were removed (though it is interesting to see that *symmetrically* in the fifth line appears without distortion, to use Williams's own term, and hence is properly poetic). The poem is an idea, it is a specifically moral idea, and it lives because this is so.

On a far broader scale and in a far more complex condition of control, *Paterson* also is a moral idea. In its substance it is, like all fine poems, a life-affirming idea. It is a defense of what is right without sanctimony. It is an acknowledgment of reality, and a confrontation as well, with no feelings spared. It is, incidentally, an explicit avowal that the poet's mind in all its faculties is an indigenous component of reality; that is what is ultimately meant, I believe, by "no ideas but in things." Finally it is not an escape into any kind of antireality, stylistic or other, but an assertion of human dignity; that is to say, an assertion of the efficacy of ideas (especially the procedural ideas of love and justice) in the face of whatever is brought to bear against us.

Certainly it is time now to say these things loudly and lovingly. William Carlos Williams was one of us, committed to our life, our reality, our enigma. He was a man of courage who required neither escape nor mystification. His poems will be our bulwark, I think, long after the antirealists have followed their inadequate doctrines into the history books.

Poets without Prophecy

From *The Nation*, April 27, 1963.

BEGINNING WITH WHOM?—not Eliot—with Arnold perhaps?—well, beginning rather a long time ago the meaning of the words *poem* and *poet* shifted finally from a matter of substance to a matter of technique. Today we can find vestiges of that older way of speaking. In the country where I live people still say, when you tell them a lie, "Oh, that's poetry," and I suppose somewhere people may still exclaim, "How poetic!" upon seeing a sunset. We do not say these things. We consider them offensive. For us a poem is a work of art, a composition of verbal materials, a thing, and the poet is the maker who makes it.

I don't want to suggest that we are wrong; certainly I don't want to excuse the sentimentality and unctuousness which were the end products of the old view. But I would like to point out that these end products were a long time in coming—centuries, in fact—and that there distinctly was something grand and ennobling in the idea that a poet was to be known not by his art but by his vision; something more than grand and ennobling, something essential. And we have lost it.

I don't know what to call it precisely. It's hard to move back into that area of old custom without falling prey to the soft, foolish terms it spawned so readily toward its close. But let's extend to one another the charity of understanding and agree on an acknowledged orotundity: "the larger vision of humanity." Once the poet was our spokesman and not our oracle, our advocate and not our secret agent, or at least he was as much the one as the other; and if he did not speak for us, all of us, fully and warmly, if his poems lacked the larger vision of humanity, we said he was deficient in one of the qualities that, virtually by definition, make a poet.

This attitude survived among the older poets of our time, though their own theories about poetry tended to suppress it; the larger vision of humanity was still a part of their poetic instinct. The *Cantos*, *The Waste Land*, and *Paterson* are alive with it; Frost's poems reveal an unmistakably general feeling; so do the poems of Cummings, Aiken, Ransom; Stevens veiled his concern under his marvelous verbal textures and his epistemological preoccupations, but it was there, especially in the later poems where a sense of brooding pity underlies almost every word. Even Marianne Moore, whose writing has never appealed to me, conveys a kind of coy consciousness of sodality in her least timid poems. The point is that all these poets came into the world at a time when the poet's direct responsibility to mankind at large still hadn't quite been laughed out of existence. They themselves were the ones who set off the final burst of laughter when, in order to discredit the impressionistic views of the previous age, they directed attention away from the representative role of the poet and toward his work as experimentalist, hierophant, artifex, oneirocritic, or what have you.

It should be clear that my topic is poetry and politics, though I have chosen to work my way into it by means of concepts which show political feeling as what it really is, rather than as mere partisanship.

Next came the thirties, the time when poetry was avowedly political, the time of Archibald MacLeish, Muriel Rukeyser, Alfred Hayes, and the British socialists, the time equally of the Southern Agrarians. I myself find this poetry refreshing to read today, especially the radical poetry; its motives and objectives were so forceful that often a kind of vividness was the result, against which our own verse, striving for greater richness, seems only muddy. I wonder if we aren't ready for a revival of interest in proletarian writing, similar to the Jazz Age revival which occurred a few years back. Serious attention is being given again to John Steinbeck, thanks to his Nobel Prize, and that is to the good. Others also deserve reconsideration. I nominate Malcolm Cowley and Kenneth Fearing. Nowadays they are scarcely thought of as poets, yet they each wrote a few first-rate poems.

At the same time one cannot avoid seeing that the larger vision of humanity became more specialized in the poetry of the thirties, narrowed and reduced, and that this constriction grew even tighter in our poetry of the war. We had some fine war poems, things like Eberhart's "Fury of Aerial Bombardment" and Jarrell's "Death of a Ball Turret Gunner"; they have become standard anthology pieces. Yet if we compare them with the poems of the First World War we see a great difference. In the poems of Wilfred Owen, for instance, or even in such a highly wrought work as David Jones's *In Parenthesis*, the larger vision is instinct in every word and very profoundly expressed in some; but Jarrell's gunner, whose remains are washed out of his turret with a hose, is a far more specialized figure. He does not live in our minds as a fully realizable exponent of our own suffering. The figures created by Bill Mauldin and Ernie Pyle, though shallow, come closer to this and closer to the Tommies of Owen's poetry. This isn't Jarrell's fault. He is a fine poet, and the reason for his narrowed sensibility (which I don't think he desired at all) lies in the cultural evolution of the century. There had been an attrition of poetic consciousness. Far too complicated a matter to be easily explained; yet I think we can all see the difference between Owen and Jarrell, and I think most of us can concede that it is connected with the increasing refinement of the poet as a self-appointed agent of sensibility in an insensible and ever more hostile society.

Since then this erosion of the larger view has reached a point at which poetry has become almost totally apolitical. The supreme political fact of our lives is the atomic bomb. Am I wrong? It is enormous; it occupies the whole world. It is not only what it is but also the concentrated symbol of all hatred and injustice in every social and economic sphere. Speaking for myself, I have lived in fear of it for fifteen years, fear that it will go off, one way or another, and kill me and my family, or render our lives so intolerable that we won't wish to go on. Maybe I am more timorous than most people; I believe there are actually some

Americans who never think about the bomb. But poets? That would be incredible. No matter how hard they try they cannot escape being included among society's most percipient members. Yet if one were to judge by their output one would have to believe that poets are the least concerned people in the world, not only on their own account but on everyone's.

Poetry, under the editorship of Henry Rago, is as representative of the various groups among American poets as any single magazine could probably be. I have just gone through all the issues for 1961, the only recent year for which I could find a complete set on my shelves. The year produced 335 poems by 139 poets, and although I skimmed through them rapidly, it has still taken me several hours to make up a count; I didn't go so quickly that my figures are likely to be off by more than a little. In the whole year I found two explicit references to the bomb, one a passing seriocomic remark, and ten poems on the general theme of suffering in war, two of which were translations from foreign poets of an earlier time. There were a great many poems on sex in its various aspects, religion, growing old, being young, thought and feeling, the uses of knowledge, themes unintelligible to me, and painting, music, and poetry.

That's it, of course, that last—poetry. The only topic poets will admit. Time after time they say so. Robert Creeley, one of the best alive, asserts his allegiance to "the poem supreme, addressed to / emptiness. . . ." At the other end of the country, Howard Nemerov, a good academic poet, speaks of himself as

> *Dreaming preposterous mergers and divisions*
> *Of vowels like water, consonants like rock*
> *(While everyone kept discussing values*
> *And the need for values), for words that would*
> *Enter the silence and be there as a light.*

Could anything be plainer? And I believe you could find statements of this precise credo—belief in the poem as an isolated act of absolutely and solely intrinsic goodness—in 90 per cent of the books published by American poets in the past ten or fifteen years. There are a couple in my own.

Not spokesmen then. But hermits, lone wolves, acolytes—building poems in the wilderness for their own salvation.

The poets will retort in two ways. First they will say that art has always been lonely work, that the artist must use his own experience, and that ultimately he must put together his vision of reality—or, as some would say, discover it—within himself. This is self-evident; but it does not require the poet to withdraw himself so far from the general experience of his time that he becomes merely a specialist pursuing specialized ends. In fact it ought to mean just the opposite: that the poet, within himself, identifies and augments the general experience in such a way that it will excite a renewed susceptibility in everyone else.

Second, the poets will say that their isolated poems are acts of an implied political significance. They will say that in evil times the individual person exerts a force for good by carrying on his private endeavor with exemplary honesty. They will say that by refining their own purity as artists and by rejecting the false values of the world they are expressing a political attitude of considerable importance and firmness, and are doing so in terms more durable than could be used in direct statements about immediate political objectives. In the past I have said this myself, and I do not think it is sophistry. But it comes close to it. Politics is practicality, and a political act is by nature an act committed in the context of immediate objectives. And isn't the "context of immediate objectives" simply a jargonistic equivalent of the "larger vision of humanity"? This context still exists, I grant you, in the very remote background of today's estranged poetry. But when the correlation between the output of *Poetry* magazine and the leading headlines of, for example, the *New York Times* is as disparate as my little tabulation for 1961 indicates, then the context has receded so far that it no longer furnishes a useful field of reference to most of the people who read the poetry.

This is the point. The larger vision has been turned over to the newspapers, to the so-called industry of so-called mass communications. I imagine there's not a single reporter covering the discussions at Geneva for whom the larger vision isn't so fully, consistently present that he must drink himself or weep himself to sleep every night. But poetry is not his job; and if he is a good reporter he knows this and steers clear of it.

The Beats are the exception to what I have been saying. At least so they seem at first, though I wonder if they aren't simply the other side of the coin. I mean the hard core of poets who still flourish their

Beat credentials. Among them we find explicitly political poems in great numbers, poems designed to incite impeachments, riots, revolutions, etc. To my mind they fail. The best of these poets is Gregory Corso, an exceedingly talented poet who has written perhaps two dozen really good poems; and that is enough to make anyone envious. But all these good poems are nonpolitical, most are apolitical, and the best are not particularly Beat. His most popular poem is a diatribe called "The Bomb," but for me it seems only a long composition made up partly of rant and shapeless anger and partly of attempts to exorcise the bomb in the name of some numinous human essence; it turns politics into a sort of gang war supervised by the old ladies from the settlement house. In short it contains no poetry, no imagined transmutation of experience, no single realized image to which our thought and feeling can cling. In this respect, that is, the reintroduction of poetry to politics, it seems to me that the Beats, whom we all hoped (some of us secretly) would succeed, have failed almost completely, and what success they have had has been on the wrong level.

Poets are never liberals or conservatives, they are always radicals or reactionaries; and today, of course, public life rejects these indecorous extremes. True, the far right has worked up something resembling a movement in recent years, but it remains intellectually disreputable. On the left, in spite of sporadic efforts in New York and California, those of us who are born anarchists have to agree there isn't much doing. In other words the political attitudes usually endorsed by poets are now amorphous, disintegrated, anachronistic, without programs. Yet this ought to be exactly the political condition in which poets can flourish and in which politically directed poems—and I mean *poems* in the completest sense—can be written without becoming debased by doctrinaire points of view. I cannot speak for reaction; but it is hard for me to believe that any radical poet in the country today lacks a point on which he can stand firm, a point from which, as the spokesman of us all, he can attack known injustices and stupidities. Isn't the bomb, our monstrous, inescapable, political absurdity, the place to begin? And why then isn't it happening?

Théophile Gautier, while discussing his fellow writers, said: "To be of one's own time—nothing seems easier and nothing is more difficult. One can go straight through one's age without seeing it, and this is what has happened to many eminent minds."

Yes, of our time too. We poets have gone straight through fifteen years without seeing them. One can think of a hundred reasons: the extraordinary burden of the poetry of our immediate past, the long evolution of formal preoccupations, the sociology of the culture hero; but none of these, or even all together, can suffice against the bomb, none can explain 2 poems out of 335. I think American poetry, to speak of only that element of our civilization, is stupefied by a massive neurosis—terror, suppression, spasmodic hysteria—and I cannot conceive of a therapy ingenious enough to cure it.

Two Notes on Experiment

From *Genesis West*, no. 3, Spring 1963.

THESE BRIEF NOTES on the nature and limitations of literary experiment originated in my thoughts about the problem of differentiating poetry and prose, which I imagine is a quaint enough problem now. Twenty years ago, when I was a student at one of our rustic universities, we used to worry our heads a good deal about this; it was the tail end of the controversy over free verse that had begun during the literary revolution of the early years of the century, and for this reason (to say nothing of our utter ignorance) we discussed it in our own terms and never thought of going to others—Aristotle, say, or Mill or Croce—for help. In the cultural isolation which was permissible and even sought after in the 1930s at second-rate provincial universities, we found ourselves, thirty years after the event, still impressed by the technical radicalism of Pound and Sandburg and Amy Lowell; and poetry's confusing expropriation of prose techniques raised in our minds the question of how to distinguish between the two; in other words, how to define each kind of writing in rationally objective terms. Now the old argument has died away and probably students no longer concern themselves about it. They are willing to let the distinction between prose and poetry rest on subjective judgment in each particular case. Nevertheless I think the old problem will be worth reviving for the way in which it may illuminate the present situation in American literature, especially American poetry. In the course of reviving it I shall need to revive also some of the commonplace ideas that have been associated with it, though I do not remember seeing them arranged before in precisely this order or for precisely this end.

Clearly the distinction between poetry and prose cannot be drawn in terms of the kinds of subject matter suitable to either. Even if anyone until now had thought that this might be the case, today we can see immediately behind us the evidence of a half century of writing during which both prose and poetry have burst all former bounds of suitability or propriety and have taken on the whole spectrum of human experience. But just as clearly the distinction cannot be drawn in terms of exterior forms either. This is what the people who debated the question of free verse years ago were trying to accomplish—the ones, that is, who clung to the old notions of necessary gratuitous forms—but the more they specified particular rules of form the more the poets and prosewriters refused to comply. Our half century of modern writing contains hundreds of specimens of undoubted poetry which break all the "rules" and against which no doctrine of gratuitous form can stand up, and the prose has been equally insuppressible. Even Yvor Winters, our most respected and probably most insistent advocate of traditional forms, has argued for them, not as embodiments of extrinsic gratuitous value, but as implements of a morality that must be generated within the poem itself. In view of this what shall we conclude? If neither "content" nor "form" offers a basis for an objective discrimination between poetry and prose, what is left?

Often in the old days the argument would come to an end with someone saying that both form and content are determined, not by the imposition of exterior, eternal, and more or less ideal models, but through the emergence of prior and internal esthetic motives; and something like this seems after all to be the answer. These motives function, I think, rather like a final cause, if a final cause can be conceived, in esthetic terms, as arising within the particular expressive complex, the work of art. In any event there are two such motives, and they are recognizable as two principles, easily stated: the principle of repetition and the principle of variety. For me these concepts come back out of the past trailing clouds of earnest ignorance. Nevertheless they are the clearest insight we have, even now, in this area of muddle. In the hands of the writer the former principle gives rise to poetry, the latter gives rise to prose. The principles work more obscurely in the realm of content than in the realm of form, but they are evident in both. Thus in poetry the rules of prosody, traditional or modern, are really abstractions derived from the functional values of repetition, working within the expressive complex and embodied in the prescriptive formulas of rhyme, alliteration, meter, cadence, stanza-form, line-structure, and so forth; while the content of poetry—the structured substance of meaning and feeling—is organized in similar patterns of repetition, namely refrains, recurrent or analogous images, connotative echoes, structures of "mood," "tone," "texture," and the like, which take shape in response to the inner esthetic motive. Prose, on the other hand, evolves in a constant irregularity of rhythm, a disparity of verbal effects, and a more or less consecutive, linear, nonrepetitive structure.

Thus all literature organizes itself in a polarization, and for this triteness we probably ought to be grateful. One pole stands for poetry-repetition, the other for prose-variety. For clarity's sake I call poetry and prose the *types* of literature. Left alone, each type will tend toward its own polar center. Thus at the lowest level of poetry, for example, we have the children's taunt—*nyah-nyah, nyah-nyah*—in which both poetic form and content have been reduced to an inflexibility of repetition, and at the lowest level of prose, similarly, we encounter every day (God knows) abundant effusions of bureaucratese from our most eminent public men, who reduce prosaic variety to the utterly drab and maladroit. This does not mean that in either type writers of genius may not create works of great distinction close to the polar centers. We have Shakespeare's songs in poetry, for example, and the pages of *The Golden Bough* in prose. But our bipolar arrangement does mean, I believe, that whenever either type, taken as a whole and under its public aegis, deviates from its polar center and strays laxly toward the opposite center, then that type is violating its own esthetic motives and is in danger of radical deterioration.

At this point the probability arises that my own motives will be mistaken. I am not saying that literary experiment is impossible or unfeasible or in any way undesirable, provided it is genuine experiment. To say any of these things in the face of recent literary history would be to play the fool or the philistine, and naturally I hope to avoid either imputation. On the contrary, I believe that genuine literary experiment is a reaching out from one pole toward the other, but a reaching in which the experimentalist keeps his work firmly attached to its own pole, so that the reaching becomes a stretching or tension between the basic polar type and the aspiration toward its opposite. This is just what unskillful poets and prosewriters, the bogus and academic experimentalists, are unable to do. Their experiments consist simply in becoming detached from their own polar centers—slipping the collar, so to speak—and meandering away without tension and more or less without purpose, in the vague direction of the other pole. Along with the genuine experiments of the past fifty years we have had a great deal of this kind of flaccid counterfeiting. Even the great experimentalists haven't always avoided it, Ezra Pound in the middle *Cantos* being a case in point.

The sharpest retort to this analysis will probably come from the devotees of "poetic prose," who will go straight to their source and say, "What about the Bible?" My reply is twofold. First, the translators of the English Bible customarily put long passages of Hebrew verse into prose, though retaining much of the syntax and cadence of verse; these passages are in fact poetry, albeit not written according to European ideas of quantitative measure, and they should be restored to their proper form. Second, large parts of the rest of the Bible are not as well written as we have been taught to suppose. They are atrociously written; but they have acquired a spurious esthetic valuation by osmosis, as it were, from their spiritual valuation as scripture, and from this misconception has flowed an extraordinary amount of bad rhetoric over the centuries. The best prosaic parts of the English Bible, for example, Genesis, the narratives, the proverbs, conform pretty well to my analytical scheme. However, the Bible is a difficult case because in its modern forms it is an amalgamation of many literary developments, in which later styles have been superimposed on earlier ones. In the evolution of the verbal arts prose seems to come after poetry, as can be shown in the scriptures of many "primitive" societies, and the whole question becomes impossibly muddled.

For our purposes a clearer example is the prose of the English neoclassical writers. Under the influence of critical precepts derived from the analysis of poetry, these writers invented a highly artificial prose *mode* (which I differentiate from personal *style*), and this mode incorporated certain repetitive devices, namely a pronounced syntactical parallelism accompanied by a kind of thumping regularity of cadence.

This is bad prose. Admirers of Dr. Johnson will say that my view is subjective, and up to a point they will be right; that is to say, the subjective element is inevitably prior in any esthetic judgment, although this does not rule out the discovery of objective criteria later on, which is just what I am attempting here. (Even on subjective grounds I suspect that most readers who take the trouble to compare the prose of Johnson with that of Hobbes before him or of Hazlitt after will agree with me.) Johnson broke contact with the prose center, except in his very best writing (the Shakespeare prefaces and some of the lives of the poets), and instead of achieving a tension between prosaic variety and the desired poetic rigor, he gave up all tension whatever in his language and ended in a drone (as in most of the *Rambler* pieces on manners and morals), occasionally enlivened by verbal extravagances of various kinds. Admirers of his prose, I feel, are attracted, so far as its attractions are a matter of language at all, by its poetic qualities, and they would be better satisfied if they gave up the prose altogether and read only the verse. From the standpoint of good prose Johnson's conversation, as recorded by a young man who cared less than his elders for critical dogma, makes better reading by far than *Rasselas*.

Is it possible to see a significant contribution to the modern prose mode in the works of American humorists of the nineteenth century? Perhaps they had something to do with the dissociation of wit from the artificial prose techniques of the Enlightenment, and perhaps through Crane, Dreiser, and others of their generation this sanative dissociation found its way into serious letters, both in America and in England. Nothing less than a vaudeville humor that relied on misspellings and bad puns could have managed the break, while at the same time preserving the values of professionalism and genuine feeling, values generally forfeited by the Victorian dilettantes of England. This break cleared the way for Twain, and thereafter for the best comic writers, as well as many of the best serious writers, of our own century. To what extent Henry James and his school are conformable to this historical scheme is not clear, although I feel that purely verbal analysis might reveal more likeness between James and Twain than has commonly been supposed to exist. Today one thinks of James Thurber, who acknowledged his indebtedness to both. He was our funniest writer. At the same time he was the person who remarked more than once that the trouble with most prosewriters today is their inability to write a simple declarative sentence.

We have now a good many writers who have not learned Thurber's lesson, especially among the schools of "poetic prose" in its various aspects. Thomas Wolfe and his followers were preeminent until a few years ago, and now we have the young Californians. All these writers are seldom good and usually bad; but universally bad, I should say, when they move, as they often do, into incantatory rhetoric, detached from the prose center. One notices that whatever other faults Faulkner's writing may have, this is not one of them, even though much of his work has been done in an elaborately experimental manner. At its most involved point, just where it seems about to founder in complexity, it renews and reinvigorates itself by a return to the prose center; by a return, in other words, to the principle of dissonant variety in diction and syntax; just as Milton's epic returns always, no matter how it may strain away from the poetic center toward a richness of variegation, to the necessary metrical root. I may seem to be saying only that a good writer always pricks his own balloon, but it is more than that: it is regularity-variety, assonance-dissonance, symmetry-asymmetry, and its examples in art, being the great ones of their kinds, are precisely those which give us the fullest sense of nature. These are the examples which most of the young Californians, among others, have failed to study. I don't say experimental writing is easy— obviously the contrary is true—but its principles are not difficult to understand. The Californian rhapsodists pay no attention to the need for establishing themselves first at the modal center, before they strike out. They offer their unattached writing as specimens of a new avant-garde; but the truth is that although they clearly have something to write about, in contrast to most academic writers, they are doomed to failure because they do not understand the modus operandi of experimentalism.

So much by way of statement and illustration. My main points follow, five conclusions (of which two are recapitulations) and a corollary remark.

1. Poetry and prose, the types of literature, each tend toward their own typical centers. Moreover this tendency transcends mode and determines, though in less obvious ways, topical organization, topical attitudes, and probably also topical substance, this last being, however, a function of custom rather than necessity.

2. Genuine experiment extends out from its own center—from which, however, it does not become detached—toward its opposite center. This extension may be straight or devious, but since all litera-

ture comprises one bipolarity, experiment probably cannot take any ultimate direction except toward the opposite pole, though I grant that some experiments, for example, those of the lettrists and other essentially antiverbal writers, have sometimes appeared to be striving for totally new directions.

3. Because a genuine experiment pulls away from its own center, it can add nothing to the central line of formal and technical development of its own type. On the contrary, a successful experiment is inevitably individualistic; it shuts off its own avenue from further creative work, leaving the way behind it open solely to imitators. Of course a successful experiment may suggest other possible avenues of experiment, but its own is forever closed off. Joyce, who seemed in his lifetime such a liberating phenomenon, tolled the death knell for his own experimental technique, as we see from the hundreds of failures who followed in his wake; whereas Ford Madox Ford or Scott Fitzgerald or E. M. Forster or James T. Farrell, all writers close to the prose center, have left succeeding writers free to go forward. Granted, this is an extreme statement, made for the purpose of analytical clarity. Actually a major experimental exertion, individual or collective, leaves a residue which accrues to the main development, thereby effecting gradual changes in grammar, meaning, and public attitudes toward language and style. *Some* of the experimental techniques of E. E. Cummings have been taken into the mainstream of American poetry. But the principle that a successful experiment puts an end to the immediate creative use of its particular technical innovation, and does so the more as it reaches farther out from its own polar center, is both obvious and important; at least so it seems to me.

4. At present every experimental avenue is shut off. The recent age of experiment, extending roughly from 1910 to 1945, is finished. Anyone who doubts this may dispel his uncertainty forever by reading the poetry written in the United States during the 1950s. It has not been experimental. Many have said that it is simply dull. Be that as it may, the fact is that most good young poets have not attempted to experiment, and this includes not only the academics but those operating in the general Williams-H.D.-Zukofsky-Rexroth orientation as well, while those who have tried to experiment have been unable to produce anything actually experimental; that is, they have been unable to think of anything actually new. My reading in recent prose has been less than in verse, but I will risk saying that I know of no young

prosewriter who is a genuine experimentalist, unless it is John Hawkes, and his *style*, which I like very much, can be considered only a quite minor experiment if it is an experiment at all. A new age of experiment will come someday. But it will come only as the concomitant of new conditions of thought and experience, something radically different from any course of social or cultural evolution we can imagine now. For this reason the new age of experiment will not come soon, even leaving out of account the question of present political insanity. From the cultural viewpoint alone, the recent period of literary revolution was so thorough, so complete, pursuing the experimental be-all-and-end-all in every direction to the brink of formal disintegration, that the new age of experiment cannot come until after a long period of recovery and assimilation. The possible avenues of experiment have all been shut off. This means that writers, or at least poets, who have begun to work since 1945 must necessarily be either centrists or imitators.

5. Since there is no point in being an imitator, today the intelligent poet will devote his energies to exploring the means of the formal center. He will seek to make his work new by extending its substantial range, in both topic and attitude.

Corollary Remark. Even though this analysis is, in truth, discouraging for the young poet of ambition—discouraging because he knows that with few exceptions (Bach, Yeats) the artists and epochs in whose works we find the qualities of supreme greatness have been characterized by experimentalism and have derived at least part of their creative force from the energies released in the coming to birth of new techniques; discouraging also because he looks upon these men and these epochs as the most exciting events of the past, whose function in art furnished a truly brilliant, socially efficacious use of talent and experience; discouraging especially because he knows that our own epoch, from Baudelaire to the present, is rooted more than any other in artistic individualism—even though all these things are true and must serve to dampen the transcending ambition required of any young poet if he is to make a start, nevertheless the young person of talent today can look forward to real accomplishment in poetry, provided he understands the nature and limitations of his task. His task is to use the means of the modal center in fashioning a newly accurate image of man in his own time. Here two points must be made. First, there is nothing to prevent the artist who works at the modal center from creating a personal style; Yeats and Bach did it, Van Gogh turned a worn-out idiom into something very much his own, and many others have done as well. The centrist need not—must not—be an academician. Using the term in its personal sense, we have always said that style is the man, the man revealed in particular expressive combinations of artistic material, in this case words. Such combinations, operating within a poem, do not require any kind of determinative form, certainly not a unique or unusual form. Second, every variety and quality of subject matter is accessible to the center at any time, provided the young centrist will divest the central mode of the stereotypes of experience and attitude that have become attached to it in its transmission from the elders. Thus the centrist, who by definition is not an imitator, possesses the two attributes that an imitator cannot possess: a personal style and a genuine subject. Using the central mode, the young poet ought to be able to think and feel in any terms he likes, and to deal with any experience he has encountered. As a matter of fact the poets of the 1950s failed to touch large aspects of that decade's experience; the image of ourselves that they gave us was worn out, something inherited from another generation. It was a case of nostalgia, perhaps excusable on psychological grounds but certainly not on literary grounds: the academicians gave us 1919, the Beats 1936. In other words the poets failed to see that the evolution of the center proceeds by means of a continual sloughing off of the previous generation's vision of existence and by a continual renewal of feeling in the perception of immediate, authentic, original experience. Hence the old definition of style may be enlarged: style, through the mediation of man, is experience. So long as this is true and so long as poets recognize it, there need be no deterioration of the central mode.

FROM WHAT HAS BEEN SAID above about the bipolar organization of literary types and the nature of literary experiment, one additional observation seems unavoidable: the supreme experiment is yet to be accomplished. I mean the invention of a mode securely fixed to both modal centers and ranging in flexible tension between the two. Is it possible? In theory I don't see why not. But in practice there may be psychological and cultural blocks that are insuperable. At all events no experiment so far has succeeded in incorporating true bipolarity in a single work. Our own experimentalists of the recent era failed to come as close to it as their predecessors who translated the Bible. (I am aware that devotees of *Finnegans Wake* may dispute this, but the point isn't essential.) This supreme experiment cannot be made now because the impulse is past and we must await the next heave, to use Pound's term. Naturally such a bipolar mode will be beyond the lyric. It will require a long form, narrative or dramatic; and this leads me to wonder if some such conception doesn't offer the best explanation of the old question of what Shakespeare was doing when he wrote his plays in both prose and verse. Certainly what we were taught in school about some styles being appropriate to particular social estates, however plausible it is historically, fails to satisfy people who know anything about the poet's creative processes. Shakespeare was moving toward a point at which the two modes would combine in one, without any clear line of distinction between them, but with both extremes still fixed at their polar centers. He did not go the whole way, probably because in the context of Tudor theatrical sensibility it wasn't necessary or because the idea didn't occur to him. Eliot, in his recent verse dramas, seems to be attempting something of the same sort; at least he has permitted his verse to relax toward prose. I use the word "relax" purposely, because I think this is just the wrong way to go about it. The necessary tension has gone out of Eliot's work, and his recent style is probably a good example of experimental writing that has become detached from its center. (This is not the whole reason, or even the most important reason, for the failure of Eliot's plays since *Murder in the Cathedral*; his notion of domesticating verse drama in the naturalistic theater prevents him from using his great talent for poetic expression, and in such circumstances it would be remarkable if he wrote anything really first-rate.) Kenneth Rexroth, in his chamber dramas on Greek themes, has done a good deal better, but has worked for a very limited effect. Most poets write stage verse in the same manner as they write a sonnet, and thus do not even begin to approach the problem.

As I say, we must wait for the new age of experiment before this final (if it is final) experimental heave can be attempted. And perhaps waiting is not such a great adversity. Once the experiment is done, to the great glory of the one who does it, it will be done forever.

A Kind of Revolt

A review of *A Precocious Autobiography*, by Yevgeny Yevtushenko, from *The Nation*, September 21, 1963.

THERE ISN'T MUCH REAL AUTOBIOGRAPHY in this book. Evidently the work was begun as an introduction to translations of Yevtushenko's poems. It was an attempt to tell Western readers about the circumstances in which the poems were written, or at least this was the pretext for a piece of writing which is in essence neither autobiographical nor literary but polemical. But the poet found he needed more space than an introduction would allow. What he has ended up with is an essay which, though still rather short, constitutes a full defense of himself and at the same time a plea for his country. Are the two compatible? At any rate Yevtushenko tries to make them appear so, while stitching his arguments to the main events of his own life, yet never in a spirit of self-proclamation. In fact he seems in this essay to be an altogether more modest and less flamboyant figure than we have been led to think by the publicity given him in the past two or three years.

Thus I suspect, though solely on the basis of internal evidence, that the English title of his book, or at least its implication, was not Yevtushenko's responsibility. And beyond that I am 90 per cent convinced his essay is not only modest but naive. If, as I believe, the best, most penetrating, most extensive definition of revolt in our time has been given by Camus, then Yevtushenko, like other Marxist writers, is tediously old-fashioned. He unashamedly uses such terms as "ideology," the "heroic struggle for the future," the "religion of the revolution." He again and again affirms his devotion to the concepts, not of 1919, but of 1921. His enemies—Stalin and the Stalinist bureaucracy—are castigated only for their suppression of those ideals; that is, for their falling away from Leninism. Lenin himself and all that he did remain absolutely unquestioned, while Marx and Engels stand dimly and patriarchally in the background. Trotsky is still referred to in orthodox terms as an "opportunist." As for Kropotkin or the Kronstadt soviet, they are not referred to at all.

In other words Yevtushenko makes a case for himself as an unquestioning party man who simply wants a return to the austerity, purity, and fervor of the olden days. In 1963 he still sees nothing of the catastrophe lurking in the heart of the Russian revolution; so he says at any rate. "A Communist," he writes, "is a man who puts the people's interests above his own, but who, at the same time, would never wantonly squander human lives in the name of those interests." For me, the inference is inescapable that the squandering of human lives is perfectly OK as long as it isn't wanton.

I do not believe for a moment that if Yevtushenko somehow found himself in authority he would carry on in the manner of Stalin, perhaps not even in the manner of Lenin. Yet there is nothing, fundamentally, in his autobiography to rule this out. Should we have expected more of his essay, some kind of genuine radical enlightenment? I suppose not. Yevtushenko is a poet, not a political scientist. Moreover, he was born in a society which, like all modern societies, has imposed a high degree of intellectual conditioning on its citizens, and his higher education, according to his own account, was sketchy. Finally he has his neck to look out for. But one can't help being depressed by the renewed evidence of failure to understand. History repeats itself—what could be more dismal? The new Russian revolutionary is like the old, and I guess like too many from still farther places and times as well, always acclaiming the chaste past, exalting the triumphant future, suffering the present like a wound.

But even though Yevtushenko's essay seems a very pat specimen of that familiar kind of Marxist literature in which one praises one's own revolutionary piety while condemning everyone else's, it still is a far more charming, even more eloquent, piece than most. And interesting and important too, one can't deny that in the present context of world affairs. Yevtushenko has been the most conspicuous of the Russian anti-Stalinist writers who have come to our attention in recent years. Ultimately his reputation will rest on his poems, whose real qualities are very difficult for us to judge in translation. For the present, however, his largest audience will probably be for his autobiography, at least in Western Europe and America. It is the bitterest anti-Stalinist polemic out of the USSR that we have so far been permitted to see, and we find it, like everything about Russian politics, fascinating.

Finally there is my 10 per cent doubt. Is Yevtushenko actually as naive as he appears to be? Is there a chance that this essay is a calculated exercise in hidden meaning, in which the author has buried an outright, sophisticated condemnation beneath his simpleminded, "constructive" criticism? I suppose the chance is even less than one in ten; it would be terrifyingly risky. But consider this: the term *dialectical materialism* is used only once and then is coupled scornfully with the grossest kind of anti-Semitism; on the other hand the words *spirit* and *spiritual* appear often, and there are a number of covert Biblical references. There is just enough of this to make the book a puzzle, something for historians of the present to play with. Sometimes Yevtushenko's control almost slips; he veers into unequivocal condemnation, only to cover his steps immediately with a new avowal of revolutionary zeal or an anti-Western platitude.

We are told that in recent months, because of this book as well as his other writing and speaking, Yevtushenko has been in hot water at home. One can only, with a whole heart, wish him good luck.

Sartre on Genet

A review of *Our Lady of the Flowers*, by Jean Genet; and *Saint Genet: Actor and Martyr*, by Jean-Paul Sartre; from the *Chicago Daily News*, October 5, 1963.

THE PUBLICATION IN ENGLISH of Jean Genet's first novel, *Our Lady of the Flowers*, raises once more the question of the literature of damnation and its relationship to literature as a whole and to society.

Genet was born in 1910, an "illegitimate" child, and was raised by foster parents who were, we are told, well-intentioned people; but as so often the experiment did not work: Genet became a thief, a homosexual, and one of the most anguished men to have lived in our anguished time. Until he was somewhat more than thirty years old he lived a large part of his life in European jails, from the Netherlands to Yugoslavia, and the rest of it in concealment, privation, and ignominy. In spite of this the withdrawal into psychosis which would have been normal in the circumstances did not occur. Genet's intelligence and creative sensibility remained operative, and the measure of their power can be taken exactly from the depth of the abyss in which they rose and flourished. Decidedly, this is no case of dandyism—which we always have to suspect in the French—no flirtation with debasement. Genet's life began in the depths and in a very real sense has remained there ever since.

He wrote his first novel in a prison cell, writing on the brown paper from which he was supposed, as part of his punishment, to manufacture paper bags. One day a jailer discovered what he was doing, took the manuscript, and burned it. Genet began again. The result, *Notre-dame des fleurs*, was eventually published in a small edition by a small publisher. Nevertheless it was quickly recognized as a work of importance, imbued not only with astonishing esthetic acumen but with great psychological and moral urgency as well. Its author was a man writing to save his life, and to find his soul.

Later Genet wrote other novels and a number of plays, and his reputation grew quickly. It was advanced momentously in 1952 when the world's greatest living philosopher (in terms at least of plain mental ability and energy) published a huge book about him. Nothing like it had ever happened before. Sartre's *Saint Genet* is enormous, magnificent, exhaustive, and exhausting; brilliant on page after page after page, leaving the reader stunned. Yet Sartre's objective was only partly an appreciation of Genet. He turns Genet into a type, a problem, and an example, in short an exercise in his own method of psychophilosophy, the "existentialist psychoanalysis" which he expounded at some length in *Being and Nothingness* (and which has begun to make an impact in America through the work of such writer-practitioners as Rollo May). Although Sartre seems to me closer to Freud than he pretends to be, it is true he throws out much of the psychiatric apparatus of complexes, neuroses, libidinal conflict, and so forth, and instead transfixes the individual as a thinking, moral being. This is refreshing. In the practitioner's office I should think it might be more than that, genuinely humanizing. On the page, however, owing to Sartre's dialectical method it has just the opposite effect, and Sartre's Genet is as puppetlike as the hero of any case history, so that we must turn back to the novel to find Genet, the human being, again.

Sartre's method begins in simplicity itself with the basic opposition of the Self and the Other, which puts him more directly than sometimes appears in the line of French ego-philosophy, descending from Descartes. But this basic opposition quickly opens into a spiraling, or helical, series of dualities: being-becoming, essence-act, eternity-time, nature-freedom, beauty-happiness, form-content, and so on. Sartre projects us through these avenues of opposites in a sequence of reverberating analytical detonations, and though each new projection seems like a single lucid clap, the reverberations become so complex and so overlaid with literary flourishes that we soon find ourselves resorting to serious note-taking in order to keep track of the argument. Always Genet, in Sartre's reconstruction, is rebounding away from experience, from life, from his own inner life, in a series of recoils that is the essence of alienation; not a fixed, graspable alienation, but instead a dynamic alienation leading ever further out or further down, from damnation to martyrdom to sainthood, the saintliness of the totally other. We follow him with a mingling of horror and admiration that I do not recall from any other book I have ever read.

Sartre's book, in its 625 pages, is unquestionably the most thorough literary, sociological, psychological, philosophical, and theological documentation of a living author ever attempted. Perhaps its magnitude may be suggested by saying that neither Dante nor Shakespeare has been the object of such a penetrating single study (which may strike some readers as an absurdity in itself). The point is that *Saint Genet* is a book which transcends its subject, or rather engulfs it, transforms it, elevates it. Aside from the question of Genet himself, *Saint Genet* is a monument of understanding dedicated to the soul of twentieth-century Europe, the criminal-esthetic-religious temperament *in extremis*; and no one henceforth should ever make the mistake of thinking that these three elements of the alienated mind—the criminal, the esthetic, the religious—are not one.

Saint Genet should be read by every lawyer, judge, penologist, psychiatrist, teacher, and social worker in the country, as well as by all who are seriously interested in literature and philosophy.

But what shall we say in the end about Genet himself? *Our Lady of the Flowers* is a book about criminality and sexual inversion which turns all morality—not merely bourgeois morality or Christian morality, but all morality—absolutely upside down. It is a novel written in the spirit of finality. At the same time it is a work of literary invention, and its quality as art is inseparable from its moral (immoral) absolutism. It is a novel felt, conceived, and consummated in the extremity of sensibility. I think it may be a great novel. At all events it is a work of undoubted integrity which will occupy a significant place in the intellectual and ethical life of modern man for a long time to come. Nothing in it is meretricious, connivant, or factitiously provocative— the qualities we have come to recognize as constituent to our definition of pornography.

Having said this, should one say that *Our Lady of the Flowers* is a good book for everyone to read? It would be like saying that tuberculosis, simply because a few people have made a good thing of it, would be a good disease for everyone to catch. In plain fact only a few readers will be able to take Genet's book at all, and even fewer will benefit from it. This is in the nature of things. I see no reason to quibble about it, but it does raise an interesting question.

Almost certainly Genet was striving, in his early works at least, to contribute quite consciously to underground literature. In our country we are accustomed to think that this in itself is somehow reprehensible; but we are wrong. Given creative honesty and seriousness, any writer may aspire for an underground, really underground, audience without the least ignobility; quite the contrary. The ignobility belongs to those who misuse his work, meaning the posturers. We have plenty of those. And it is just possible that the publishers and editors who in our time have striven so courageously and energetically to bring underground literature before the general public, including preeminently the publisher of *Our Lady of the Flowers*, have played into the hands of the posturers and done the authors of this literature an ultimate disservice. In the case of Genet, quite obviously the light of his life above ground, which must seem blinding, makes him extremely uncomfortable, as Sartre is at pains to demonstrate.

In short there is a case, a strong one, for esoterica of all kinds. But the first premise of that case is the self-evident proposition that an esoteric work is changed in its modality and its essence when it is removed to an exoteric status.

Multiple Disguises

A review of *Love Declared: Essays on the Myths of Love*, by Denis de Rougemont, from the *Hudson Review*, Autumn 1963.

THE WORK of Denis de Rougemont, taken as a whole, seems to me obsessed, conventional, disorderly, and unprofitable. Such was my opinion formerly, and since this new book adds nothing exceptional to what de Rougemont has said before, such my opinion remains. I state it in these somewhat vehement terms because I find I more and more resent authors who believe that they may serve the modern world by offering it exercises in analytical simplification. Many of these authors are extremely clever; de Rougemont of course is much more: a finely gifted, beautifully learned man. But to me our culture is so obviously not simple and so obviously never was simple that anyone who suggests he can explain it to me in one book arouses my indignation. By now a great many people have made exactly this suggestion, and my tolerance is about gone. I am perfectly willing to grant my animosity: the work of de Rougemont is an intellectual fraud, and it makes not one whit of difference that it is also a pious fraud.

Is there any other way to describe a piece of cultural analysis which is so driven by enthusiasm for its schematic concepts that it denies not only history but what everyone knows to be true from the experience of daily living?

Love in the Western World, the book in which de Rougemont first attempted a full-scale account of his ideas, was published in France in 1939 and has enjoyed a considerable vogue ever since. I imagine the main points of it are known to most readers, but a summary will be useful. Human experience, according to de Rougemont, is ruled by two types of love: first, agape or Christian love, which is a love between equal persons and which is typified in a marriage undertaken for purposes of procreation; second, eros or passion, which is a love between unequal persons, which shuns marriage and thrives on separation, which is ultimately not love of a person at all but love of Love, and which ideally ends in the death of the lovers. The two arise from fundamental religious sources. Agape is a development in human

terms of the Christian theories of Incarnation and the absolute quali-
tative separation of God and man; these ideas, in spite of the doctrine
of sin, permit holiness on earth and happy love in life. Eros, on the
other hand, springs from the oriental and specifically Manichaean belief in a totally divisive conflict between evil and good, in which evil is
identified with the world and the body, and good with heaven and
the spirit. Eros entered the main current of Western civilization, still
according to de Rougemont, with the Catharist heresy of the twelfth
century, and its primordial Western literary expression was in the
songs of the troubadours. De Rougemont suggests that most Provençal love poetry was disguised devotional poetry of the Catharist
church, in which the lady of the poet's song was a stereotyped representation of the Lady, Maria Sophia, Eternal Wisdom, the Light of
Heaven, to whom the poet vowed allegiance, for whom he swore
himself (hypocritically or not) to chastity, and with whom he hoped
presently to unite himself in death. The whole apparatus of *cortezia*,
the laws, the courts, the rituals, the prescripts for *vray amor*, was no
more nor less than a consciously disguised analogue of the Catharist
rites—so de Rougemont suggests, although he tempers his historical
radicalism by saying that he is more interested in the cultural intent of
his analysis than in the determinable history of ideas. After the Al-
bigensian Crusade, the Catharist heresy was fragmented and driven
even further underground, and its literary counterpart, now beginning to lose its conscious ground in religion, moved to the north and
became linked with Celtic literature. The result was the Arthurian cycle, and the epitome of this cycle was the legend of Tristan and Iseult,
in which de Rougemont finds all the necessary ingredients of the
erotic myth par excellence: the love of Tristan and Iseult is an adul-
terous relationship of unequals, it thrives on separation (to such an
extent that the lovers invent needless obstacles whenever external cir-
cumstance fails to provide them), and it ends in the blissful death of
the lovers. From this point on, de Rougemont traces the Tristanian
myth as it becomes further and further dissociated from its religious
source, through Faust, Don Juan, the romantic upsurgence, and into
our own time, when in an almost wholly profaned but very widespread form it has issued in the cult of the movies, the commercializa-
tion of sexual imagery, and especially the breakdown of marriage; its
political corollary is the totalitarian passion. This summary greatly
truncates de Rougemont's schematism, and in particular his analysis

of the Tristan legends, which in itself is a marvelous, though unoriginal, study in critical exegesis.

The new book, *Love Declared*, adds nothing essential, though it refines and extends some of the concepts. The principal change is the elevation of Don Juan to a mythical status equal and opposed to that of Tristan within the erotic hierarchy. Thus Western culture is now seen to vibrate between serious, sacramental Tristanism and comic, impious Juanism, depending upon its periodic *rapprochements* with the religious sensibility; all this, of course, still being subordinate to the broader antinomy of eros and agape.

A thoroughgoing critique of de Rougemont's theory of love would be valuable except for one consideration: we have had our fill of critique. What we need now is affirmation. And this is my first comment on de Rougemont: he writes from the point of view of a committed Catholic, he praises agape and blames the world's ills on eros, and yet almost his entire work is devoted to a critical discussion of eros. He returns to the articles of his disapproval again and again, obsessively, and without adding anything new. His hope lies, apparently, in some unrealized synthesis of eros and agape, but he is exceedingly vague on this point, and his discussion of agape consists solely of statements that it derives from the Christian commandments to love God and love thy neighbor and that it is good. Yet the problem of married love is far more important and probably far more difficult than the historical analysis of heresy, as some Catholic philosophers are beginning to recognize. Certainly in the modern world the complex "institution" of marriage can no longer be reduced to the prescriptive formulas of the historical Church.

Second, like any good Catholic de Rougemont anathematizes the Manichaean dualism, and yet his thought is formed in the same mold. It is interesting to note that in the revised edition of *Love in the Western World*, which was published in 1956, de Rougemont introduced a number of terms from existentialist philosophy as well as the word *existentialism* itself, applying them to his own position. I don't mean to suggest that this was conscious trimming; de Rougemont acknowledged his debt to Kierkegaard, for instance, from the first. Yet there does seem to have been some attempt to shift the philosophical tone of the argument. In spite of it, and in spite of the essay in the new book devoted to a definition of the person, de Rougemont remains as far from the existentialist attitude as anyone could be. His work is built on dualisms—eros-agape, Tristan-Don Juan—and more-over he insists that Tristan and Don Juan are not persons but forces. (Compare the humane Juan of Montherlant or the absurd Juan of Camus with de Rougemont's eternalized sex maniac.) This is what I mean by analytical simplification; its sign is the dualism and its direct provenance is absolutist idealism. This seems to me a far more insidious and pervasive aspect of fundamental Platonism than the ambiguities which may persist in our sex mores. And the manipulating of ideals in de Rougemont's manner seems to me far less satisfactory (questions of religion aside) for the person who is *rationally* concerned with the predicament of modern civilization than the realism and relativism of writers like Camus, whatever other shortcomings they may have. At this stage of intellectual history we have no need to be reminded of the determinative power of myth. What we need are suggestions for ways to escape it.

Third, the question of ordinary experience. In one of his most recent statements of the distinction between agape and eros, de Rougemont writes, "Eroticism begins where sexual emotion becomes, beyond its procreative goal, an end in itself or an instrument of the soul" (*Love Declared*, p. 35). This sounds very neat, which is what makes me suspect it. Agape equals Christian marriage which equals sex for the purpose of procreation; eros equals adultery which equals sex for its own sake. But at this point, though I suppose it is indiscreet to say so, I begin to wonder if de Rougemont, who has set himself up as the leading philosophical authority on love, has had any experience of it himself. Is anyone who has ever gone to bed in order to make love unaware that the *primary* motive for doing so is immediate, sensory pleasure?—susceptible to almost endless refinement no doubt, and thank God for that, but sensory and thus immediate nevertheless. In other words marriage, so far as it is definable at all, is a combination of eros and agape, or better yet a tension between them, immensely rich and changeable, and any writer who denatures the complexity of this fusion is doing marriage a disservice, not a service.

Fourth, de Rougemont says that the decline of poetry and the rise of the novel, that is, the shift from lyricism to drama, begins with the transference of the erotic literary center from Provence to the north and with the loss of eroticism's sacral meaning. In other words *Tristan* is the first novel and de Rougemont's work, as he says, is in one sense an investigation of the novel as the preeminent Western literary discipline. But what are we to say about a critic of the novel who doesn't mention, for instance, Dostoevsky? Is it possible that the crucial importance of Dostoevsky and the line of sensibility descending from him cannot be explained in the terms de Rougemont has invented?

Fifth, the historical pivots of de Rougemont's theory are the twelfth century and modern times. The twelfth century was "precisely," as he insists, the time when the erotic myth entered Western civilization; sometimes he pins it down even more narrowly than that. But is this likely, considering what we all know about love? Is it possible, considering what we know about Augustine, Scotus Erigena, the schools of Chartres and Arras, to keep solely on the philosophical side? Were human beings all continent up till A.D. 1130? Does the work of Reinach, Cornford, Schroeder, Dupouy, Stoll, Hoernes, et cetera, et cetera, mean nothing? Fertility and procreation have been powerful ideas, of course, and we have had many explanations of their role in ancient and medieval religions; but there is plenty of evidence also that mankind has nearly always made a place for the sex urge as such, for pure eroticism, in religion, life, and art. Indeed if this is not the meaning of Paul's "better to marry than to burn," then it has no meaning. De Rougemont asserts further that the twelfth and twentieth centuries are notable for the breakdown of marriage which occurred in each era, under the influence of ascendant eroticism. But here he is venturing into the area which he otherwise excludes from his philosophico-literary analysis, namely, social history. If he mentions the breakdown of marriage at all, then he is obligated to investigate the social factors—for example, collapse of feudalism, collapse of capitalism—which probably are more important than the cultural factors. At least he ought to acknowledge that, without history, his literary or even mythological criticism of human behavior is in the realm of fantasy. No poet, but only a critic, would arrogate so much responsibility to his own discipline. For that matter, why didn't the modern breakdown of marriage occur during the great upsurgence of erotic romanticism from Kant to Wagner, rather than a hundred years later when almost the entire Western cultural leadership was in revulsion against it? I don't say these matters cannot be explained; I only say they are wonderfully, magnificently complex. I repeat: any simplification is a degradation.

De Rougemont's accomplishments are praiseworthy. He has given us, for example, a modern definition of the soul which seems practicable from almost any point of view, and though this is implicit among other writers, I know no one else, off hand, who has done it explicitly. It is useful work, as is much of his mythological exegesis and some of his comparative analysis of oriental and Western religions. But all these accomplishments are ancillary to his main objective. Let us proclaim the end of the age of critique; it has lasted long enough. A cultural philosopher who adopts the methods of critique is living off the work of the past and hence is circumscribing the range of his achievement even before he begins. The change won't be easy. It will require a mental insurrection. It will require the displacement of knowledge—at any rate secondary, derivative knowledge—by invention. But if obsolescence is the mother of revolution and necessity the mother of invention, I'd say the only thing lacking now is an obstetrician.

The Dry Heart of Modesty

A review of *Notebooks: Volume 1*, by Albert Camus, from the *Virginia Quarterly Review*, Autumn 1963.

ALBERT CAMUS BEGAN to keep his notebooks in 1935 when he was twenty-two years old. He continued until he died three years ago. The notes, written by hand in cheap copybooks, were not at first intended for publication; but in 1954 Camus gave the first seven notebooks to a typist, and then, with care, revised the typewritten copy. The first three of these revised notebooks were published in France last year, and have now been translated into English by Philip Thody. The remaining four, according to the French editors, will be published in France in two separate volumes during the next few years, and thereafter will be available to Mr. Thody for translation; but the literary trustees of the Camus estate are undecided at this point about the advisability of publishing the notebooks for the period 1954 to 1960, which Camus left unrevised at his death.

We are told that the revisions made by Camus in preparing his *cahiers* for the press were chiefly deletions of personal references to his feelings and experiences, and that in any case the original copybooks were remarkably free of such motifs. The copybooks never contained, for instance, any mention of his work as a journalist, of his political activities, or of his family life. In other words the notebooks served almost entirely as literary workbooks, which means that those who are interested in learning about the life of Camus will be disappointed: the notebooks have virtually no direct biographical value.

On the other hand we are not told precisely what it was that Camus did delete. One hopes that eventually we shall be able to see not only the unrevised notebooks of the final six years but all the notebooks in the original, unrevised state. The comparison of unrevised and revised texts would be at least instructive, and possibly much more.

Meanwhile we may legitimately guess the motives which led to the revisions. By 1954 Camus was an exceedingly successful author. In a corner of his study, let's say, was a little stack of seven notebooks. The question was, why not destroy them? The temptation must have been great; to preserve the personal enigma is almost every writer's desire, and I think Camus especially would have wished it. But although he was not an academic Camus was a scholar, a good one, and he knew and respected scholarly technique. He could not have been unaware of the value his literary workbooks would have for students and critics. Could they be revised? Not rewritten, not polished—that would be evasive; but edited to remove materials which applied solely to the man and not to the author? This, one imagines, is what Camus decided to do.

He was not only modest, you see, but systematically modest. The evidence is here and also variously elsewhere. But what inferences one may prudently draw from it are still unknown.

At any rate Camus succeeded marvelously in being his own editor. He did not cut too much. The man is in these pages as he is in all his pages, given wholly but impersonally, the craftsman fashioning his own life for our use and leaving the work unsigned. The notebook entries for the seven years given in this first volume are short, mostly a few lines or a paragraph, and in general they comprise three categories.

First, passages written out and then transferred, virtually unchanged, to one of the works in progress. Many such entries ended up in *La mort heureuse*, a first novel which Camus withheld from publication, and others are in *L'étranger, Caligula, L'envers et l'endroit,* and other essays, stories, and plays from the early years. Mr. Thody claims to have tracked down all these entries to their final appearances, and to have given the proper cross-references in his notes. He hasn't quite done that much, as a matter of fact; but his failure is not important, especially since his translation seems excellent. What is important is the proof these literary entries offer of an extraordinary ability to extemporize in prose of an assured, lean, classical purity. Camus could do this when he was twenty-two years old, and his talent merely sharpened as he grew older. Camus the writer has been eclipsed, for some readers, by Camus the theorist or Camus the analyst, but these notebooks make the balance clear. Beyond this, one sees from the notebooks that the novels and essays were neither written nor plotted with the kind of methodical effort one might have supposed from reading the finished works. Instead they grew by fragments, whole episodes emerging from a chance sentence struck off without premeditation. That these fragments fell together so exactly is another evidence, if any were needed, of the spontaneous synthetic power of the creative imagination.

Second, a good many entries are philosophical, psychological, political; in other words, thoughtful. Camus was a natural aphorist; he was wise enough not to attempt publicly a mode which had been so thoroughly consumed by previous authors, especially in France, but one can see that the novels and essays are built from sentences and paragraphs which, in isolation, take on a distinct epigrammatic quality. In the notebooks these sentences and paragraphs stand alone, and readers who delight in books that provoke reflection—writers, for instance, in search of ideas for poems and stories—will find no one better than Camus for their purpose. Possibly someday an enterprising editor will abstract from these notebooks and the novels and essays sentences which may be collected and published separately. In general one despises such literary jobbery; but if any author can justify the attempt it is Camus.

Third, many entries are brief notations of places seen, conversations overheard (often in the streetcars of Algiers), people and animals observed. Some of these are frankly sentimental—in his notebooks Camus gave way to the impulse, well regulated in his finished work, to idealize natural objects—but most are to the point, concise vignettes depicted for their own sake and all the more meaningful for that. He gives us an imagination that is explicitly visual. Even the essays are blocked out like pictures in a gallery. Scenes, or rather fragments of scenes, meant much to Camus.

Scholars will find less in these notebooks than they had hoped to find, but we knew all along that in his stories, novels, plays, and essays Camus is complete. In one entry he speaks of the "dry heart of the creator." It is true; everything has been transferred to the page. The notebooks are scraps and leavings. But the general reader, in the presence of one of the great founders of the age, will be grateful for such remnants.

Poetic Mythology

A review of *Shelburne Essays on American Literature*, by Paul Elmer More (edited by Daniel Aaron); *The Widening Gyre*, by Joseph Frank; *Fables of Identity: Studies in Poetic Mythology*, by Northrop Frye; *To the Palace of Wisdom: Studies in Order and Energy from Dryden to Blake*, by Martin Price; *The Artistic Transaction and Essays on Theory of Literature*, by Eliseo Vivas; and *What Is Poetry?*, by John Hall Wheelock; from *Poetry*, September 1964.

WHAT AND WHO were the New Critics? The question has been asked many times, and as our era recedes into historical view it will be asked many times again. For even though the New Critics themselves disclaimed the title that had been fastened on them, and even though they were careful to point out the disagreements and disparities in their ranks, the title, after more than twenty years, persists. No doubt it will continue to persist; it has been found useful. Something was in the minds of the New Critics, after all, something new, something impelling; and now that their work is entering the phase of historical hindsight, we see this "something" gradually take form. We see also, of course, a certain blurring and shifting of the distinctions that we who lived through the New Criticism held dear, the variant evolutionary lines which produced Ransom's ontological criticism, for instance, or Burke's theories of symbolic consciousness. But what appears to have lain at the center of the New Criticism was the idea, quite distinct from humanistic or naturalistic ideas of previous ages, that the individual poem is in some sense an autotelic phenomenon. It was a disturbing idea: disturbing to poets, who felt an incipient displacement of their bardic or prophetic roles, and disturbing equally to critics, who saw their discourse withering into the irrelevant pastime of old men that Yeats decried. The poem suddenly—and apparently quite inevitably—had become divorced from life, from reality. In consequence the most aggressive criticism of the last few years has been an attempt to restore to the autotelic poem some mode of transcendant efficacy, without reverting to former naturalistic concepts of art as communication, art as expression, or art as the affective embodiment of ethical derivatives. To such an attempt the ordinary reader can attend only in breathless anticipation, for the critical texts which now tumble from the presses like acrobats from a paper drum surpass, in their quickness and acuity, any ordinary competence. Sometimes it is refreshing to return to the texts of former ages.

Paul Elmer More is now a legendary figure of criticism in the twentieth century, known to all, but read by few, who study in the field. So it is good to have the *Shelburne Essays on American Literature.* Readers who wish to become acquainted with More's qualities and accomplishments will find the book a handy means of doing so. It contains seventeen of the hundred-odd Shelburne Essays which More published in eleven volumes from 1904 to 1921. More, as he said repeatedly, was interested in the definition of standards: not literary standards in our sense of the term, but rather standards of literature drawn from other sources, chiefly from ideas. He applied himself with great intelligence to thought as a cultural manifestation, and he was adamantine in his rejection of anything—idea or work of literature—that seemed in the slightest degree mushy or nebulous. This, in combination with the simplistic lucubrations of T. E. Hulme, was the beginning, as we know, of the longstanding antiromantic bias which influenced Eliot, the Southern Agrarians, and the whole school of New Critics, clamping modern literary taste into the Draconian schematism of romanticism v. classicism, from which it has not entirely freed itself even today. In the context of our present dilemmas More's strictures seem largely inapplicable, especially since they rest, at bottom, on nothing more cogent than his belief in what he called "character"; at some points More sounds remarkably like Theodore

Roosevelt, whom he probably despised. Nevertheless, within his limits More worked at a pitch seldom attained by his successors. His elucidation of the follies and the great strengths of Puritan America lies at the root of nearly all our present knowledge in this area, and he is equally good in tracing the descent of Puritanism through the eighteenth and nineteenth centuries. His fault, from our point of view, is his lack of concern for technique, for form. Thus he fails to understand the importance of what we consider the primary achievement of the nineteenth century in America: the development of an indigenous symbolism. His discussion of Hawthorne, although superb in defining the relationship between Hawthorne and his Puritan forebears, nevertheless seems to miss the point, and on Melville and Emily Dickinson he has nothing to say. More's best essays in this selection are those on Jonathan Edwards, Philip Freneau, Whittier, and Thoreau.

In addition to the example of a splendid intelligence at work More offers the reader a style: dry, fluent, highly modulated. He knew what most critics cannot know: that the critic, wherever he finds himself, in the academy as elsewhere, is a writer. (Blackmur knew this too, and I now wonder if More, rather than James, as I have always supposed, was Blackmur's guide.) More took pains to write well. His writing was by no means crabbed or cold, but flashed with genuine anger at times, as when he lit into Mrs. Eddy, for example, whom clearly he would have been obliged to see in the stocks on Boston Common. One remembers that More's principal antagonist in his time was not a fellow academician but H. L. Mencken. Now that so much of what each man had to say has fallen from contemporary relevance, we can read them both without taking sides; and it is a real pleasure to do so. Theirs was a period of vigorous expression, rhapsodic wit. Today we have a species of imitators, literary punks who try, through vociferation alone, to resuscitate that grand asperity; but the time is gone. It takes more than crowing to make a cock.

But style is after all the least important element of criticism. Nor can the palm be given solely to the ancients; quite the contrary. Our own critics today, driven by the spectre of the autotelic poem, have taken on a brilliance of concentration that would be frenzied if it were not technical. Fortunately, the techniques vary a good deal. Northrop Frye, for instance, disclaims More's insistence on standards, saying that scholarship logically must precede evaluation; and he demonstrates his point, though he does not prove it, by confining his exertions to texts whose values have been long established. The wonder is that, after a century or more of previous criticism, Frye can still say something so startling and informative about Shakespeare's sonnets, for example, that he leaves the reader's literary consciousness virtually re-formed; which suggests the ineluctability of standards, or at least of values. Joseph Frank, at any rate, asserts not only the necessity but the propriety of critical judgment, and offers in his discussions of such "new" texts as Djuna Barnes's *Nightwood* and Mann's *Dr. Faustus* truly first-rate specimens of what technical criticism can do, not only to propound but to enforce standards of appreciation. Meanwhile Martin Price, who has read Frye, appears to be conducting more or less the kind of scholarship Frye has in mind; his *To the Palace of Wisdom* is an investigation of the conflict between concepts of order and concepts of energy as it descends from Pascal to Blake, a meticulous, modest, honorably academic work, aimed more at the establishment of a true account than at the promulgation of interpretive judgments. His book is sure to underlie much that will be written about the eighteenth century in decades to come. Finally Eliseo Vivas, the philosopher, stands somewhat aloof from the critical fray, affirming standards but disdaining to create them, intent rather upon the refinement of esthetic theory as it applies to the functioning of the autotelic poem.

But exactly how do these men proceed?

The Widening Gyre contains nine essays by Joseph Frank, five of which are crucial to an understanding of the contemporary critical mind. Frank begins with the commonplace observation that modern literature, both poetry and fiction, has broken with the old order of linear narration, replacing it with the method exemplified in *The Waste Land*, in which discrete fragments of poetic experience are juxtaposed, so to speak, on a plane surface. Drawing on the analogy of painting (and he could as well have chosen music), while at the same time working through the content of German esthetic from Lessing to Cassirer, Frank defines this structural technique, which in years gone by was always called the associative method, as "spatial form." It is a conceit, of course, not a literal statement; language remains by nature consecutive, not extensive. But Frank's metaphor works neatly as a paradigm of what the modern writer is up to, and it permits him to exhibit the technique of the modern poem with particular vividness.

Beyond that it permits him to show how the poem, as it abandons narration, falls from the stream of history and becomes ahistorical or at least superhistorical. And what is superhistory but myth? Thus Frank joins up, rather unexpectedly, with Northrop Frye.

Frye has been the bad boy of modern criticism. Brooks and Wimsatt, in their "Short History," gave him a cautionary tap on the wrist, but he has forged ahead undaunted, producing an extraordinary spate of books and essays in the past few years. The present example, *Fables of Identity*, contains sixteen essays drawn from the whole period of his critical activity, including several that have become famous. Together, they offer a brief, somewhat simplified view of Frye's theory and practice; the view is less adequate and more restricted, especially in the region of social applications, than in the *Anatomy of Criticism* and the more recent *The Educated Imagination*; but for readers who wish a quick dunking and who are willing to put up with the atrocious writing of the early essays, *Fables of Identity* will be useful.

The beginning, for Frye, is simply the conflict of literature and life. He accepts it, welcomes it, revels in it. The poem is a thing apart, he says, taking up where the New Critics left off; considerations of person, the author's feelings and experiences, have no place in the critic's work, however interesting they may be as biography. Literature evolves solely within itself and by reference to itself, a cultural Leviathan sloughing off authors as it goes. In a word, literature is conventional. Here is where the scholarship begins, the investigation of conventions, and for Frye the process is coextensive with culture itself—that is to say, endless. For Frye also the study of conventions has little to do with the elaboration of *genres* practiced in former times, but is rather the discovery and explication of archetypes. Myth, in other words, is the structure of literature; and the highest form of criticism is anthropology, the only technique which can turn criticism from a mere appanage of literature into a self-sustaining discipline, a consummation which Frye suggests is greatly to be desired. At first the reader feels that Frye says nothing which was not contained, quite explicitly, in Maud Bodkin's *Archetypal Patterns in Poetry*, which appeared exactly thirty years ago and which was itself a compendium of former investigations (Weston, Harrison, Cornford, Raglan, Frazer, and others) filtered through Jungian hypotheses. But this is unfair to Frye; he has certainly given his materials a force and direction that are original. In his own applications of his theory he has concentrated on the quest myths and on various cosmological archetypes of recurrence (lunar, seasonal, theocratic), with results which, as in the essay on the Shakespearean sonnets, are genuinely revealing.

Eliseo Vivas is the most abstruse of the present company. The untrained reader is likely to lose confidence. In his extreme revulsion from philosophical naturalism in all its shades and disguises, Vivas has asserted and defended the authority of the autotelic poem through an ever more refined analysis of the esthetic act, until an impossible feat of jugglery is required to keep all his distinctions in mind. The writing of philosophy, somebody has remarked, is an exercise in the art of hedging. Vivas defines the esthetic object as that whose meanings are immanent, not referential, and the esthetic act as that which is vividly (that is, affectively) self-contained and intransitive, not transitional to other acts, as is the case, for example, with cognitive experience. In short, esthetic knowledge functions solely within esthetic experience, the whole complex of actions being as shut off as life in a goldfish bowl. Yet the word *functions* leaves a loophole; nonesthetic knowledge may impinge in a nonfunctional way upon the poem, both before and after the act; this *must* occur, in fact, if the poem is to have any meaning at all, immanent or not. Hence the knowledge of beauty which is the product of esthetic experience has a certain osmotic persuasiveness—Vivas would deprecate the term—extending beyond the poem into the realm of practical or moral action; and perhaps—perhaps—this connects up with what Frank and Frye call myth.

The poet is vindicated. Through the nexus of myth, so to speak, he is reintroduced to humanity; culture becomes, not the historical objective expression, which is mere ethos imprisoned in museums and anthologies, but the eternal syntax of the categories of imaginative experience; and it is lived. Criticism, if it cannot attain complete independence, at least ranges farther and farther afield, battering on the walls of philosophy and social science, enjoining the fealty of more and more legions of amateurs; an outcome only to be applauded in an age burdened with leisure. At one time it had seemed that the earlier euhemerists, from Frazer to the author of *The Hero with a Thousand Faces*, had exhausted myth as a topic for useful discussion; now we see that its surface has barely been scratched, at least in connection with the application to higher culture. But who will speak for poetry? We notice the poets themselves take to criticism chiefly at times of technical onrush, as in the cases of Dante, Wordsworth, and Pound; and then their criticism is devoted to the mere utilitarian, to prosody and the assassination of dullness. Betweentimes, they fret and pout, but that is not criticism. Who cannot sympathize with John Hall Wheelock's fears for poetry in a critical era? Who cannot rejoice with him in the lofty or insinuating passages of great poetry which we normally have no time to read? Sipping the polished sentences of his essays, collected in *What Is Poetry?*, is like a taste of champagne after the critics' horrendous slug of moonshine. But alas, the critics have ruined us. We are as strong as oxen, as drunk as lords. Mr. Wheelock's twice-watered Emersonianism, not to say thrice-watered Catharism, cannot awaken our palates. Yeats, who knew something of spirits, said that the artist's life at best is an endless "preparation for something that never happens." So be it. At least it is a facing forward.

Pursy Windhum Lucigen

A review of *The Letters of Wyndham Lewis*, edited by W. K. Rose, from the *Hudson Review*, Autumn 1964.

PERCY WYNDHAM LEWIS WAS BORN in 1882 and like the rest of us began by sponging off his mother, the difference being, however, that he refused to be weaned and kept it up till he was nigh on to thirty; whereupon the poor lady, who was none too well nourished herself, died. Percy's hysteria when no one, and more especially his "mother country," would offer a surrogatory tit continued the rest of his life, or nearly; and a more pitiable, childish, and ultimately tedious spectacle is unlikely to be found among English men of letters, or among the latter-day Parnassians generally.

Unflattering as it is and even, if you like, "dirty," this is all that the reader of Lewis's correspondence can conclude. Or almost all. The book itself, handsome and substantial, has been edited with scholarly care and also with a certain warmth and imagination; but beyond that, since the selection Professor Rose has made from the extant correspondence comprises, he says, only about a fourth, we must, being ignorant of the rest, reserve final judgment of his editorial skill. Nevertheless he appears to have done a good job. More important, we are told that the selection is representative, we notice that the book is dressed up with baby pictures, footnotes, copious prefaces, etc., and we conclude that the project is attended with scholarly earnestness and an air of quasi finality. Hence I see no reason why we should withhold our judgment of its subject, Lewis himself. Like all collections of letters, this is a book about a man. In this case the man was also a painter, a novelist, and a critic; but it was not the painter, novelist, or critic who wrote these letters, it was the man. Those who offer us the letters are, by so doing, inviting us to judge the man alone. Nor is this judgment trivial: first, because the man happened to be a figure of some importance in his time; second, because the man indubitably did create the paintings, novels, and works of criticism.

Percy was born on board his father's yacht, which had been tied up for the occasion at Amherst, Nova Scotia. His father was a wealthy young Canadian, his mother a goodlooking young Englishwoman. Not long afterward, however, they separated, and the mother took Percy to live in England, where she sent him in due course to various public schools. She had a hard time, it appears. Percy's father was frequently in default of the cash remittances customary in such circumstances, and we are left with the impression that he was squandering his substance in the fleshpots of the Maritimes; though for that matter as far as I know no one has troubled to investigate his side of the story. At any event Mrs. Lewis maintained herself and her son through her own ingenuity and hard labor in various shoestring enterprises, chiefly shopkeeping. Percy was at the same time washing out of the schools to which he had been entrusted, and at age sixteen, when he stood twenty-sixth in his class of twenty-six at Rugby, he gave it up as a bad job. Later he attended the Slade School of Art, where his talents for drawing were recognized and encouraged. In 1902 he went abroad, and until 1910 lived in Paris, Madrid, Munich, and the Netherlands, attended occasional lectures, made paintings and drawings, dressed in a black cape, and generally pursued *la vie de bohême*, as it was still properly called in those antediluvian days. The only letters offered us from this period are those to his mother. They are filled with cheerful condolences for her hardships, both physical and financial, and with reports on his expenditures for lodging, food, and models. During most of this time he apparently sent his dirty laundry home to London to be washed, and his letters often contain requests for books and other articles to be enclosed in the returning packages. Most of the letters also contain requests for money. In 1907, when he was twenty-five, he wrote: "Chère Maman, Well, so long as you give me enough to keep me in food, etc. and pay for the stove, etc., it's all I can expect. . . ." Etc., etc., etc. At the same time one ought not to deprecate the affectionate tone of these letters; it seems clear that mother and son were held in a close if desperately unequal relationship by a deeply felt mutual need.

Lewis had always mingled writing with his art studies, but it is difficult to tell how serious he was in his first attempts, of which we have no specimens. They were poems, apparently, and were destroyed by Lewis, or perhaps suppressed by his executors after his death. In 1909, however, he sold a story to Ford Madox Hueffer's *English Review*, a success which led him, in 1910, to return to England and establish himself in London. Quickly he became engaged in the ferment of the new esthetics, along with Pound, Hulme, and the rest; the story is well known. The part played by Lewis is somewhat difficult to assess. Certainly he was not the leader; but he brought from France a genuine Fauvist and Cubist enthusiasm, and no doubt his knowledge of the plastic arts contributed something valuable to the program. Beyond that his personality must have been congenial to the others. The word *biting* as applied to intelligence has lost its meaning through overuse, but it can be momentarily restored by saying, emphatically, that this was the quality which distinguished Lewis from Pound, acerb as the latter could be and often was. In later years Lewis disputed with Pound for the credit of having originated vorticism. The truth seems to be that although Pound invented the term and contributed several characteristic pronouncements to their joint magazine, *Blast*, it was Lewis who did most of the work and furnished most of the ardor. And without doubt he was the one responsible for exporting the new sensibility from the literary to the artistic centers; he was busy during these years with exhibitions, workshops, art publications. Concurrently he kept up his other writing. He was extraordinarily productive, in short, as he continued to be for the rest of his life. In 1914 he began serious work on his first novel, *Tarr*.

The war was, for Lewis as for everyone, a waste of time, yet he took to it with aplomb. After casting about for any easy commission, he enlisted as a common soldier, trained in an artillery batallion, and won a second-lieutenancy in the regular way. At the front, though he grumbled eloquently over the military snafus, he was a fearless and even enthusiastic soldier. Those who have read Mitchell Goodman's fine novel *The End of It* will have an illuminating cross-reference for the following two sentences from a letter to Pound dated September 1917: "Ainsi, I was F.O.O. (forward ob officer) of the Group three days ago, and on that occasion had the extreme gratification of seeing, in the midst of our barrage, a large Bosche fly into the air as it seemed a few feet beneath me. From the ridge where I was observing things I looked down into the German front line as you might into Church Street."

Tarr was published in 1918. It was the beginning of a maniacal spate of activity which produced, in the next twenty years, more than twenty books, a great many paintings and drawings, and a steady outpouring of pamphlets, little magazines, manifestoes, reviews, and other ephemera. The letters during this period tell us nothing about Lewis himself; he is a disembodied epistoler. We know, for instance, that he was married in the late twenties, but the letters contain no mention of it, and at this moment, having just read his lifetime's correspondence, I cannot think of his wife's name. I find it hard to imagine anyone else's letters that would leave me similarly uninformed. We do not know where he lived or in what circumstances. We know nothing of his tastes in clothing, food, landscape, climate, architecture, music, or manners. During much of this period he wrote his letters from a safe deposit box in the Pall Mall. In short, Lewis's desire for secrecy became a mania, the private half of the mania which, in public, expressed itself in delusions of persecution. The letters we have in this volume are chiefly of three sorts. A small number are affable but impersonal communications to friends who were so staunch that they refused to quarrel with him, for example, Augustus John and Roy Campbell. A larger number are requests for money. And the largest number of all are simply a flood of disputation: insults, vituperations, cavils, a sea of self-fomented troubles. His enemies were publishers, rival authors, critics, agents, gallery and museum directors, bureaucrats, the entire cultural community; his Enemy was Anglo-Saxon civilization from top to bottom. Well, many of us might agree, but not, decidedly not, in Lewis's terms. He belonged, or wished to belong, to an "elusive but excellent community," the "party of genius," "outside any milieu or time"; but it was too "elusive," it didn't exist, and this nonexistence, thrust continually into his face, exasperated him to the point of unabated bad temper. But more than bad: evil.

Why? What was it all about? In one of his more temperate remarks Lewis spoke, late in his life when he was reviewing a new sculpture by Henry Moore, of "how important it is to know how to circumvent the natural platitude of the dimensions of life." There it is; he had been saying it for thirty years, and he continued till his death. Whatever other faults he had, he was neither dishonest nor obscure, and his style, though complex and overheated, hit with ringing clarity upon the crucial words. When he said "circumvent" he meant precisely that; and when he said "platitude" it was like a snarl. Life was unbearable, reality was unbearable, nature and the body were totally corrupt; their adherents, the naturalists of every camp, were not only corrupt but conspiratorial; only art and the mind could preserve the "aristocracy of intellect" from the nihilism which had resulted, paradoxically, from an emotionally charged misreading of Nietzsche. And thus Lewis joined the antirealists, those who would invent Being from the misapprehended dynamisms of esthetics. He became for England what Gottfried Benn was for Germany—the parallel is astonishingly exact—and if his course was the opposite from that of Céline's in France, they both had begun at the same point and their effects were strangely similar: Céline destroyed the body through exercises of nauseated lust, Lewis destroyed it through the annihilating decrees of his revulsed and frigid mind. These and their allies created the New Parnassus, which their disciples have turned into the New Philistia. Lewis's novels are peopled by Ideas, beings of Style, creatures as sexless as himself, for only these could exist in the unreality of the devalued and denatured universe; and if as a painter he acquired among the elite a certain reputation as a portraitist, it was because he bestowed upon his sitters a firm, machinelike flesh, which sometimes seemed desirable in the thirties. He was England's Léger, but totally without Léger's humor and compassion. Politically Lewis's course was predictable and remarkably similar to that of his continental comrades: outspoken, unqualified support of Franco and Hitler.

When the second war came Lewis left England and went to North America, boarding ship the day before England declared war on Germany. No matter how Professor Rose minimizes this escape, the inference is unavoidable that Lewis left his country because he feared for his safety after his years of Nazi vociferation (even though he had publicly changed his mind about Hitler the year before). But once in North America, where he suffered grievously from the climate, the people, and the restrictions of the war, he gradually slipped into a new self-delusion, namely, that he had left England solely for financial reasons and now wished nothing better than to return. If only he could raise the fare for the clipper flight to Lisbon and thence to London. . . . Of course he could not.

Frankly I was so nauseated by these wartime letters that I skipped over to the final section of the book: Lewis at home again, the grand old man ensconced finally in the admiration of younger writers, critics, and publishers. The metamorphosis at last occurs. The tone of his attacks softens, though the attacks continue until the end, and he now spends a good deal of time writing in kindly condescension to his disciples and well-wishers. He resumes friendships with Eliot and Pound on a much more equable basis than formerly, and he keeps up a steady though ineffectual campaign to secure Pound's release from St. Elizabeth's. He dispenses generous and chiefly sound advice to younger writers. He becomes, in short, Le Vieux, the only role he could conceivably play with any degree of charm. It was during this period that those who are now his advocates, including Professor Rose, first met him and corresponded with him. What accounted for the change? One can't be sure. I doubt that the tragedy, a very true tragedy, of his blindness was enough to bring it about, or even his eventual knowledge that the loss of vision was caused by an inoperable growth inside his head which was methodically killing him. Lewis had been quite critically ill in the thirties (though the nature of his illness, like everything else about his personal life, is darkly hidden) without any moderating result, and his suffering during the war had merely changed him from a blaster into a whiner. More likely his mellowing was simply an effect of the new sympathy he detected in the reactionary intellectual milieu of postwar England, coupled with the natural decline of energy in his advancing years. The old battles were over, after all, and if he had abandoned his outposts, so had his adversaries. Stephen Spender, who only yesterday had been the young radical, was one of the first to offer his services as a reader when news of Lewis's blindness became known.

This book of letters gives us a man who grew from adolescence to senility in one movement. Emotional maturity and that part of intellectual maturity which rests upon emotional factors were denied him. He belonged, without a doubt, to the Party of Genius; we look back on that Party only with regret, first that its brilliance was so perverse, second that we lack its means in pursuing our so much more serious ends. What estimate the years to come will place on Lewis's works I do not know, of course. I shall be surprised and sorry if his writing comes to be valued as art, that is, as something necessary to the life of man in a condition of civilization. But I won't be surprised if a few of his many works, especially *Childermass* and *The Revenge for Love*, retain a reputation as glittering examples of what can be done within a convention of sterility. In either case I refrain from judgment. I don't say a man may not create his own reality from considerations of style. So may a man raise himself by his own bootstraps, speaking in terms of the inner synthesis. But for the onlookers it remains merely a feat of levitation, a curiosity, a sideshow which exists simply by virtue of its a priori irresponsibility, and in the present instance the performer happens also to be a remarkably ugly man. I am content to pass on to the next attraction.

Scales of the Marvelous

A review of *Roots and Branches*, by Robert Duncan, from *The Nation*, December 7, 1964.

THE NECESSITY of gathering one's forces before sitting down to write poetry: what prescription could be simpler? And what more stupidly, arrogantly violated in most current practice—poems thrown out upon the face of reality like discarded candy wrappers! Decidedly this is not the case with Robert Duncan. I know nothing about his methods of composition except what I infer from his published work, and one of my inferences is this: his poems are gathered to him, slowly or quickly I do not know, from many sources and by procedures which are at least in part deliberative. I find this admirable. His poems have a completeness, an inextensibility that is rare in an age devoted to scraps and shards.

Duncan has been called a man of learning. It may be true or not; perhaps he possesses much knowledge, from which he has selected the materials of his poems, or perhaps he simply puts everything he reads into his writing. It is of no consequence. But richness of texture is of consequence, and so is the wisdom that should accompany it, of which there are several kinds: wisdom that is the ghost of poetic language, wisdom that is the ghost of acquired data, wisdom that is the ghost of experience, and a fourth, wisdom that is the ghost of wisdom, otherwise called humility before one's task. Duncan has them all. He writes:

> *There is no life that does not rise*
> *melodic from scales of the marvelous.*
>
> *To which our grief refers.*

The "scales of the marvelous"—a column of opposites from which life emerges reverberantly, as the tune emerges from the air column of a horn: the present and history, the seen and the unseen, nature and reason. From these life arises melodically, and more especially the life of a man, his individuality, his identity as a person. His own present and history double against the present and history of the race. The poet is the musician who evokes this life, or in another sense the mediator who elicits from these opposing values the continual compromise which is a man. It isn't easy, for the marvelous scales are those of justice as well as those of music, and in addition are the scales that cover our eyes. This difficulty is what occasions the poet's "grief," while his knowledge that his task is endless, that it will wear him out and cause him to relinquish it, still undone, to others, is what occasions his humility.

Duncan announces his purpose, or at any rate one of his purposes, early in his book:

> *O to release the first music somewhere again,*
> *for a moment*
> *to touch the design of the first melody!*

If the vitality of art originates in inner tension, as it evidently does, then one source of this tension is the balance of old against new. Much recent American poetry has lost it; some poets have domesticated themselves in the old, others have abandoned everything and run off with the new; dullness and wildness exhaust themselves in their own gluttonies and their mutual recriminations. Duncan is one of the few who have striven to keep the tension in their work, and who have recognized that in occidental poetry it is chiefly a question of the crossfire between religious and secular ways of speaking. There is nothing limiting about this; Whitman and Donne, Emily Dickinson and D. H. Lawrence took their styles from a reinvention of liturgy; this is the root of our verbal sensibility. In Duncan's case, as in all others, it is a question of finding a way to touch again the old sources and keep the poetic impetus—not a particular mode, but the impetus—alive.

The tricks by which one summons modernity and antiquity are simple enough for a skilled poet. On one hand, abrupt line breaks, a touch of scatological diction, contemporary references; on the other, allusions to mythology and history, archaic words and spellings (*governd, lockt*), reworkings of poetic structures used in other times. But these are only tricks, and though they may be used beautifully, as Duncan mostly uses them (he likes to experiment with sonnets and to rewrite in his own manner famous poems from the past), the vitality of a poem comes not from surface effects but from its inner movement, that is, from its meter. Duncan's metrical usages are extremely various, extending from tight lyrics to looping paragraphic constructions; yet in them all the ear detects the *ostinato* of standard English measure and the falling intonation of liturgy; the masculine and feminine of our poetic tradition. Because his poems diverge widely from one another, it is hard to find a typical example. The following, which is the last of his "Four Songs the Night Nurse Sang," is a brief elegiac song and a coda, part of a longer sequence; slighter and prettier than most of his other writing, but showing what he can do.

> *Let sleep take her, let sleep take her, let sleep*
> *take her away!*
> *The cold tears of her father*
> *have made a hill of ice.*
> *Let sleep take her.*
>
> *Her mother's fear has made a feyrie.*
> *Let sleep take her.*

Now all the kingdom lies down to die.
   Let sleep take her.

Let dawn wake her, if dawn can find her.
   Let the prince of day take her
from sleep's dominion at the touch of his finger,
   if he can touch her.

The weather will hide her, the spider will bind her

   : so the wind sang.

O, there she lay
in an egg hanging from an invisible thread
spinning out I cannot tell whether

from a grave or a bed, from a grave or a bed.

The uses here of repetition, inversion, internal rhyme, assonance and consonance are obvious, and probably some readers, inflamed by exorbitant applications of poetic novelty, will wonder if the poem is modern at all. It is; these devices are not tricks of fashion but the craft forced on the poet by the language itself in its whole speaking historical weight, and they are therefore as undying as language (or as undying as the theme of this poem, beauty and the beast). Moreover, the freedom with which Duncan has moved within the evolving shapes of language, relying on his ear alone, is perfectly evident. In fact the touchstones of modernity are poems like this, things which have the contemporaneity of the life thread, and readers who cannot recognize them are those enslaved by fashionable effects, that is, those who have lost their freedom. But the most important critical points to be made about this poem are two: first, Duncan has touched, in these lines unscannable by any customary method, the deepest metrical sources of the language; second, he has done so with variety and firmness, giving each word a value that cannot be obscured.

Of the three poets who brought Black Mountain College its brief poetic renaissance a decade ago—the others were, of course, Charles Olson and Robert Creeley—Duncan has been the last to attract a larger poetry-reading public. Indeed he has not attracted it yet. Maybe this new book, his most substantial so far, will bring him the audience his work merits. I hope so; for although Duncan's writing lacks Olson's intellectual ferocity or the immediately ingratiating quality of Creeley's erotic lyrics, it has its own distinct virtues. Beyond his obvious verbal gift (a musical sense standing halfway between Williams and Pound, with something of the former's tenacious suppleness of phrasing and a good deal of the latter's versatility) is the ease of Duncan's ranging through the cultural complex. After all I think he *is* a man of learning, though a poet not a scholar, an amateur and certainly not a dilettante. His fault, aside from the apparent and at present allowable quirks of personality that issue in occasional poems either too exquisite or abstract, has been his need to evoke the "first music" in a too-personal service; but his new book contains a chamber drama of twenty pages, "Adam's Way," that plunges deeper into the "scales of the marvelous" than anything in his past work, leaving the simply private sensibility farther behind. So much the better. To sound from the scales of the marvelous not only the melody of the poet who sustains the world of sensibility but the melody of the men and women who sustain the world of action—of anyone and everyone—is a work of bewildering difficulty in this age of literary over-self-consciousness. "Adam's Way" is evidence that Duncan may be the man to do it.

Upon Which to Rejoice

A review of *Collected Poems 1909–1962*, by T. S. Eliot; *Knowledge and Experience in the Philosophy of F. H. Bradley*, by T. S. Eliot; and *Notes on Some Figures behind T. S. Eliot*, by Herbert Howarth; from *Poetry*, June 1965.

Mrs. trollope's opinion of American religion was low—uniformly, doggedly low. And nowhere did she speak more to the point than in her footnote describing the effect of American religion upon American writers: "The mind of a man devoted to letters undergoes a process which renders the endurance of the crude ignorant ranting of the great majority among the various sects of American preachers intolerable; and accordingly they have taken refuge in the cold comfortless stillness of Unitarianism." Mrs. Trollope's pen was not always up to her ambition, as here in the first part of her sentence, but in "the cold comfortless stillness of Unitarianism" she surpassed herself. I came across it in my copy of her *Domestic Manners*, the fifth edition published in 1839.

The first edition had appeared in 1832; and in the fall of the following year a young graduate of Harvard Divinity School, William Greenleaf Eliot, emigrated from New England to St. Louis, where he founded—or rather helped to found—three institutions: the St. Louis branch of the Eliot family; the city's first Unitarian church, which became one of the strongest in the West; and Washington University, where Hegelianism, in the teaching of W. T. Harris and his colleagues, rose to its clearest and most orthodox American expression a few decades later. (Harris, who was a distinguished philosopher and educator in his time, founded and edited the *Journal of Speculative Philosophy*, was appointed United States Commissioner of Education, was associated at various times with Peirce, Royce, Bronson Alcott, and William James, and was largely instrumental in adapting German idealism to the service of American free education, free westward expansion, and free enterprise generally.) When William Greenleaf Eliot's grandson was born in 1888, he came into an intellectual environment that combined Eliotean gentility, Unitarian cold stillness, and Hegelian cosmic rationalism into a mood of petrified expectancy. He did not like it. Yet exactly one hundred years after Mrs. Trollope's remark, T. S. Eliot was writing of "the still point of the turning world," and doing so, moreover, in Mrs. Trollope's own England. Mrs. Trollope would have objected to the current notion that the poet went there to discover his "still point." She would have said he brought it with him.

Professor Howarth has written at length about this early environment in his study of the influences exerted upon Eliot by relatives, friends, and others. Since Howarth does not actually know, any more than the rest of us, what was happening inside Eliot's head at the various stages of the poet's work, his book, from a scholarly point of view, must be classed as an entertainment; but it is interesting and in part suggestive. Howarth's conjectural slickness, as a matter of fact, can set off whole chains of it in the reader's mind. For instance, Karl Jaspers and Gabriel Marcel were both born in the same decade as Eliot. What would have happened if Eliot had gone to Europe, to Ger-

many, for his education, instead of to Harvard? Like his two contemporaries, he had a penchant for spiritual philosophy and an attachment to concrete experience. Taken together, these suggest, at that
time and with that background, a young man extremely likely to have
been impressed by the new currents stirring in European philosophy.

Practically speaking, the opportunity did not exist. Eliot was an
American, and an American at that time was still a provincial, and a
provincial was still an idealist in the academic sense. At Harvard Eliot
wrote his doctoral thesis on the idealism of F. H. Bradley, performing
adroitly in a worn-out epistemological mode. Now that it has been
published for the first time, fifty years after it was written, we can see
both Eliot's superior philosophical gifts and the dead end to which he
applied them. Certainly he would have become a poet in any case; but
his recognition of this dead end must have corroborated his natural
tendency. For the young American idealist of 1915, the way of philosophy, temporarily or not, was closed; but the way of poetry was
open.

The poems are what we have, a new collected edition that is hand-
somer than the familiar green volume of 1935, to which it adds the
Quartets and a section of short poems written since 1940. Reading it is
a great pleasure, and a slow one, not only because the poems demand
one's close attention but because so many issues have consolidated
around the poems that from line to line, sometimes from word to
word, one must make new judgments. I shall omit my own particular
observations, which are probably those of many readers in recent
times. What they come to is this: 90 per cent of the critical profusion
surrounding Eliot's poems is wrong; the commentators must begin
again. A number of the most celebrated poems are his worst (for he
was quite capable of bad writing), and some passages upon which the
sensibility of our era is thought to rest simply do not mean what most
people think they mean. Eliot's gravest defect, I believe, has been his
apparent lifelong temptation as a poet to write for an effect; in each
phase of his work there are brilliant, hollow-sounding lines, places
where we miss the genuineness of Yeats, for instance, the sense of
complete emotional commitment. Yet for me the power of the writing
is still there, mounting steadily until almost the last word, and I find
myself remembering the defects for reasons which do me, I think, no
great credit. Eliot's chief virtue has been his willingness to experiment; this is not what most people think now that Eliot has become so
firmly a figurehead of the Establishment, but it is perfectly plain on

the pages of the book. Every major poem is not only a technical advance over previous work, it is a technical *departure*—a movement into something completely new. I am not sure that this can be said of any other important poet in English. And Eliot is important; he always will be, there can be no mistake about this. His departures give us our clearest examples of responsibility in art. These, and not his opinions, justify his leadership. Beyond that, he has enlarged our poetic diction enormously and made it consonant with the whole range of contemporary experience, which is the first and perhaps the only universal criterion of importance that we can infer from the history of poetry.

The point raised by Mrs. Trollope is a confusing one. I who have never been in England find myself on her side, at least in this instance: I do not care for coldness and I take small comfort from stillness. Yet these are what another American has transplanted to England, and enforced there chiefly through his poems, although partly through his essays and other literary activities. Eliot's coldness is the aspect of his work that repels me: his idea of authority based on literalness; and I see no way to pretend that it is not as much a part of the poems as of the essays. His stillness, considered abstractly, is for me fantasized post-Nietzschean nihilism. Yet like thousands upon thousands of others who share my feelings, I find these elements in his poems, though not in his essays, harmonious and esthetically moving; and this I think is the ultimate criterion not merely of importance but of greatness.

Wasting His Talent on Finks and Funks

A review of *The Bit between My Teeth*, by Edmund Wilson, from the *Chicago Daily News*, November 27, 1965.

IN A MEMOIR of his fellow critic Paul Rosenfeld, whose gifts were to a certain extent unrecognized during his lifetime, Edmund Wilson has commented bitterly on the repressive tendencies of American journalism, apparently without seeing that the same point may be made with equal justice about his own career. Now the third volume of Wilson's collected reviews has come out. It covers the years from 1950 to the present, is entitled *The Bit between My Teeth*, and is uniform in format with the previous two volumes, *The Shores of Light* and *Classics and Commercials*. It is the dullest of the lot. And it proves without question the harm that has been done to Wilson, and thus to all of us, by his submission to the standards of journalism in this country.

When Wilson began his critical vocation in the 1920s he was associated with the young magazines of that era, particularly *Vanity Fair* and the *New Republic*. His reviews were pointed, brief, touched with exuberance, generous yet sharply intelligent; and what is especially noteworthy, they dealt almost unerringly with the important figures of the time, young novelists and poets who were creating a new literature—Hemingway, Fitzgerald, Joyce, Eliot, and the rest. But in the 1940s, when he began to write for the *New Yorker*, his reviews became longer, more obtuse, crotchety, often downright ponderous. His attention was diverted—whether or not at the behest of his editors, it makes no difference, since he at any rate acquiesced—to detective fiction, horror stories, books of etiquette and cookery, or to secondary authors like Thomas Love Peacock and W. S. Gilbert. Granted, he brought to these topics more critical acuity than one was accustomed to find in reviews of ephemera. But what a waste of talent.

The new book is in effect more of the same. It contains a few fine pieces, such as those on André Malraux and the Marquis de Sade. But must Wilson, in the years of his greatest maturity, expatiate on George Ade and Stephen Potter? And how shall we explain his protracted enthusiasm for such finks and funks as Max Beerbohm and James Branch Cabell? You may look from end to end of his new volume without finding the name of a single writer who has contributed prominently to the literature of the years in question; I have in mind such American novelists (never mind the poets!) as Algren, Mary McCarthy, Bellow, Warren, Malamud, Roth, Mailer, Tennessee Williams, Baldwin, Flannery O'Connor, Bradbury, et cetera, et cetera—the list can be extended to include virtually anyone's choices. Wilson might as well have been writing in Timbuktu.

There were omissions in the earlier work too: Faulkner, for example, who is not mentioned until the publication of *Intruder in the Dust* in 1949. And we would have liked to read Wilson's views of such interesting and, at the time, young writers as Anaïs Nin, Djuna Barnes (has he an antifeminist bias?), or even Thomas Wolfe. In the entire 1,981 pages of the three volumes, moreover, Thomas Mann does not occur once—a default which is hard to account for. Hence to subtitle his sequence a "Literary Chronicle" of the period, as he does, is to commit a breach of good faith, both critically and journalistically.

Edmund Wilson derived his critical method chiefly from that of Hippolyte Taine, who a century ago attempted the first serious correlation of literature with the larger events of social evolution. If his English is not as good as Taine's French—for Wilson has always written a curious hash of Macaulayan rhetoric and chicken-track syntax— he nevertheless brought to this socially oriented critical technique a considerable depth of learning and sensitivity as well as a wide-ranging contemporary view. He can read many modern authors, including the Russian, in their own languages, and he has put his linguistic accomplishments to good use. Yet at the same time his sense of literature as a social phenomenon has held his proclivities for cultural refinement in check, so that he has never fallen into the error of ingrown esthetic analysis that has damaged the so-called New Critics. This does not mean, of course, that Wilson has no critical defects of his own. As a case in point, his judgments of poetry are far less reliable than his judgments of prose, a deficiency evidently arising from some imbalance of temperament that we cannot see. Moreover, in isolated essays Wilson is patently and unexplainably unfair; see, for instance, his remarks on Kafka, who draws Wilson's fire not for any inadequacies of his own but quite transparently for those of his commentators.

Nevertheless Wilson's original keenness and devotion to artistic values cannot be doubted. He has given us fully articulated critical statements in such books as *Axel's Castle* and *The Wound and the Bow*, which show him to be a critic in the highest sense—scholarly, humane, passionate. All the more unfortunate, therefore, that his journalistic output, which should have been the heartbeat, so to speak, of his lifework, has been enfeebled by the American journalistic ethos as it affected both his editors and himself, with consequences of the utmost significance to American literature in the past twenty-five years. This has been just the period when we needed a clear, powerful critical voice on the side of social responsibility in the arts. If Wilson had continued to write with the seriousness of his early work, he might have furnished such a voice. And where could he have spoken to more purpose than in the daily or weekly press? Wilson would have fared better in Europe, where eminent critics have done some of their best work in brief essays for the newspapers. Instead he has suffered the debilitating effect of American journalistic standards, according to which only what sells is of value and only what entertains can be sold; and to my mind the result is a folly, a pity, and a shame.

People in a Myth

From a review of *The Educated Imagination* and *A Natural Perspective*, by Northrop Frye, from the *Hudson Review*, Winter 1965–66.

. . . THE CRITICISM of John Crowe Ransom and Allen Tate was deeply moral in tone and intent, essentially Arnoldian in this respect, even though their concept of the poem led them inevitably toward a split between art and experience, between esthetic and moral values. Northrop Frye, coming later, has resolved that split in one of the possible ways, that is, by denying the moral factor altogether. For him art is simply and totally conventional, and has neither moral content nor moral application.

Both Frye's new books are series of lectures that add little to the basic views developed in such earlier books as *Anatomy of Criticism* and *Fables of Identity*. *The Educated Imagination* comprises six lectures originally broadcast by the Canadian Broadcasting Corporation, which accounts for their chummy tone. They end with a plea for schools that will teach children to read imaginatively. Nothing wrong with that; people have been saying it for generations, if not for centuries. It would be easy to conclude that if Frye's lectures have had any good effect on public education in Canada, so much the better. My own feeling is that the possible good which the final lecture may produce in education will be more than offset by the harm resulting from a general public absorption of the pernicious ideas about writing and writers in the earlier lectures. However, since these ideas are more fully and I think more seriously exploited in the second of the two new books, I shall write chiefly about that.

A Natural Perspective consists of four lectures delivered at Columbia in 1963. They are subtitled *The Development of Shakespearean Comedy and Romance*, and are an attempt to rehabilitate the comedies as texts for critical attention and to show how they, and indeed all Shakespeare's works, lead inevitably and reasonably to the consummation of the final romances. I use the word *consummation* intentionally because Frye believes that *The Winter's Tale*, *Cymbeline*, and *The Tempest* are the real climax of Shakespeare's imaginative life, not *Hamlet* or *King Lear*.

Frye's reasoning is based on his general theory of literature, which is that all works of imaginative writing are conventional structures. Perhaps the sense is conveyed better by saying that they are structures of convention. They have no meaning apart from convention. However, the meaning of convention itself is deeply rooted in the past, or in the Jungian primitive consciousness. Convention, in short, is what is left over from myth when people stop believing the myth; and myth in turn is what is left over from magic when people stop performing magical acts to induce fertility and stave off disaster. This is the progress of literature: magic to myth to convention; and it is essential to Frye's concept that the progression is upward, not downward. The refinement and manipulation of convention is the artist's role, and his success is judged by the ease and sophistication with which he performs it.

No one would think of denying that Shakespeare's plays are conventional. Aside from their rhetoric, they are full of oracular voices, changed or disguised identities, people risen from the grave, interpolated masques and revels, and so on. Frye elaborates this theme by showing that the comedies are in fact versions of regenerative myth. Each has three phases: an opening, in which society is characterized as tyrannous and irrational; a middle, in which social chaos prevails (mixed identities, frustrated courtships, imprisonments and exiles); and an ending, in which a stylized revel (a multiple wedding) signals the birth of the new society—a higher, ideal society that now becomes the "real" society, while the convention of the play casts the old, objectively known society of unreason into the shade of illusion. I cannot comment on the anthropological parts of Frye's theory, but within his framework of discussion I find many of his remarks about individual comedies genuinely enlightening, and I suppose this is the first test of criticism.

But it is not the last. Frye pushes his insight too far; he turns it into a system and permits himself to be ruled by it, with the result that Shakespeare becomes for him simply a fabricator, an entertainer, albeit one who works with the whole span and depth of emotional values. But the plays have no meaning, and the poet had no aim in writing them beyond the creation of conventional structures. At one point Frye resorts to the remark that Shakespeare wrote for money, and that when he had made his pile he quit and retired to the country. But this is terribly unscholarly, not to say inhuman. No one knows how much money Shakespeare had, or how much he needed. He was a successful playwright, and conceivably he had enough money to retire five years before he did: he could have gone to the country with the romances unwritten, in which case Frye would have been left without the consummation on which he pins his theory. The point is that if there is a movement, a shape, in Shakespeare's career as an artist, then something in the man must have been responsible for it—unless the artist's life itself is simply a convention!

Frye writes, "The theme of wearing the horns of the deer in *As You Like It* and elsewhere may have more to do with this myth [Actaeon] than with stale jokes about cuckolds." Thus Frye manipulates his own convention theory. Why is the Actaeon convention any more worthy than the cuckold convention, equally ancient and equally valid mythologically? Certainly it was not a stale joke, unless all the comic conventions were stale jokes. But Frye's whole point is that convention is timeless. He is betrayed by his own enthusiasm, and he betrays the reader with his sarcastic rhetoric.

Again: "The assumptions of a dramatist or the expectations of his audience may readily be translated into opinions or propositions or statements. If we do this to Shakespeare's assumptions, they turn into the most dismal commonplace. Hence the feeling expressed [by many critics] that, great poet as Shakespeare was, his philosophy of life, his opinions, standards, and values were bewilderingly shallow. The obvious answer is, of course, that Shakespeare had no opinions, no values, no philosophy, no principles of anything except dramatic structure." Could any critical theory be reduced further toward meaninglessness? Here is a Shakespeare who is a kind of theatrical automaton, dead to everything but the conventions of his art, a mindless poet. Frye says this not once but repeatedly. In the book on education: "Literature has no consistent connection with ordinary life, positive or negative." And here the context makes the sneer in "ordinary" quite evident.

Elsewhere: "Shakespeare seems to have had less of an ego center than any major poet of our culture, and is consequently the most decent of writers. It is an offense against his privacy much deeper than any digging up of his bones to reduce him from a poet writing plays to an ego with something to 'say.'" But Shakespeare—I'm completely certain of it, though I know I am going out on the same limb that breaks under every Shakespearean critic—would have considered this statement itself the greatest possible offense: the statement that the relationship between a poet and a man (an ego with something to say) is one of reduction.

One more quotation: "In tragedy we recognize the importance of catharsis: pity, like terror, is raised, but it is ultimately set aside. In watching the ups and downs of York and Lancaster in the *Henry VI* plays we feel an automatic sympathy for the losers, qualified by all the evidence that one side is no less cruel and revengeful than the other. The losers are humanly vulnerable in a way that the winners are not. But sympathy for them, while it may be morally superior to contempt for them, would still coarsen and blunt the dramatic point. The dramatic point is tragic, and tragedy presents the event: this [particular action of fate] happens, whatever our feelings or moral reflections about it may be. If we ask why tragedy's presentation of this event is important, the answer takes us back to the myth of tragedy. Pity and terror are moral reflections about the tragic characters, and tragedy is not dependent on moral qualities." And still one more: "*Macbeth* is not a play about the moral crime of murder; it is a play about the dramatically conventional crime of killing the lawful and anointed king."

It is simply a misstatement of fact to say that *Macbeth* is not a play about a murder. What once gave the murder of the lawful king its efficacy as a ritual act was precisely the pity and terror evoked by it, the same pity and terror evoked by every repetition of it, in life or in art. The moral consideration is itself the timeless element, that is, the convention. This has nothing to do with sympathy or contempt for the characters, but a great deal to do with our inability to define or to recognize, much less to discourse about, any action whatever except in the categories of experience: no more is known to us. How can we understand the dramatic event, the particular blow of fate, if we do not first understand the essential injustice, the immorality, of human existence: that is exactly what we mean by the tragic view; that is the substance of the play. And considerations of justice and injustice are moral considerations. Without morality, no myth; without experience, no convention.

I cannot for the life of me comprehend why a work of literature cannot be both conventional and moral, rooted in both myth and experience. Admittedly I am writing now more as a working poet than as a critic or reviewer. Yet I notice that throughout Frye's criticism he has worked more easily with Renaissance texts or courtly texts—texts highly conventional and by authors personally obscure—than with modern texts. Yeats too was a poet of bewildering and silly opinions, and a poet in many respects strongly conventional; but in the face of his letters and memoirs, to say nothing of more explicit avowals in the poems themselves, it would be difficult to call him a man without values. I cannot think of a poet worth his salt since the beginning of time who was not a man of values, a man with "something to say." Naturally they said it in terms of the categories of human understanding. How else can you frame a discourse? How else, for that matter, can you frame an experience? Life itself, loving, hating, murdering, being murdered, is in its whole actuality conventional. We are all people in a myth.

Ezra Pound and the Great Style

From the *Saturday Review*, April 9, 1966.

To READ THE CRITICISM of Ezra Pound's poetry is to subject oneself to a bewildering experience. Most of it, certainly the best of it, has been written by people who are, or were, Pound's disciples; people who have gone to him as to a sage, seeking to immerse themselves in the influence of his compendious mind. And yet these people, in the books they have written about Pound, are the very ones who cast us most rudely into bewilderment.

Almost in one voice they announce, as if they had made an immense discovery, that Pound's great work, the *Cantos*, is a failure, that his economic and social opinions are pigheaded, that his scholarship is not only full of error (all scholarship is full of error) but actually stolen and faked. But then why do these people bother to write about his poetry? Why do the rest of us go on reading it all our lives long? Why, decade after decade, have we continued to be interested in this man, who has been such a peevish critic of our civilization and whom most Americans believe to have committed treason, at least technically, against our country—though this has never been proven juridically. Bigger traitors and acuter critics vanish into oblivion overnight, but Pound has held the American imagination for fifty years, and scarcely a month goes by without some new revelation of his celebrity in our popular press.

The answer is simple yet seldom, and almost never simply, stated. In great works of art we recognize a great and splendid light; perhaps not *in* the works but *behind* them, a luminosity beyond the realm of art which only artifacts of the first magnitude permit us, still darkly, to descry. It is a radiance we discover in the ceiling frescos of the Sistine chapel, in passages from Dante and Shakespeare, in some of the music of J. S. Bach; or occasionally in stranger places, like the final part of *Gulliver's Travels* or certain episodes in *Huckleberry Finn*. Always we stumble when we try to define this light. Even the words we apply to our own state of consciousness when we are seeing it remain inexact: wonder, exaltation, the gentle shock of sublimity. Yet we know what it is; and of all the poets in our time who have written in English none has revealed it more clearly and consistently than Ezra Pound.

Because we are unable to define the light we often speak of it in terms of style, the concrete appearance of works in which the light is present; and because style too, in its fully realized entirety, is indefinable, we often choose to speak of inferior examples, which give themselves more readily to analysis. Here are four lines from Pound's translation of an ode from the *Shih-ching*, which is the Chinese anthology of ancient poems and songs.

> *Wen, like a field of grain beneath the sun*
> *when all the white wheat moves in unison,*
> *coherent, splendid in severity,*
> *Sought out the norm and scope of Heaven's Decree*

These are a long way from Pound's best. They show him at work in a conventional mode that impedes the characteristic movement of his verse, yet they are still quite good, especially the first couplet. And how daring. How closely Pound courts prosodic absurdity. For here he has used a device that tempts all poets from time to time, usually with comic results, and he has brought it off: the "perfect" rhyme. Not only that, he has used two perfect rhymes, since *Wen* and *when* are almost indistinguishable, at least to those who cannot speak Chinese. Pound has bracketed his couplet in two monumental chords, like two strokes of the tonic in a fugue, between which the separate elements are allowed their intricate play. And notice the intricacy: the narrowing or funneling parallelism in "field beneath white wheat," the syncopation of "all the white," the sudden retardation of "moves." Indeed one could write at length about the prosody of these two lines alone.

But are they true? Only great learning and patience could say with any pretense of authority, and even then the answer would be only that—a pretense. Thousands of factors, and I am not exaggerating, impinge on this single judgment, or for that matter on almost any literary judgment. But as nearly as I can tell after giving the matter reasonable attention, these lines are in fact true: true to the original poem, the coherence, splendor, and severity that Pound names in his third line; true to the legend of King Wen; and true above all to Pound's vision of the light. The real question is: What is Pound's vision?

All told it is extremely complicated, as we should expect from so complicated a man. But in essence, like the visions of all great men, it is a vision of goodness, the good that exists somewhere in the universe, the excellence at the heart of experience, which is obscured from us most of the time by the imprecision, not to say chaos, of our human arrangements. Pound himself rarely speaks of the good, but more often of equity, order, an honest wage, the importance of ceremonial observances, and the like. In fact his vision is close to the idealization of human nature that was found on the nineteenth-century American frontier, where Pound was born; it is a pastoral vision, and today it seems almost quaint—or would if Pound hadn't shaped it in his magnificent style.

Ancient Chinese civilization and particularly the Confucian tradition have been important to Pound for several reasons, but chiefly because he found in them the ideal of a just secular order. On this account he has been accused, by those who miss the point, of mere secularism, which is preposterous. What Pound is interested in is not secularism but wholeness and union: of spirit and form, mind and body, man and nature. He connects the Confucian ideal with many scriptural and mythological counterparts in Asia and the Near East, and with a long line of religious feeling in Europe. If these Western connections begin in the temple at Eleusis rather than in the temple at Jerusalem, this is not because Pound denies biblical wisdom—that of Abraham or that of Jesus—for he has expressly confirmed it, but rather because he believes this wisdom to have been distorted and vitiated by the political, economic, and military policies of the Church and the Christian rulers. This may or may not have been the case, but it is at least an arguable view, and certainly one held by many historians more exacting than Pound.

Thus Pound's affinities in European civilization have been with Eleusis, the Roman mystery cults, the ritual marriage to the corn goddess, with Gnosticism, the Cabalic tradition, the Albigenses, which in turn connects him with his second consuming passion, the marvelous and heretical literature of the troubadours, or rather the entire development from the Provençal poetry of courtly love, with its close though possibly unconscious paraphrase of Catharist liturgy, to the crowning works of Cavalcanti and Dante. In these areas Pound has made important contributions to scholarship.

One cannot say the same for some other enthusiasms into which his quest has led him, the chief of them being, of course, his long excursion into economics. For two decades or more his vision of light appeared to have dwindled to his own personal, not to say eccentric, interpretation of Social Credit, the perfectly respectable system propounded by C. H. Douglas. Many people, owing in part to Pound's dilations on the subject, and probably also in part to those of certain Créditiste members of the Canadian parliament, will be surprised to learn of the respectability of Douglas's theories; but whether or not one accepts them—and I do not—they are at least serious and well intentioned, and they have been elaborated with a considerable degree of technical competence. Undeniably Pound's enthusiasm for economic solutions has borne results that have been sometimes ludicrous, as in his blunders concerning American history and monetary theory, and sometimes extremely sad, as in his blind appreciation of Mussolini. The effect on his poetry is unmistakable; it appears in the fourth line I have quoted from the Chinese translation, where the words *norm* and *scope*, which Pound used to give precise technical meaning to Confucian economic hypotheses, fail to work poetically. On a much larger scale the *Cantos* give us whole pages of political rant that serve no poetic purpose whatever, and this has induced some critics, among them Noel Stock, whose *Poet in Exile* is perhaps the best and toughest general analysis of Pound's writing that we have had so far, to explain the "failure" of the *Cantos* by saying that at some point Pound abandoned poetry and the objectives of poetry, and turned instead to an attempt to rewrite history and impose his own political ideas. But even if this criticism weren't based on a too-narrow definition of poetry, the charge would be untrue, and for two reasons.

First, even though much of Pound's political writing and nearly all his political activity have been wrongheaded and wasteful, they derived without question from his vision of the good: that has been his obsession. It would be hard to imagine a social critic more disinterested than Pound. Hotheaded, impulsive, irascible, yes; but you may search as you will through his poems, essays, prose fragments, and personal correspondence (as far as it is available) and you will not find a scrap of a personal motive—no private ambition, not even a general desire for power, since he has continually thrown away the power he actually had. Indeed, after saturating oneself in the enormous variety of Pound's writing, one begins to realize that although at first one had thought the image of Pound himself stood out clear, in the end it is only a series of masks, almost caricatures: the man himself is evanescent. And because his vision of the good is a unitary vision, in which poetry, agriculture, and economics are all expressions of the same generative force in the human spirit, no separation of fundamental human activities is possible. The only separation is the light from the darkness. Pound is our most farsighted poet; he sees poetry in a treasury report, provided the report is true and signifies a just distribution of the products of men's labor.

Secondly, to say, as Stock does, that Pound could ever become a nonpoet is simply absurd. It couldn't be, any more than a peach could become a watermelon. I don't mean that he was born a poet, or was endowed by the gods with poetry; no Platonic inference is required. He began with great verbal talent, obviously; but he was formed as a poet in his youth, between the ages of fifteen and thirty, when he studied poetry as I think no one ever did before, unless it was Dante. It is said that once he wrote a sonnet a day for a year, and then destroyed them all. He studied nine languages, seeking the poetry in each of them; he wrote and rewrote his own work every day, insisting on the necessity of labor and thought and continual experiment. I cannot believe that any genius so sculptured in a poetic attitude—to use one of his own favorite similes—could ever change. And in fact it didn't; in spite of the history and politics, his poetry is there on the page, right up to the last cantos and the most recent translations.

A great deal of nonsense has been written about the *Cantos*. Much of it comes from a misapprehension for which Pound himself is partly responsible. When he began the *Cantos* he announced that he was at work on an epic, and later hinted at parallels with the *Divine Comedy*; from time to time he indicated that his work was going according to plan, that it had a comprehensive formal structure. Well, his forty years' labor did not turn out quite that way. Whether or not this is regrettable is a meaningless question, since we cannot imagine what the *Cantos* might have been under some other dispensation. But we can see readily enough what they are, once we put aside our preconceptions. They are the second half of Pound's collected poems, the first half being the volume called *Personae*, which contains the poems he wrote before he began the *Cantos*. If the *Cantos* have more unity than the collected poems of other poets, this is what we should expect, for they embrace persistent themes and they do proceed, though waywardly, from a hell to a purgatory to, in the last cantos, a kind of paradise; but at the same time they remain, as we should also expect, miscellaneous: good and bad, lively and dull, important and unimportant, like anyone's collected work. We need a *Selected Cantos*, just as we have selected editions of the works of other famous poets, eliminating their less interesting productions. As a matter of fact Pound himself has made such a selection, which will be published in due course if all goes well, and no doubt other editors will eventually make other selections. Whether any of these, including Pound's, will be good or bad remains to be seen; but in principle nothing prevents them from being at least useful, or possibly much more. Meanwhile we have the *Cantos*, numbered 1 to 109, plus a few later fragments that have appeared in magazines. They are an epic, yes; but only in the sense than any man's lifework is epical.

Can they be finished? A friend of mine who is also a good friend of Pound's was visiting him once not long ago when Pound suddenly opened a drawer, took out a sheet of paper, and thrust it into my friend's hands. "There, that's the ending"—to be tacked on wherever the main text ultimately stops. Then the paper was snatched back, and my friend's memory of it remains naturally somewhat vague. But I shall be surprised if, when the ending is finally given to all of us, it turns out to be the precise, climactic statement that Pound's admirers expect, and I even hope it will not be: I cannot believe that any brief passage could sustain Pound's entire vision of light. In one sense the *Cantos* were finished some years ago, perhaps at the end of the Pisan section, when the main areas of feeling and substance had been distinguished and exploited, or in cantos 90 and 91 with their recapitulation of the main themes and their beautiful vision of a culturally united world. Pound himself has suggested that the paradisal elements in the last cantos may be unavoidably weak or insecure: "It is difficult to write a paradiso when all the superficial indications are that you ought to write an apocalypse." In another sense, of course, the *Cantos* will never be finished. And their unfinishability is, like that of a few other momentous works—Kafka's *The Castle*, Mahler's Tenth Symphony—an intrinsic and indispensable part of their meaning.

It is a question of style then; but this too has been muddled. There are styles and there is Style. Styles are objectified artistic embodiments of personality, elaborations of manner—style is the man, as somebody, I think Rémy de Gourmont, has said. Among Pound's famous contemporaries we have many such styles, transmitting to us their authors' various selfhoods, to which we respond variously. I can read Wallace Stevens and William Carlos Williams with pleasure, T. S. Eliot with a certain reluctant sympathy, and Marianne Moore in utter coldness; but I believe my responses have less to do with the merits of their writing than with the equations of temperament existing between these poets and myself. Even Yeats, who wrote poems that affect me with a kind of crippling delight, remains a stylist only in this smaller, personal sense. Pound alone in our time has created Style— the huge, concrete, multiform artifice that transmits to us the impersonal light beyond art, and from which the artist himself drops away. Pound's best poetry attracts every literate sensibility without reference to temperament or sympathy; it transcends taste. The *Iliad* was written by a man who is a myth, *Hamlet* by a man so uncertain that people spend lifetimes arguing about who and what he was. So with Pound: he is evanescent, and his work—*Personae*, the *Cantos*, the translations—stands as fully self-sustaining. If parts of it are boring, is that the unforgiveable sin some critics have averred? Of course not. We forgive, gladly, Homer his catalogues and his endlessly repeated epithets, Shakespeare his *Henry VIII* and *Merry Wives*.

Pound well understands the difference between himself and his contemporaries (though his relationship to Williams is more complex than the others). For him it was the difference between symbolism and realism, and he chose the latter. Where Yeats and Eliot had looked for an "objective correlative," an image upon which to impress their partial feelings, Pound insisted that the observed detail must stand by itself, an image in the concreteness of its own meaning. Hence his poetry is detailed, and set out in beautifully exact language, for exactness is the key to his sense of beauty.

Pound once said, speaking less than half in jest, that if he had the means he would build a temple to Demeter in Fleet Street. That is primary: the goddess sought through so many incarnations: Isis, Cythera ("crystalline"), Dione, Sophia, Eleanor, and all the others. The good: meaning proportion, plenty, the spirit of earth at work in man's heart. "Nothing matters but the quality of the affection"—so he has written. Homer began it and Pound—what shall we say, has he ended it? This only, I think, is the question to which critics and poets must address themselves now. What meaning has Homer or Ezra Pound in an age of inverting values? What role is left for the goddess of fertility when fertility itself has become a nuisance? How shall our children live in a world from which first the spirit, then history, and finally nature have fled, leaving only the mindless mechanics of process and chance? Will any place exist for a humane art in a society from which the last trace of reverence—any reverence—has been rubbed out? As a matter of fact I think a place will exist, will be made; but it won't be easy. Revolutions of sensibility have occurred before in the world, overturning whole libraries of masterpieces, though none so swift as ours.

To create beauty from sterility, value from meaninglessness, this is the work to be done, and less the philosopher's than the artist's (if ultimately a distinction may be made between them). One way to begin is by investigating Style. But although our studies of how Style works, how it recurs and is transformed, inevitably become abstruse and absorbing, they must not be permitted to obscure the fact that it does work—the reality of Style in our lives. The great Style, the Vision of Light. In this respect Ezra Pound's poetry is certain to be more and more important to us as time goes on.

Natural Elegance

A review of *History of My Life* volumes 1 and 2, by Giacomo Casanova, translated by Willard R. Trask, from the *Chicago Daily News*, November 12, 1966.

IN THE YEAR 1740 and in the city of Venice a fifteen-year-old boy who was a student for the priesthood found himself one night, owing to certain domiciliary exigencies, lodged in the same chamber with two sisters, both younger, though not much, than himself. In an instant he saw his duty. With remarkable dispatch—indeed, as nearly simultaneously as the laws of nature will allow—the transition from innocence to experience of two more of God's humble creatures was effected.

And that's it, the whole story in a nutshell. You might think there would be little more to say. But on the contrary it was only the beginning, and many things remained to be told. For one, the two sisters were absolutely delighted, so much so that they invited the young man back for further *combats à trois* at every opportunity for a number of years without the least trace of jealousy, either between themselves or toward any of the dozen additional girlfolk with whom he was soon disporting himself from one end of Italy to the other.

And so it went, year after year after year. As the young man grew older, the range of his operations extended. He was expelled from Venice. He was expelled from Paris. He was expelled from Vienna, from Warsaw, from Rome, from almost everywhere, always leaving behind a considerable lacuna in fashionable society and a cortege of ladies who had been, by and large, enchanted to make his acquaintance. Of course the priesthood was also left behind; even in that day of ecclesiastical ambidexterity, when the cardinals' mistresses were the arbiters of Rome, the Church was not his vocation. Nor were the other professions to which he incidentally applied himself: the army, civil service, espionage. His only constant passion, except the ladies, was poetry, and even that took a decidedly second place.

His name was of course, Giacomo Casanova, or as he later styled himself, Jacques Casanova, Chevalier de Seingalt. The world knows him simply as Casanova. Without any idea of who or what he was, millions use his name every day as a synonym for the promiscuous lover. It's a pity in a way, for he was a man of wit, a man of learning, and a man of good sense, and a better than fair hand as a writer too, whose poems, historical essays, and even mathematical treatises were widely respected in his time. But his notoriety was of his own making.

When Casanova set out to compose his memoirs he was an old man living in exile in Hapsburg Bohemia, bored and alone. His purpose, he said, was to amuse his declining years by rekindling in imagination the amorous excitements which his failing prowess no longer permitted him to enjoy in reality. At breakneck speed, using inaccurate French because it was more widely understood than his native Italian, relying on his astonishing memory for the details, he set down an account of his many sexual adventures, interspersed with recollections of travels, business affairs, and observations of life and culture generally. When he died in 1798 he had carried his *History* only as far as 1774, his forty-ninth year.

The manuscript disappeared at his death. When it turned up twenty years later it was published first in a German translation, then in an edition prepared from the original French by an editor named Jean Laforgue, who omitted certain passages and altered others in conformity with the new decorum of the nineteenth century. Laforgue's version has been the standard one for a century and a half. Then in 1960 a new unexpurgated edition, taken with scholarly care from Casanova's original manuscript, which had miraculously survived in the basement of a Leipzig publishing house, was issued in a joint undertaking from Paris and Wiesbaden, and the present translation by Willard Trask is based on this text.

Laforgue has long since been consigned among the bowdlerizers, and Mr. Trask and his publisher are assiduous to demonstrate his infamy, but it seems in the present case at least a little exaggerated and unfair. True, Laforgue made many verbal changes in Casanova's text, but most were only corrections of grammatical and stylistic errors. Laforgue rarely needed to tone down the original language, because Casanova, although always candid, was never obscene and was seldom indelicate. A graver charge is that Laforgue omitted completely a few important passages, and the gravest of all is that he added passages of his own, ascribing to Casanova motives and sentiments that the memoirist never actually entertained. Yet all told Laforgue's editing did not change the flavor of Casanova's work—perhaps nothing could—and the claim in the present edition, at least by implication, that we are being given a new and bolder Casanova is unsupported by the text.

Of course this does not mean that our finally possessing Casanova's memoirs as he actually wrote them is an unimportant event. On the contrary it is part of the great work of reclamation which is the chief scholarly ornament of our time, the emendation and decontamination of virtually every modern European classic. But it does mean that readers who go to this new edition in the hope of finding particularly titillating disquisitions *de arcanis amoris et veneris* will be disappointed. Adventure, intrigue, spice—yes, and in plenty. But no pornography. In this respect certain passages are astonishing; one would scarcely credit that a man could discuss the relative sizes of clitoris encountered in a widely ranging experience, and do so in a spirit of complete erotic enthusiasm, yet without the least pornographic effect. But Casanova did it. He came a generation before de Sade, and the difference is immense.

Then what kind of man was he? Simply a rogue, a rakehell? Not at all. He was far more complex than that. His learning and taste are evident on every page. He was a friend of Voltaire, he corresponded on equal terms with most of the leading intellectuals of the mid-eighteenth-century Enlightenment. He was a rationalist, an optimist, a realist, a sophisticate. At the same time he was a man of nature, as it was still possible for men of refined abilities to be in that distant epoch; a natural man in a society of natural men—and women! He believed, deeply and quite consciously, that pleasure is innocent. He was an advocate of what his age called Good Sense, a kind of natural elegance of mind. And why should we not call it the same today? His preface to his memoirs ought to be required reading for every public moralist and educator in the country. In short, Casanova was a gentleman, but in a sense of the term that we have lost, almost certainly forever.

Yet having said this, one remembers that just these gentlemen comprised the society against which the poor people of Paris uprose in 1789 in the greatest eruption of human misery the modern world has experienced. For if most of the people in Casanova's memoir resembled him in their tastes and social roles, certainly a few did not; and the few of his world were the majority of the actual world. It is one thing to engage in the sexual intrigues of the *haut monde*; it is quite another to seduce a young girl of the working class with promises respecting her future, and then to leave her without a thought when the next attraction presents herself. Casanova was capable of either action, and he carried them off with equal aplomb. Such conduct, enlarged to the scale of social and political reality, is not only despicable but tyrannous. We read Casanova's memoir with curiosity and amusement; we are grateful for his historical insights, his liveliness, and his delineation of a world which in some respects we cannot help but envy, just as his fellow aristocrats were grateful for so witty and elegant a conversationalist to enliven their Parisian and Viennese salons; but we are aware too of what that wit and elegance meant in the larger scene, and of what was seething beneath that brilliant social surface. We can read his book with pleasure, but we would not care to make Casanova our friend. And in point of fact he reveals himself in his memoir as a man who had many lovers but never a friend, and who did not suffer in the slightest from the lack. This was the flaw of his age, which could elevate the values of mind and manners above ordinary human concern, just at the beginning of the modern industrial and commercial era. It was a terrible flaw and it exacted a terrible penance, which I think has still not been performed in full. I wonder if it ever will be.

Materials from Life

A review of *The Nature of Love: Plato to Luther*, by Irving Singer, from the *Hudson Review*, Spring 1967.

MAN'S EFFORT TO CONCEPTUALIZE his love must have begun nearly as soon as his first conscious recognition that lying together is warmer than lying apart—I am not facetious—and in the millenia since then it has generated thousands upon thousands of works, theoretical and imaginative, which most people agree are among the finest products of the human mind and heart. In the face of this it is difficult to decide that a new book, just received and just read, makes a significant addition to what has gone before. It is doubly difficult when the work in question lacks the flair for expression and the versatility of feeling which the topic has inspired in the great minds of the past—Plato, the Psalmist, Ovid, Plotinus, Augustine, Bernard: this is a formidable company. Too formidable; and although our minds inevitably do draw comparisons, surely their doing so betrays the unamiable side of our character. The fact is that Irving Singer, in his book called *The Nature of Love*, says what no one has said before, or at all events what no one has said explicitly and systematically. And if his writing is neither as graceful nor as assured as one might wish, nor always perfectly lucid, it is still good enough; it has wit and verve; it is far better than what we normally find in professional philosophy. Above all Singer writes with no ostentation of technical virtuosity, and his book will be understandable to any reader who has even a passing acquaintance with philosophical aims and methods. Certainly it is an important book, and certainly a very good book. It has the kind of goodness we associate with originality and modesty and a genuine desire to serve.

Of course one may be mistaken. Perhaps somewhere a book exists which duplicates Singer's. The theoretical literature of love is immense, even the recent parts of it, and I have read no more than a little; I imagine no one has read it all. Theologians of every persuasion, including the pagan, have been especially productive in our time. Such books as Martin Buber's *I and Thou*, Etienne Gilson's study of Héloïse and Abelard, Simone Weil's *Waiting for God*, the essays and sermons of Paul Tillich, and even, in its implications of new human discoveries of love, Teilhard de Chardin's *The Phenomenon of Man*— these and many others are popular and doubtless have helped great numbers of people, although all such works, I think, including the last named, suffer from the necessary ultimate regressiveness in Christian thought. The secularists have been less prolific, if you do not count the quacks and semiquacks—the sexologists—who have enjoyed such a field day with their manuals. Secular philosophers have been impeded and embarrassed by the great burden of Freudian and other naturalistic apparatus which was handed to them years ago. Albert Camus, for instance, had an *attitude* toward love, which may be worked out in more or less detail from suggestions contained in *The Fall*, but I doubt that he had a *concept* of love. Most philosophers simply evade the issue. Jean-Paul Sartre, more serious and more rigorous, has given us his "theory of existential psychoanalysis"; but it is an awkward, difficult theory; and although few of us would care to reject his notion of the importance of choice as validating our theoretical human "authenticity," at the same time the famous "freedom" that goes with it remains elusive and obscure in the experience of our lives, particularly in the experience of falling in love.

Singer performs a more useful service. Where Sartre began his discussion of being with a consideration of man in alienation, Singer begins with man in love, and what he has produced is a phenomenology of love, having all the credibility and simplicity that Sartre's work lacks. (The sheer tenebrosity and poundage of Sartre's book on Jean Genet seems especially needless in the light of what Singer has done.) I do not mean of course that Singer has out-performed Sartre; his aim is both narrower and shorter. But within the limits of a discussion of man's affective experience Singer, from a general philosophical orientation similar to Sartre's (so the reader deduces, although Singer himself does not say it), has moved in a direction both more fruitful and more easily verifiable than Sartre's.

The heart of Singer's conceptualization lies in his first twenty-five pages. He begins with the accepted notion that "love is a way of valuing something," either a thing or a person, although we agree generally to confine the discussion to love of persons. Singer then analyzes love-as-valuation into two functions. The first he calls appraisal, which in turn he divides into two types. "Objective" appraisal is the discovery in the beloved of values which are commonly and publicly agreed upon. It is objective, of course, only in the sense that it is publicly verifiable, since a change of taste may easily overturn it: the objective value of Gina Lollobrigida is appraised differently, at least in some respects, from the objective value of Jean Harlow. The second type of appraisal is what Singer calls individual appraisal, this being the private valuation made by the particular lover who finds in his particular beloved values corresponding to his needs: she is blonde and he dislikes brunettes, she is rich while he disapproves of poverty, and so on. (I apologize for sexing the lover and beloved; it is a flaw built into our system of pronouns, and it plagues every discussion of love. But naturally the affective mechanisms work both ways, equally.) Both objective and individual appraisal are merely the *discovery* of values which already exist in the beloved, and by themselves they do not, according to Singer, suffice for a description of love.

What is needed is the addition of the other half of love-as-valuation, which he calls bestowal. Bestowal occurs when the lover assigns or ascribes to his beloved values which she does not necessarily possess in objectivity, but which in a sense she comes to possess as a consequence of her lover's act. For them the bestowed values are real. Thus loving consists of three forms of valuation, of which two are incidental while the third—bestowal—is essential. The beloved may be good-looking, which is a commonly held value discovered through objective appraisal; she may speak Chinese, which is a value only in respect to her lover's particular needs and is discoverable only through individual appraisal; and she may suffer from a hideous speech defect, which her lover turns into a charming mannerism by bestowing upon it a value it does not possess in "reality." Through the act of bestowal, in other words, the lovers transcend considerations of mere desire, convenience, and need, which may be requisite to their love but which can never constitute it. Bestowal is the essential element of love.

Many important consequences issue from this conception of bestowal, it seems to me, but I shall keep my discussion to three.

First, bestowal is always and essentially gratuitous. It may occur with rhyme—it often does—but never with reason. It is the free invention of value, emanating solely from the lover's affection and directed solely toward the beloved. It has no end or object beyond her, not even the gratification of the lover's needs, since these require an appraisable value; it proceeds directly and solely to her, to her as a *person*, a *someone*. This is important. It is one means by which Singer attacks the Freudian deterministic concept of love as sublimated narcissism. Singer gives love a content beyond necessity. His argument is analogous to Sartre's, of course, since both men are concerned to restore autonomous selfhood to the human animal, but it seems to me that the idea of gratuitous bestowal is a sharper, simpler counterfoil to nineteenth-century naturalistic determinism than Sartre's ideas of choice and a mankind "condemned to be free."

Second, because bestowal is always and essentially gratuitous it is always and essentially creative. From feeling, the lover creates value, which he bestows upon his beloved, thus creating in her an augmented being; or rather, more strictly, an augmentation of being. At the same time the lover's act is self-creative, an augmentation of his own being, because it enlarges his capacity for response: clearly it would be impossible to create a *value* to which he did not respond. Being as such, then, is the consequence, if not strictly the product, of love, and what could be more creative? (Singer's concept of bestowal is thus closer in some respects to Jaspers than to French sources.) The meanings of all this for secular philosophy are fairly obvious, and some are obviously dangerous, but for the moment I shall simply say that one important meaning is the freedom of love. Not so much a freedom of choice, as Sartre would have it, for the "selection" of the beloved is always hidden, even if it is not ultimately adventitious; but a freedom of invention, of creativity. It is the freedom of making rather than the freedom of affirming, of initiative rather than response. Thus the lover's freedom is a continuing enrichment, not a source of anguish, and surely this interpretation is closer to our real experience of love than Sartre's.

Third, because bestowal is always and essentially creative it is always and essentially imaginative. That is to say, love is functionally esthetic. Here is where one chief danger lurks. For human imagination operates inevitably in terms of ideals, call them what one will—forms, models, gestalts, universals, noumena. Any artist knows from his working practice that it is impossible to create a representation of anything without the intrusion of prior knowledge; we cannot so much as "see" anything as it actually is—certainly not our beloved. Hence idealization is an inevitable part of love. But we know too that the processes of idealization tend to place the image of the beloved under this or that sign, to lead away from a consideration of her as a person and toward a consideration of her as a meaning; ultimately they may end in aims and objects totally separate from her. The trick is to show that this need not be the case, that idealization need not inevitably or necessarily lead away from the person, but on the contrary may lead back to the person and may, so to speak, reinforce the person; and to my mind this is a point which Singer has failed to make with sufficient force. On the other hand this volume is only the first of several he intends to devote to his theory of love, and I am sure he will have much more to say about idealization later on.

The 350 pages which follow this introductory section of Singer's book are devoted to a critique of the principal theories of love from the beginning of the Greco-Hebraic tradition to the end of the middle ages. Although he obviously has an enormous knowledge of the literature and does not hesitate to bring in obscure texts when he needs them, Singer concentrates on Plato, Aristotle, the Old Testament writers, Lucretius, Ovid, Paul, Plotinus, Augustine, and the medieval writers from Bernard of Clairvaux to Thomas Aquinas, ending with the radical revisionism and reversionism of Martin Luther. Much of this material will be familiar to Singer's readers; any philosopher who decides to proceed in terms of systematic criticism, historically arranged, runs the risk of boring his audience. Singer's reading of the texts in question is acute and clear, but not strikingly original. What comes through most prominently from his discussion is an impression of sweetness in the intellectual tone; not so much in the writing as in the sympathy of mind he brings to great writers in the religious tradition. Clearly, although he works from a standpoint outside that tradition, Singer finds much that is attractive in the Christian philosophers, and in the saints and mystics. And who can doubt that their great effort of love, prolonged in intellectual jeopardy over so many barbarous centuries—right if it was right, or wrong if it was wrong— did in fact save the world?

Singer makes two exceptions to his rough chronological arrangement. The first stems from an embarrassment in his materials. Since all his texts come from the period of Western religious flowering, Singer lacks naturalistic texts to use for foils. The incipient naturalism in parts of Aristotle is not useful for his purpose, and Lucretius is too elementary, while Ovid is a special case. Hence Singer displaces Freud, who on other counts as well is his bête noire, from a comfortable niche in our own era, and takes him back to the Middle Ages to act there as the foremost theoretician of naturalistic love. This is no injustice to Freud, it may even be a kind of honor; yet sometimes the juxtaposition of Freud and Saint Thomas or Martin Luther seems a trifle odd. Perhaps in the circumstances it isn't surprising that the Viennese doctor always comes off second best.

But the ultimate point of the critical parts of Singer's theory is that both traditions, religious and naturalistic, not only fail to explain love, as we understand it now, but impede it, misdirect it, and even destroy it, at least conceptually. In both cases this happens through the misuse of the processes of idealization. For both philosophies, through their idealizations, direct love away from the person and toward an ideal object existing outside the competence of human valuative faculties, on one hand toward God and on the other toward Nature; and thus they both deny to human love the function of bestowal which, as Singer has argued, is the indispensable constitutive element. Reduced to this brevity, the argument is full of holes, of course. God is conceived in many ways; so is Nature; the entire evolution of man's loving relationship to both is marvelously intricate. Yet Singer's argument, detailed but not difficult, holds up throughout, I think. It is sound intellectually and experientially, and it points always back toward ourselves. It is the first step toward the accomplishment of the task we must perform for ourselves, an absurd but imperative task: to find a way for modern man to love without external sanctions. This is the essence of Singer's book.

But in addition Singer's critique performs another valuable service, the rigorous redefinition of the chief terms in Christian theories of love, *agape* and *eros*, as well as the reintroduction of two important subordinate terms, *philia* and *nomos*. All these have been seriously muddled by religious popularizers for centuries. (A case in point is a new book by Ralph Harper, who however is no popularizer, his *Human Love: Existential and Mystical*, to which we turn with good will and a certain sympathy for the author's intention; but we find in it the same woolly use of terms, particularly the reduction of eros to a virtually meaningless animal impulse, and the same glib religious and idealistic concepts that have already estranged us from most of the speculative literature of modern love.) Singer has done well to bring semantic precision back to the discussion. He has done it by tracking his terms to their philosophical sources in ancient texts, then by analyzing their evolution. I don't say this is a unique distinction, but such rigor is unusual, and we are glad to find it in a book of this kind.

Singer's second departure from his chronology is the omission of the entire episode of courtly love in the twelfth century. This, he says, together with its effluence in the romantic tradition generally, will be the subject of another volume; or possibly two—he does not state his plans exactly. The heresy of *vray amor* and its subsequent influence upon European civilization down to our own time has been for years the special province of Denis de Rougemont, and has been muddled by him, both conceptually and historically, almost beyond belief; so that for this reason alone I should think many people must look forward with agreeable expectation to Singer's next book. But I, for my part, look forward even more enthusiastically to the final volume of his projected series, the one which he will devote to modern love; for then, it seems to me, he must come at last to an end of critique, and must shift his aim to an affirmative philosophy of love—especially, I hope, to the consideration of the role of existential idealization in human love and in life generally.

For isn't the real significance of Singer's work the fact that it is open, at least implicitly, to immense possibilities? By now I am sure many readers of this commentary wonder why I began it by calling Singer's book new and original. What is original about the idea of gratuitous and creative bestowal—except perhaps the term? Isn't it a common part of our attitude to life now? It is; and when I began to read Singer's book I said to myself, "But of course, this is what I have thought for years." Love for its own sake or for *our* sake, creative human love as a condition of unsanctioned being, is part of our overwhelmingly secularized culture; we find it everywhere—in our movies, poetry, fiction, in the hortatory materials that are thrust at us continuously from every moral stronghold, including the religious—to which it ought to be anathema. Love, despite the state of the world, *is* our existence, and creativity is its touchstone. This is how our loves now work if they work at all; this is the idea we try to impress on our frolicsome children when we tell them what is really meant by making love, not war. But all good philosophy takes its materials from the life in which it is born. Singer has crystallized our attitude toward love. And in doing so he has searched out its elements systematically and has made them into a good instrument for criticism. He has a long way still to go. I, no more than another reader, have access to his plans, and all I can say to him is that I hope he won't be deterred by the professional objections his colleagues are sure to raise to his work—objections I would not raise myself, even were I competent to do so. I confess I have a kind of vision: the final overturning of the Cartesian applecart. We have known for a long, long time that the *Cogito* was a false hope, with all its supervening burden of self-divisive consciousness. We have seen it as a vitiating element in all Western culture, including much of our own existentialist thought. We know perfectly well, from our whole experience of intellectual, social, and military history in our time, that if we have any virtue in meaninglessness, it is our capacity, not to think, not to feel, not to "see ourselves," but to love; and hence to imagine, for love, not necessity, is the mother of invention—to imagine, meaning to bring together, to synthesize, to act undividedly in the existential wholeness of the human spirit. Yet for two thousand years no important new philosophy has begun with love as the explicit starting point, and I can't help asking myself, naively or not: Wouldn't it be wonderful if it happened now?

Poetry of Abstraction

A review of *Birds*, by St. John Perse, translated by Robert Fitzgerald, from *Poetry*, June 1967.

SOME TIME AGO St. John Perse described an encounter with his friend André Gide: "He told me of the attraction that an exhaustive study of the English language was beginning to exert over him. I, for my part, deplored the denseness of such a concrete language, the excessive richness of its vocabulary, and its pleasure in trying to reincarnate the thing itself, as in ideographic writing; whereas French, a more abstract language, which tries to signify rather than represent the meaning, uses words only as fiduciary symbols like coins as values of monetary exchange. English for me was still at the swapping stage."

Is this why we have so few good translations from French poetry? Is it perhaps also why we are so tempted, puzzled, and charmed by that barrier? Our books are full of adequate translations from the French, virtually everyone tries it, and yet not more than a handful of French poems sit really comfortably in English: one or two by Lang, one or two by Rossetti, a dozen others here and there; whereas we have hundreds of easy, authentic versions from the Chinese, Hindu, Spanish, Persian, and almost every other big language in the world. Even as fine a translator and poet as Robert Fitzgerald cannot quite achieve it, for I find in *Birds* a quality of embarrassment, a verbal apologeticism, of which I see no trace in *Oiseaux*.

If we accept the common notion of translation among modern poets, to re-create the original poetic impulse in another language, we see at once why translations from the French so often fail. What re-creation can there be when the entire order of thought and feeling is different? We have no meeting-point with the French. On the other hand if we resort to the earlier notion of translation as a carrying over of literal content from one language to another, we know that except in very lucky instances we get only a crib. And indeed this now seems to me to characterize the whole attitude of English-speaking poets toward French poetry: from Chaucer to the present, and in both senses of the word, it has been cribbing.

Here at all events we have a splendid French poet, very likely a great French poet, *deploring* the *concreteness* and *excessive richness* of our language, and recommending that poetry should *signify*, not *represent*, its substance. He is willing to accept words as *fiduciary symbols*, to accept them on trust without pinning them down; he is willing to be *abstract*. Of course for centuries English-speaking poets have been saying exactly the opposite. Beauty is truth, and no ideas but in things.

This antithesis is in the poetry. Perse writes a kind of pure poem of sensibility, an analytic of the heart, a conceptualizing poem. Without meter, without any rhythm except the self-sustaining verbal flow, his poetic principle, as one would expect in so abstract a composition, is pure grammar. It is a poetry of syntax, not cut to any particular rules of practice, although the general rule seems to be this: use every syntactical resource, and make it move. The result is a Ciceronian concision, elegance, and thrusting vigor which some previous translators have tried to render in a kind of Dickensian sonority. This is wrong; Fitzgerald does much better with his clean, classical style. Yet the embarrassment I spoke of is still present. In English the poem seems to lead, through agonies of conception, up to something concrete, the thing itself, but just there, where we expect the object upon which to pin our feelings and our hopes for the poem, the translator is left hanging, the poem relapses into conception, into "fiduciary" symbols. In French it works, but in English . . . at any rate it does not work as well.

Hence we have a poem that begins like this, reaching toward a cry we cannot hear:

L'oiseau, de tous nos consanguins le plus ardent à vivre, mène aux confins du jour un singulier destin. Migrateur, et hanté d'inflation solaire, il voyage de nuit, les jours etant trop courts pour son activité. Par temps de lune grise couleur du gui des Gaules, il peuple de son spectre la prophetie des nuits. Et son cri dans la nuit est cri de l'aube elle-même: cri de guerre sainte à l'arme blanche.

Yet I for one find this cry, not only as it winds abstractly through this rather long poem but as it "appears," unsounded, here at the beginning, somehow—I admit I don't entirely know how—precise and effective.

And I must point out that the poem itself is "about" the problem I have raised. Its "occasion" was the bird lithographs of Georges Braque, four of which are reproduced in this very handsome volume, and in effect its "subject"—quotation marks being necessary because in another sense this distinctly modern poem is "about" nothing but itself—is the relationship between Braque's abstractly particular birds and the poet's universalizing ambitions. I don't know what American poets can learn from it; but if we submit ourselves to it we may begin to suspect that in spite of our doctrinairian and prescriptive tendencies any poem which works is a good poem and there is room in the world for them all.

Delmore, 1913–1966

From the *Texas Quarterly*, Summer 1967.

POETS THINK A GOOD DEAL about words and the qualities of words, naturally enough since in the broadest sense words are their livings (though ultimately it comes to more than that). I have been thinking lately about the word *ruth*. A discredited word, marked "poeticism," in the dictionary. It turns up commonly in poetry written on the most amateur level, where it rhymes invariably with *truth*, but you seldom see it anywhere else. In my own case it is well known to me yet doubly discredited, because it rhymes with—indeed is part of—my own name, as I discovered when I was a schoolboy and whiled away the tedium by fiddling with the meanings of *hay, den, car,* and *ruth.* But with one exception I can think of no serious writer of the twentieth century who has used the word. You might expect it would be a very useful word, rooted firmly in the Anglo-Saxon origin of our language, an active word, meaning mercy, compassion, Aristotelian pity, yet more vigorous than any of these. Ruth suggests not merely a passive state of sympathy, but the compassionate attitude as something outgoing and efficacious. Perhaps this is because when we think of ruth we think also of the story of Ruth in the Old Testament: "Whither thou goest, I will go," though as nearly as I can tell by consulting the etymological dictionary there is no linguistic connection between the English word and the Hebrew feminine name.

Is it significant that in our society today we use the word only in its negative form: *ruthless?* Delmore Schwartz would have thought so.

He is the exception I spoke of. He used the word *ruth* again and again, trying, with the kind of poetic courage that comes close to folly, to find the combination of prosodic and thematic factors that would allow a rehabilitation of the word. It went with another favorite word of his, equally unfashionable, the word *hope.* How well this rehabilitation succeeded in individual poems is a matter of taste. To my taste some of the poems are masterpieces. But in his whole work and his whole life, Delmore failed. He had to fail. His vision of a world of ruth and hope was shattered again and again, and no poet shows us more clearly the ruthlessness of our own society. Incidentally I make no apology for calling him Delmore, because it is impossible to call him Schwartz; he was always just "Delmore" to everyone, friends and strangers alike.

The truth is that our society today, in spite of all our recent cultural pretensions, is as hard on poets as it ever was. Granted, many poets are fed and housed better than they were thirty years ago, and their work is published more promptly and sometimes more effectively, but only provided that they teach, recite, perform, expound, exhibit—in short, that they tickle the institutional vanity of the age. Those who cannot or will not do this suffer in one degree or another the tyranny of a social machine more highly institutionalized, more ruth-less, than ever. Delmore suffered it in the greatest degree. It destroyed his life.

Then there is a complementary truth, which is even more depressing. Simply this: that the smaller society within the larger—the society of poets which ought to be the reverse of the larger society, which ought to be the society of almost pastoral grace and creativity that Delmore envisioned—is instead racked by its own desperate tyranny, the tyranny of competition, envy, vanity, professional avarice. This is what destroyed Delmore's work. Not all of it of course, for his best poems and stories and essays make a little group of splendid pieces. But Delmore never produced the body of fine work that he could have produced and that he would have produced, as we cannot avoid recognizing, in other circumstances.

Delmore's terrifying, lonely, evil death in the summer of 1966, when he fell gasping with a heart attack at 3:00 A.M. in a hotel corridor, and the wrong corridor at that, significantly enough, because the room he was looking for, his own last home, a tawdry, littered cubicle, was two floors above: this rotten death nevertheless brought, in a wry, unhappy way, a sense of release to his old friends. For the first time in years they could speak publicly of their affection and admiration for him without fear of immediate recrimination. Not one of them, as far as I know, had escaped the wild accusations that Delmore issued during the years of his deepening psychopathological crisis. Some of his paranoid delusions were so outrageous and complicated that everyone laughs at them, even people who have the best reason to understand the depths of anguish from which they sprang. Delmore's aggressions had the fantastic quality of an invention by Rube Goldberg. And of course his old friends were silenced by them. They had no choice but to withdraw in the face of such unappeasable hostility, though they continued to help him, silently and indirectly, when they could.

Now during recent months we have seen a number of tributes written by Delmore's old friends. Invariably they recall him as a young poet, someone fun to be with, a bright talker, hard-minded and humorous, tireless, looking for a good time, full of the élan of being a poet in the company of poets. In the eyes of these people he seems an attractive, lively, gifted, romantic figure.

I never knew him well, though I saw him off and on over the years.

He was somewhat older than I. When he was poetry editor of *Partisan Review* he published some of my first poems, and we had an amiable correspondence. He was always helpful and interested in his dealings with younger writers, I think. He had many teaching jobs, including some real plums at posh universities, and although often he was unable to last out the term of his contract, his students felt warmly about him and frequently went to look him up later in New York. Toward the end these young people, students and others who found him in the bars around town, were apparently the only ones who were close to him.

In the early fifties I took a job in a publication office on Fifth Avenue overlooking the park, where Delmore worked too on a part-time basis. He came in one day a week to write paragraphs and blurbs and do other little chores. He did not like the office, and although I worked there every day for a year I never felt comfortable in it either, and often on "Delmore's day" he and I would take off in midafternoon and go to one of those bars on Madison Avenue where the woodwork is darkly polished and the mirrors are shadowy. These places would be empty at that time of day; the bartenders would be setting up for the five-o'clock rush; Delmore and I would lean on the bar with our big, expensive highballs that neither of us could afford, and talk about . . . almost anything, I suppose. Poetry and baseball, since we shared these interests, and then I recall one time when I tried for an hour to explain to him my devotion to jazz and to the musical qualities of jazz. It didn't work. Like most poets—I have always been especially annoyed by the poems on jazz that William Carlos Williams wrote— Delmore continued to think of jazz in essentially nonmusical, that is, sociological, terms. But what I remember most of all is his appearance. He still looked rather boyish, like that old photograph in the Oscar Williams anthologies, but his features were somehow softened, hazy, blurred, and his voice was so quiet that I had to bend my head to listen. I had the impression of great sadness and sweetness. It was as if he was lost and knew he was lost, and had given up caring about it. The exhilarated spirit his older friends remember was never apparent to me, but rather a quietness and a desire to cling to little things, little actions and objects, as if from a simple attachment to littleness for its own sake. He looked and spoke like a defeated shipping-house clerk. I could almost imagine him on the point of adopting some far-out hobby, like growing dwarf trees, to occupy his declining and withdrawn years.

Impressions of lost afternoons! And who knows how many of those expensive highballs set off fuses that detonated in catastrophe twelve hours later?

Anyway Delmore was lost—it wasn't just my imagining. Not long afterward the roof fell progressively in, the nightmare of his final decade began. When he died he was fifty-two years old.

What we have left is his work. He began very early—his first published writing appeared in *Partisan Review* when he was twenty-two years old—and he won almost instantaneous success. His poems and stories had a romantic warmth that seemed more than appealing after the "proletarian verse" of the deep depression, and at the same time they were vigorous and fresh, products of a strong personal vision; they offered a sense of direction at a time when the defeat of human aspirations in Spain and the build-up for a new world war were creating anxiety and jaded sensibility everywhere. Here was a proper romantic. Delmore acknowledged his model—Shakespeare—and it seemed almost unheard of. He wrote sonnets—how strange!—and gave them high-powered first lines in the proper sonneteering tradition. It was a part of his almost foolish poetic courage. Yet it worked; the sonnets were good, and they still are—some of them probably among the best of their kind in American literature.

There was a charming simplicity about Delmore's early work, though never simplemindedness. He was, of course, a product of his time. He claims somewhere that he began studying existentialism in 1935, three years before Sartre published his first book, in which case Delmore was one of the most precocious philosophers in America; but of course he was exaggerating, he often did. The point is that he was aware, with his quick, intense mind, of the main currents of thought in the intellectual world of which he himself had so rapidly become a part. He was aware, too aware for his own good, of anxiety and nihilism, of obsessive guilt and responsibility, for these themes formed much of the substance of his work for years to come. He was not only aware of these elements of the time's sensibility, he fought against them—in his own way. Always he clung somehow to his concepts of ruth and hope. He turned them and twisted them, he did everything he could to rescue them from the absurdist denials of

Sartre, Camus, and their American followers. Hope was reasonable, damn it!—so he insisted. It was the only value which could bring mankind through the incredible horror of the war and the whole stupidity of modern life.

In almost no time at all Delmore found his work in great demand and found himself in a position of considerable power in the literary world. He was an editor of *Partisan Review,* which without doubt was the best connection a young writer could have in those years. The pages of other reviews opened to him as if like flowers; teaching offers came to him; he was lionized and studied. He entered what must have been a period of insanely intense activity. New poems, stories, and essays appeared frequently. Plans were announced by his publisher for a long autobiographical poem and for a translation of Baudelaire's *Fleurs du mal.* But then came the probably inevitable collapse. For whatever reasons—and although I am sure they were complex, still the simple pressure of sudden success must have had a lot to do with it—Delmore began producing work so bad that one can hardly believe it was written by the same man. The long poem was abandoned before it was finished, though parts of it were published, and the translation, when it came out, was so poor and so riddled with error that it had to be withdrawn from circulation. Consider how great a blow that must have been. And the decline that set in then continued for a long time, for years. A new collection of poems in 1950, *Vaudeville for a Princess,* contained so much poor work that Delmore himself was able to include only three poems from it in his selected poems of 1959.

The old models had disappeared, the ones that had guided his first work, Shakespeare, Keats, Kafka, Baudelaire. Instead Delmore's poetry began to look more and more like a pastiche of his contemporaries and rivals. Auden, Thomas, Roethke, Lowell—for a while Delmore's work was like a roll call. He seemed to be trying to beat everyone at his own game. It was hopeless, ruthless, as Delmore himself must have begun to realize. Then at last he found his own voice again, a drier voice than formerly, running in longer cadences and in a rhetoric of bitterness that burst out of itself continually toward joy. These were his last poems. Above all they spoke of endurance:

> *Poetry is better than hope,*
> *For Poetry is the patience of hope, and all hope's vivid pictures*

It was not a reconciliation, we cannot imagine that in Delmore's case; but at least we can trust that his last work gave him moments, perhaps hours and days, of rest in his turmoil.

Delmore's stories, perhaps because he took them less seriously than his poems, were always good. He was a marvelous storyteller. His prose was real prose, not a poet's typical posturing, but straight and clear and strong and flexible, and he could manage a complicated story line without stress. He never wrote a bad story, as far as I know, and he wrote some that are superb; the only trouble is that there are so few of them altogether. He could have been one of the great masters of the short story. Then finally there is his criticism. He wrote a lot of it, mostly magazine reviews but also some longer essays, all intelligent, lucid work. Like all criticism much of his is ephemeral, but some has permanent value. I remember especially a long review of Faulkner's *A Fable*. Perhaps it took a poet to do justice to that so often unjustly criticized masterpiece.

The personal factors in Delmore's illness are largely unknown to us, and will remain so until somebody—I hope a very intelligent somebody—writes his biography. But the public factors in his failure are not. To be a young Jew and a young poet in America in the thirties and forties was a brutal experience. We know this because so many others were hurt by it. Delmore was simply one of the most gifted. He wrote splendid poems and stories, but how much more good work he might have done if he had been given the chance to escape from the pressures of racial tension and competitiveness, a chance to create a consistent, integrated body of writing. I wish that somehow he had gone away when he was about twenty-five, had gone out West perhaps, to live on the desert or in the mountains. He wouldn't have liked it, he was too much a city boy. But if he had been forced to stay until he learned to like it, until he learned to recognize the strength he possessed within himself . . .

Well, maybe it would have been no better for him. We can do nothing to help him now at any rate. We can only take steps to secure and distinguish his work. I hope some publisher will soon bring out an intelligently edited selection of Delmore's best poems, stories, essays, and reviews. There are enough, I should say, to make one good-sized and extremely fine volume, and it is a book we cannot afford to do without.

A Meaning of Robert Lowell

From the *Hudson Review*, Autumn 1967.

A BOOK REVIEWER looking at Robert Lowell's new book, *Near the Ocean*, for the first time would find good reasons to be annoyed with it and to say so forcibly. The book itself, for one. It is a pretentious volume; printed on expensive paper, bound in heavy cloth and stamped in three colors, decorated with twenty-one drawings by Sidney Nolan, designed lavishly and wastefully in an outsize format, jacketed in varnished sixty-pound stock: in short, a very self-conscious-looking collector's item, which might easily provoke a reviewer into a little investigation. He could learn without difficulty, for instance, that publication of the book had been postponed several times, and that the price had been announced progressively at $4.95, $5.50, and $6.00. Why? Our reviewer would soon discover that the longest piece in the book, a translation of Juvenal's Tenth Satire, had appeared in a magazine version, in *Encounter*, only a few weeks before the book came out, and he would see significant differences between the two texts. He would surmise that last-minute revisions had been made in the poem—hence, very likely, the delays in publication—and he would wonder if other equally impetuous revisions had been made in other poems, especially the personal ones whose texts are spattered with ellipses. He would wonder also if the resetting of so much type had required the increases in price. He would read the note at the front of the book, in which Lowell, speaking of Nolan's drawings, says, "May my lines throw some light on his!"—apparently meaning that the poet hopes a certain reciprocity of example will ensue between texts and illustrations. But what a curious way to say it, what a slip of the two-edged pen. As for the drawings themselves, would indeed, our reviewer might exclaim, that the poems could illuminate them, they need it! Next he might look at the table of contents, where he would count the titles, seven poems and six translations, and wonder if readers should be asked to pony up six dollars for so small an offering of untried work. Finally our reviewer would turn to the texts themselves, where he would find, first, an ill-assorted group of translations from classical and Renaissance poems, not Lowell's best, and second, among the original pieces—the slight heart of this slight book—one conventional tribute to Theodore Roethke and six personal poems: strange poems, not poorly written in the usual sense, on the contrary fairly glittering with the acuity and verbal panache we expect from Lowell, and yet so awkward nevertheless, so fragmentary, devious, elliptical, and even stilted that they seem—well, to make the best of it, bewildering.

How could our reviewer fail to give the book an angry notice? Highfalutin ostentation: nobody likes it. All the less do we like it in contrast to Lowell's other books, which, in their quiet formats and with their modest crosshatch illustrations by Francis Parker on the title pages, make an attractive and more reasonable appearance. *Near the Ocean* looks unmistakably like a "big production" that was supposed—if not by Lowell, by someone—to catapult the poet into the cushiest seat in stardom, as if he weren't sitting there already. But by its own overreaching, it has failed.

Our reviewer, if he had an inquiring mind, would not be satisfied simply to blast the book's appearance, however. He would wish to find out why Lowell wrote these strange new poems, and what purpose their new style is intended to serve. In short he would change himself, if he were able, from a reviewer into a literary critic. He would study all Lowell's work, he would divide, classify, elucidate, analyze, and compare, and he would give us a schematic judgment which might or might not be useful to us, and which might or might not have something to do with the poems.

Incidentally, if he were a proper scholar, he would begin his essay with a review of previous critical opinions, which in the case of Lowell's poetry comprise a truly splendid range: from servile adulation (in the New York clique) to contumelious rejection (among the West Coast paradisiacs). Obviously this hodgepodge offers a great opportunity to a critic who fancies his own rhetorical prowess.

For my part I am no critic. More's the pity perhaps, because I do find, like our hypothetical reviewer, that I am unwilling to rest on the simple distaste aroused in me by Lowell's new work, a distaste which is uncertain at that, inconsistent and unformed. I would like to know more. In consequence I must attack the poems in the only way I can, namely, as a fellow poet, someone who has worked the same side of the street for roughly the same period, and who presumably knows something about the difficulties of the job. This is what I propose to do, that is, to look at the poems less as finished works than as objects coming into being. Indeed, for reasons I shall elaborate, I think this is the only way one can look at Lowell's work of the past fifteen years.

The risks in my method are great, of course. One is that I shall stray from my literary topic into what is normally considered personal or biographical. To those who may charge me with this, I give two answers. First, I shall not stray far because I do not know Lowell personally, having met him only twice, for a few minutes each time and at an interval of more than a decade. My knowledge of the man comes either directly or by inference from his own writing, and from what I have heard during twenty years on the edge of the literary world. Secondly, in dealing with poetry as personal as Lowell's, or as personal as most poetry written nowadays in America, the risk of infringing upon the poet's privacy is properly speaking no risk at all. An invitation has been extended to us: why shouldn't we accept it?

THE PLACE TO BEGIN, then, is with a biographical datum. Robert Lowell is, and for some years has been, the most envied poet in the country. The consequences of this are many, but for the moment I wish simply to enforce the fact. I envy Lowell. Everywhere I go among literary people I meet only others who envy Lowell. The reasons for it are obvious enough: his great advantages. First, the advantage of his birth in a distinguished family. One does not wish to insist on this, but at the same time it is not negligible. No doubt being born with a ready-made cultural and social status is sometimes a hindrance, but often it is a help too, and in our hearts most of us would be glad to put up with the one if we could thereby attain the other. Secondly, the advantage of talent and intelligence. I am not speaking of the particular concrete expressions of these properties, but of the properties themselves. From the first Lowell's poetry has had an inner force bespeaking his great native gifts. It has put him in the class of wonder boys, along with poets like the early Auden and Dylan Thomas who, however idiotic they may sometimes look in other respects, were simply unable to write a trite or flaccid line. Most of us must cultivate poorer gardens. If we console ourselves with the idea that the best crop sometimes comes from meager soil, nevertheless we yearn often enough, in our adverse labor, for the facility of mere brilliance. Thirdly, the advantage of success. Let anyone say what he will, Lowell is our leading poet. It is a fact. He has power, influence, and an enormous reputation. His books, for example, are kept in print and they sell steadily—what a joy that must be! We all, I know, are reasonable creatures, and we realize that success is more often a nuisance than a blessing. But are we so inhuman that we deny our envy of those who have it? I hope not.

Of course envy is a tricky thing. It takes many directions. At bottom it accounts, I believe, for 90 percent of the critical response to Lowell's work, the wide range of opinions, and it accounts too for the concentration of responses at the extremes of the scale: adulators at one end, detractors at the other. As for the adulators . . . but why not call them by their right name, the flatterers? In their multitude we dismiss them; and we need add only that although their opinion in the long run may turn out to be right, and Lowell's poetry may be seen to be precisely as great as they say it is, if this happens it will be not because of, but in spite of, what they themselves are saying and doing now. The detractors, whose motives may be equally disreputable, are nevertheless forced by the nature of their position to take a more discriminative view, and hence their expressions of opinion may be actually helpful to us in making discriminations of our own. At least I shall go on that presumption.

Myself, after discounting as well as I can my own factor of envy, I find that my uncritical, working man's response to Lowell's achievement changes from time to time but generally hovers between the two extremes. In each stage of his poetic evolution Lowell has written a few poems that seem to me extremely fine, and he has also written poems that seem to me mannered, pointless, incomplete, and obscure. Indeed, try as I may—and I have tried again and again over the years—some of his poems, particularly his earliest and then again his latest, remain incomprehensible to me, as dark and profuse as a pot of Bostonian whistleberries. Moreover I cannot escape the feeling that some of this obscurity has been purposely, even crassly laid on.* For me, this is the single largest detracting element in his work.

One point, however, I wish to make perfectly clear. Lowell's position of leadership seems to me not only to have been earned but to be altogether suitable. I say this on two counts. As a man, Lowell has given us more than enough evidence of his firmness and integrity— one thinks of his conscientious objection during the war and all that it

*Lowell has admitted as much. See his *Paris Review* interview.

entailed, his refusal to attend White House sociables, and many other such actions—to substantiate his moral fitness for the role. As a poet, he gives us this same integrity in art. When I read his poetry, however negative my response may be to its effect, I know I am in the presence of an artist *in extremis*, operating, I should say struggling, at the limits of sensibility and technique. This is a quality which we consider peculiarly American, a kind of hardrock Yankee pertinacity, and to me it is peculiarly attractive. Who was it that said he would fight it out on this line if it took all summer? An American military man, I believe. When I read Lowell's lines, I feel that he has fought it out upon them for years. This is tough and homely and American. It is admirable. It is what leads me to place Lowell alongside William Carlos Williams, rather than in the company of other older poets to whom he bears a closer superficial resemblance. It is also what leads me, in the perennial confrontation of artists with the world, to rest content under his leadership. If my standing behind him will add to the strength of his position, he may be sure I am there.

So much for preliminary considerations. The phases of Lowell's poetic evolution are so well known that I need indicate them only briefly. We may dismiss his first book, *Land of Unlikeness*, which was published in a limited edition that few people have seen; Lowell himself effectively dismissed it when he republished its main poems, considerably revised, in *Lord Weary's Castle*, the book that established him with one shot as a leader of his generation. Written in the first flush of enthusiasm after his conversion to Catholicism, the poems were highly charged devotional lyrics mixed with autobiographical elements, presented in an elaborate formal dress: close rhymes, exact meters, a heavy reliance on couplets, and an equally heavy reliance on the rhetoric of allusion. It was a virtuoso performance. At its best, in perhaps a fourth of the poems, it showed a young poet writing with genuine spontaneity in the strict forms of the English metaphysical convention, while bringing to them his own distinct voice and idiosyncratic manner. In short Lowell had done what everyone had been saying could not be done: he had invented a new style. In his next book, *The Mills of the Kavanaughs*, he stuck with it, but most readers considered the book a falling-off, especially the long title poem. What this poem, a dramatic narrative in monologue, showed was that the ability to sustain narrative tension across the librations of discrete pentameter couplets is lost to us: the suspension bridge has replaced the viaduct.

Lowell waited eight years to publish his next book. Then, in 1959, he presented us with a change of appearance so radical that it seemed a reversal. The formal manner was gone; no pentameters, no rhymes, no ornate rhetoric. The book, called *Life Studies*, which more than re-couped his reputation, gave us instead poems in open, loose mea-sures, without rhyme, in a diction that seemed easy and almost in-souciant. The heart of the book was a group of autobiographical poems so intensely candid that critics immediately called them "con-fessional," an unfortunate choice of terms. It implied that Lowell was engaged in public breast-beating, a kind of refreshing new psychoex-otic pastime, or in a shallow exercise of "self-expression," long ago discredited; whereas in fact his aim was far more serious than that.

The following two collections of poems, *For the Union Dead* in 1964 and *Near the Ocean* this year, have continued to explore themes of au-tobiographical candor, but have gradually reverted toward formalism. Not the conventional formalism of *Lord Weary's Castle*, however. Now the meters, though basically iambic, are cast in rough lines of trimeter and tetrameter, punctuated with purposefully inexact rhymes. The diction is more extreme, more peculiar and concise, than in *Life Stud-ies*, and the syntax has become progressively more taut, split up into smaller and smaller units. This has gone so far in the latest poems that one can scarcely find a complete sentence from stanza to stanza, but only phrases, expletives, stabs of meaning. The effect, although en-tirely different from the high style of *Lord Weary's Castle*, nevertheless brings us back to an obscurity and artifice that seem to denote an-other reversal; the simplicity of *Life Studies* has been jettisoned.

In effect Lowell made, in *Life Studies*, a considerable leap into a new area of poetic experience, which he has been exploring since then through increasingly elaborate means. Why he did this, what was in his mind, are questions readers must try to answer if they would un-derstand the actual meaning of Lowell's experiment.

I have said nothing about the translations, perhaps because they are a source of embarrassment to me. Over the years Lowell has made a good many, including a couple of long ones and a whole book of short ones, from many languages, called *Imitations*. When this book was published in 1961, I reviewed it enthusiastically. The density and tonicity of the best translations took hold of me and persuaded me that Lowell had reached far toward the intrinsic qualities of the original poems, especially in his Baudelaires. Since then my friends who know Baudelaire better than I have informed me with cogency that this is not true, and that I had no business reviewing such a book in the first place. Of course they are right on both counts, as I have ruefully come to see. Aside from the intended alterations of sequence and literal meaning which Lowell acknowledges, there is, for instance, the way in which Baudelaire's characteristic elegance, deriving from the fluent, almost sinuous build-up of stanzas and longer passages, is fragmented and rigidified in Lowell's choppy phrasings. And there is the way, too, in which Baudelaire's tainted postromantic sense of beauty is both reduced and roughened in its passage through Lowell's anguish-ridden, New Englander's sensibility; the flowers of evil become merely evil flowers—a considerable difference when you stop to think about it. Lowell's detractors seize on these points, and others, as ammunition for their campaign, which is made easier by the evident inferiority, when judged against any standard, of some of the other translations. The Villons are quite bad, the Rimbauds and Pasternaks barely passable. But I continue to feel that the best of the Baudelaires, Rilkes, and Montales are excellent Lowells indeed, and this is all he had claimed for them. He does not call them translations, but imitations. Perhaps he should have gone further and specified that what he was imitating was not the poetry of Baudelaire or the rest, but the poetry of Lowell; perhaps he should have chosen another title, for example, *Appropriations* or *Assimilations*. No matter; the point is that Lowell has made a perfectly legitimate effort to consolidate his own poetic view of reality by levying upon congenial authentications from other languages and cultures. The best of his translations go together with the best of *Life Studies* and *For the Union Dead* to make up the nucleus of his mature work, the organic unity of which must be apprehended by those who wish to form reliable judgments.

EVEN AT THE MOST SUPERFICIAL LEVEL of technique, the prosodic level, Lowell's evolution, both his successes and his failures, offers a fascinating study to people who are interested in the disciplines of poetry. This is usually the case when important poets change styles. Consider Lowell's commonest prosodic device, the suspended or Hopkinsian upbeat produced by ending a line on the first syllable of a new unit of syntax, a phrase or sentence. He made it work well, not to say famously, in his early poems, but when he abandoned strict pentameters he had more trouble with it. How do you employ this very useful concept of metrical enjambment when your line-structure has been purposely unfixed? It is the old story: you can't have your cake and eat it too. Simple as it appears, this is a crucial problem, perhaps *the* crucial problem, of contemporary unmetered poetry, which different poets have met in many different ways. Some have adopted the practice of reading their poems with abrupt pauses at the end of each line, but this is an oral stratagem that seems to have little connection with the actual dynamics of the poem. Denise Levertov has gone further by rationalizing line length and rhythm in terms of "organic form," a concept which appears, however, to be incompletely worked out at this stage. Like her, Lowell has preferred to work on the page, that is, within the poem's prosodic structure, but with indifferent success in many instances. Conceivably such a simple matter as this, which is nevertheless extremely important in terms of Lowell's natural style, lies behind his recent return to more exact, or more exacting, meters.

But that is a topic for another discussion. What I am interested in here is something prior to poetry. Before a man can create a poem he must create a poet. Considered from the limited perspective of artistry, this is the primal creative act.

Imagine Lowell seated at his work table on some ordinary morning in 1950. *Lord Weary's Castle* has been out for four years; already its triumph is a burden. The poems in *The Mills of the Kavanaughs*, now at the press, have been finished for a year or more, and are beginning to slip into the past, to seem stale, remote, and incidental—like the verses of one's friends. Now I have no idea what Lowell would be doing in such circumstances, probably brooding and daydreaming like the rest of us, but for the moment let me ascribe to him a simple, orderly, godlike self-mastery that neither he nor you nor I nor Charles de Gaulle can claim in actuality. In 1950, given that marvelous perspicacity, he would have had to ask himself two questions. In essence, what is my theme? In general, what is my defect?

One does not ask these questions once and then go on to something else; one asks them over and over, as one asks all unanswerable questions. A serious poet moves progressively toward his essential theme, though he can never reach it, by means of exclusions, peeling away, from poem to poem, the inessential, working down to bedrock; and he examines every word he writes for clues to his defect. In the case of Lowell we cannot doubt that he works in such a state of constant tension and self-interrogation. Yet it seems clear to me, even so, that at some point around 1950 he must have asked these questions with special intentness. Nothing else can account for the change of poetic stance so strikingly evident in *Life Studies*.

What had Lowell set out to do in his first poems? He had set out explicitly, I think, though ingenuously, to build on the Donne-to-Hopkins tradition of devotional poetry in English, to write poems of faith. The evidence, in the poems themselves, is unmistakable. Consequently he had produced a rather large number of set pieces in a high style, such as the poems on Jonathan Edwards and other historical figures or events, affirming a public, devotional aspiration. This is what all young poets do, isn't it? They begin, or at least they try to begin, where the mature poets they admire left off. They do this in the compulsion of their literary zeal, in spite of the evident unfeasibility of it, owing to the irremediable disparity of experience. At the same time Lowell interspersed among his devotional pieces various autobiographical elements, usually disguised and highly wrought, set out in the same taut, allusive, difficult style as the rest, but genuine autobiography nevertheless. I think it must have become evident to him by 1950 that in spite of the very great but purely literary success of the devotional set pieces, these autobiographical poems were the more alive, the more interesting, and ultimately the more comprehensible.

Poems like "Mr. Edwards and the Spider" and "After the Surprising Conversions" are good specimens of their kind, but like all their kind they are sententious. That is to say, a large part of their meaning is a stable and predictable element of the general cultural situation, with which the poems are, so to speak, invested. (And under "meaning" I intend the entire affective and cognitive experience of the poem.) But the autobiographical poems or partly autobiographical poems, like "Mary Winslow" and "At the Indian Killer's Grave," work themselves out in their own terms, within their own language; and in spite of the high gloss of artifice that remains upon them, they speak with urgency.

All this is even more evident today, fifteen years later. The most prominent motifs of the poems in *Lord Weary's Castle* are the Christ, the Crucifix, and the Virgin; they are repeated on almost every page.

Yet they remain inert. They are not personal realizations, they are not symbols, they are merely tokens (which perhaps, in the tradition Lowell had chosen, is all they can be). The personal motifs on the other hand—personal guilt, personal death, personal time, personal violence and desire—are what carry the poet along, and they are connected, not with devotional aspirations, but with his experienced life. He returns to them again and again in poems about himself, about his mother and the Winslow family, and about his father, Commander Lowell. In *Life Studies* he simply relinquished one set of motifs, the former, and took up the other. The resulting augmentation of his poetic stature—his personal stature as creator within the domain of his poetic materials—was enormous.

As I say, Lowell cannot discover the precise specifications of his theme, which is lucky for him. If he were to do so, he would be clapped into silence instantly. Nor can we do it for him, which is equally lucky. All we can do is brood, as he does, over his lines and the shadows behind them, tracking down the motifs to see where they lead. In my own recent brooding I turn especially to two lines from the poem called "Night Sweat" in *For the Union Dead*:

> *always inside me is the child who died,*
> *always inside me is his will to die*

Simple enough; explicit enough. They are one expression of the radical guilt which seems to lie at the base of Lowell's poetic nature. It is a guilt which took form like any other, leaving aside psychoanalytical factors: first from elements of generalized cultural guilt, in Lowell's case the New Englander's shame over the Indians and the Salem women, which has exercised an obviously powerful influence on his imagination; then from guilt that all men feel, with deep necessity, for the deaths of their own fathers; and finally from the horrendous events of contemporary history. But what is the punishment for the crimes that produce this pervading guilt? It is personal death. We all know this, from the first moment of our mortal recognition. Yet against this Lowell casts again and again his instinctive belief in the remission of sin, or rather his knowledge, his feeling, of his own undiminished innocence. Then what can our death be? What is our guilt? There is only one answer, outside of absurdity. Our death is our sin, for which we pay in advance through our guilt. Our death is a crime against every good principle in the universe: nature, God, the human heart. And we, the innocent, are the responsible ones—this is the idea Lowell cannot forego. We bear this crime, like a seed, within us. Our bodies are going to commit it, do what we will. They are going to carry out this murder inexorably, while we stand by, helplessly and aghast.

This is the ultimate Yankee metonymy, you might say. Puritan death as punishment for sin contracts, under the paradox of benign transcendentalism, to death as sin. Naturally it is a theological monstrosity. It is impossible. Yet in the human and poetic sphere, it is a validity of staggering force. And it lies at the heart of the American sensibility, a far more cogent explanation of our attitudes, including our racism and violence, than, for example, Leslie Fiedler's mythologized sexualism.

Well, all this is highly conjectural. There are scores of other, doubtless better ways to approach Lowell's theme, I'm sure. Yet I feel this progressive identification of sin, guilt, and death can be traced fairly directly from such poems as "At the Indian Killer's Grave" to "Night Sweat" and beyond. The two lines I have quoted strike close to it. They are literal. When Lowell says "inside" I think he means inside: he is carrying this sin-death around in him like a monstrous illegitimate pregnancy. I would almost bet that if he suffers the common nightmare of artists, the dream of male parturition, it is a dead thing that comes out (at which point, if he hasn't awakened, his dream may be suffused with bliss).

Meanwhile Lowell has his defect, for which he should give thanks. It permits him to relax into the mercy of technical self-criticism. Not that it is easy to deal with; quite the contrary. Like all fundamental defects, it is a function of his personality, and hence wears many faces. I call it the defect of pervasive extraneity; but it could have other names. One aspect of it is quite clear, however, in *Lord Weary's Castle*: the laid-on metaphysical obscurity. This was the fashion of poetry at the time, and Lowell accommodated himself to it easily and naturally, and without the least poetic infidelity. We must bear in mind in considering fashion that a fashion during the period of its ascendancy is not a fashion; it is merely what is right. In composing the poems of *Lord Weary's Castle*, Lowell had no sense, I'm certain, of doing anything but what was necessary. He had no sense of *doing* anything at all, except writing poetry as it is written. Nevertheless the obscurity, like the ornate style and the use of inert figures from a general cultural conspectus, was clearly extraneous to his main themes and objectives, as he could see five or six years later, and he gave it up; this was his defect and he chopped off its head. But it sprang up elsewhere, hydralike. Other aspects of it were more difficult to see. For instance, in the title poem of *The Mills of the Kavanaughs*, he had shown his inability to sustain the long units of poetry, and at the same time his great talent for the short units: the line, couplet, phrase, and isolated image. These are his forte. Lowell can rap out a single sharp line with extraordinary facility. The trouble is that these brilliant strokes may contribute nothing to the whole fabric and intention of a poem; they may be merely extraneous—pervasively extraneous because in spite of their irrelevance they do sit within the total structure and they cannot be eradicated once the poem has acquired a certain degree of distinctness.

In a poem called "The Scream" from *For the Union Dead*, Lowell writes of the time when his mother gave up her mourning:

One day she changed to purple,
and left her mourning. At the fitting,
the dressmaker crawled on the floor,
eating pins, like Nebuchadnezzar
on his knees eating grass.

We have all observed this, of course, a woman crawling on the floor, her mouth full of pins, to adjust another woman's hem—at least all of us have observed it who are over a certain age—and we are struck, consequently, by the originality of Lowell's simile. It seems to me absolutely genuine; I have never encountered it before. Hence the pins and grass collapse together spontaneously in my mind like a perfect superimposition of images. I am charmed. Only when I stop to think do I realize that Nebuchadnezzar and what he stands for have only the remotest connection with this passage, and that the dressmaker herself is a figure of no importance in the poem. As an image, this is a brilliant extraneity: the defect at work.

And what shall we say about the appearance of the new book, its crass and confused ostentation? This is gross extraneity and nothing else.

In short, Lowell's defect is a temptation to mere appearance, to effects, trappings—to the extraneous. And it arises, I believe, from a discrete imagination, that is, an imagination which works best in disjunctive snatches. I suppose some people would call it an analytic, rather than a synthetic, imagination. His problem as a poet during the past fifteen or twenty years has been to continue digging toward his essential theme, while at the same time turning, if it is possible, his defect into an advantage.

So FAR I have been writing about Lowell as if he were an isolated case, but the reverse is the truth. He is a poet of his time. The shift of focus in his poetry has been one part, a very small part, of a general shift in artistic values and intentions during the past quarter-century.

When was the last time in our Western civilization that a writer at his work table could look at a piece of writing and with complete confidence call it finished, self-enclosed and self-sustaining, autonomous—a work of art in the original sense? I'd say in poetry it must have been at the time of Pope, and in fiction, since the novel lags behind, perhaps as late as Flaubert or Turgenev; but actually no one could draw the lines so precisely. The change from one notion of art to another was very gradual. All we can say with certainty is that sometime during the nineteenth century—that changeful time!—the old idea of the enclosed work of art was dislocated in the minds of serious artists: Heine, Rimbaud, Strindberg. Such men began to see that art is always unfinished; and from this arose the concept of its a priori unfinishability, that is, its limitlessness. For a time—quite a time—the two concepts ran side by side; many artists tried by various means to combine them. In the forepart of our century, for instance, we got the idea of the circularity of artistic structure, from which derived the work of art that was both limitless and enclosed: *The Waste Land* and *Finnegans Wake*. These were grandiose conceptions. They made art into something it had not been before, a world in itself.* They were helped along by the general collapse of values in the post-

*An extreme statement; in one sense art had always been a world apart. The "immortality" of the poem was a desperately held notion of the Renaissance, and was transmitted through succeeding generations of poets—poets of every school—down to recent times. But in another sense the enclosed *and* limitless masterpieces of 1910–1940 did introduce something new: the possibility of an art that was not only distinct from "objective reality" but contradistinct, a plane of being divorced from and better than the corrupt world of nonart; and this engendered a philosophical departure far more serious than, for instance, the shallow Yellow-Book estheticism from which it partly sprang.

Nietzschean cultures of Europe. Some artists, despairing of their own painful nihilism, even tried to substitute for the reality of the world the antireality of art—or of style, the word, or whatever—believing that only by this means could they create a bearable plane upon which to enact human existence and build a consistent scheme of values. I am thinking of such men as Gottfried Benn, Céline, and Wyndham Lewis, or in a different way of Breton and the surrealists. Of course Hitler's war smashed all that, proving the ugliness and irresponsibility of it. Reality was reality after all. We came out of the war badly shaken, clinging to the idea of existential engagement. Henceforth, contrite as we were, we would be responsible and free, creative within the real world. Yet what could this mean in a reality over which we had no control, a reality in which we, the conscious element, possessed nothing but the lunatic knowledge of our own supererogation, to use Auden's terms? If antireality were denied us by our own responsibility, and if reality were denied us by our own alienation, what could we create? We decided—and to my mind the inevitability of it is beautiful—that what we could create was life. Human life.

It was not a retreat into antireality. In looking back we saw that, after Nietzsche, we had been living in a crisis of intellectual evolution, a terrible blockage and confusion; we had been absorbing what Jaspers calls "the preparing power of chaos." Now we were ready to go forward. Now, in freedom and responsibility, we began to see the meaning of what we had known all along, that a life is more than a bundle of determined experiential data. (For the biggest horror of our crisis had been the complex but empty enticements of Freudian positivism.) A life is what we make it. In its authenticity it is our own interpretation and reorganization of experience, structured metaphorically. It is the result of successive imaginative acts—it is a work of art! By conversion, a work of art is a life, *provided it be true to the experiential core.* Thus in a century artists had moved from an Arnoldian criticism of life to an existential creation of life, and both the gains and the losses were immense.

The biggest loss was a large part of what we thought we had known about art. For now we saw in exactly what way art is limitless. It is limitless because it is free and responsible: it is a life. Its only end is the adventitious cutting off that comes when a heart bursts, or a sun. Still, the individual "piece" of art must be objective in some sense; it lies on the page, on the canvas. Practically speaking, what is a limitless object? It is a fragment, a random fragment, a fragment without intrinsic form, shading off in all directions into whatever lies beyond. And this is what our art has become in the past two decades: random, fragmentary, and open-ended.

Hence in literature any particular "work" is linear rather than circular in structure, extensible rather than terminal in intent, and at any given point inclusive rather than associative in substance; at least these are its tendencies. And it is autobiographical, that goes without saying. It is an act of self-creation by an artist within the tumult of experience.

This means that many of our ideas about art must be reexamined and possibly thrown out. I have in mind not our ideas of technique, derived from the separate arts, but our esthetic generalizations, derived from all the arts. Such notions as harmony, dynamism, control, proportion, even style in its broadest sense. How do these criteria apply to a work which is not a work at all, conventionally considered, but a fragment? I do not say they do not apply; I say the applications must be radically redetermined.

As readers, where does this leave us? In a mere subjective muddle? Sometimes it seems so. For that matter why should we read another person's poems at all? Our life is what concerns us, not his. Is he a better observer than we, a better imaginer, a better creator? Can his self-creation of his life assist us in ours, assuming a rough equivalence of human needs and capacities? Perhaps; but these too are subjective criteria. What then?

All I can say is that the most progressive criticism we have now *is* subjective, resolutely so and in just these ways. It asks what a poem can *do* for us. The reason we have so little of it is that we are unused to such methods, we are fearful—justly—of the sentimentalism and shallow moralism such methods might reintroduce into our frameworks of sensibility, and we do not know upon what principles to organize our new subjective criteria. Our critics are still years behind our artists, still afraid of the personal, ideal, practical, and contingent. For strangely enough, these four properties are just what we preserve in fragments but often destroy in wholes. Working philosophers know this. In a grave correspondence to human limits, an apothegm is better philosophy than an organon.

Still, I see some evidence, here and there, that the critics are beginning to stir themselves.

WHAT LOWELL THINKS of all this he hasn't said. He has written almost no criticism, and apparently does not intend to write any. I salute him! But at all events we know that he has been working for twenty years in the heart of the movement I have described, among eastern writers and artists. He has been associated with the painters who gave their work the unfortunate names of abstract expressionism and action painting, and with theatrical people who have used such concepts as the happening and nonacting acting; these being half-understood designations for the artist's life-constructing function. This has been Lowell's milieu. Of course he has shared it with many other writers; what I have been discussing in terms of Lowell's work is a shift or tightening of artistic intention which cuts across every line. And one thing more is certain. Whatever the rationale, or whether or not there is any rationale, we cannot read Lowell's autobiographical writing, from *Life Studies* to *Near the Ocean*, without seeing that we are in touch with a writer who is in fact making his life as he goes along, and with a degree of seriousness and determination and self-awareness that surpasses the artistic confidence of any previous generation. He has resolved to accept reality, all reality, and to take its fragments indiscriminately as they come, forging from them this indissoluble locus of metaphorical connections that is known as Robert Lowell. No wonder he is enthusiastic.

Hence we see that in his translations, and for that matter in all his work, Lowell's methods are distinct from those of Ezra Pound. This is a distinction we must be careful to draw, I think, because Pound's methods have become so much second nature to us all that they blur our recognition of the principal fact about the two poets, namely, that the historical gulf separating them is enormous. Thus when Pound wrenches and distorts Propertius in the translations from the Elegies, or when he capsulates writing from many sources in the *Cantos*, he does so in the interest of a general program of cultural aggrandizement conducted from a base of personal security. There is no uncertainty of values in the *Cantos*; in this respect the poem is as old-fashioned as *Candide* or Boethius. Nor is there any uncertainty of poetic personality. The writer—*ego, scriptor*—is a steady and reliable, if sometimes rudimentary, presence. Pound's work, in effect, is an Arnoldian criticism of life on a very grand scale, which is only possible because the critic looks out from the secure bastion of his own personality founded on a stable scheme of values. Lowell on the other hand is a poetic ego without fixtures: in a sense neither being nor becoming, but a sequence of fragments, like the individual frames of a movie film, propelled and unified by its own creative drive. This does not mean that Lowell's work lacks values; his poems are as strenuously moral as anyone's. But his objective is not critical, nor even broadly cultural; it is personal; and the moral elements of his poetry are used, not as precepts, but as the hypotheses of an experimental venture in self-validation. In his autobiographical work, both translations and original poems, Lowell employs many of Pound's devices, perhaps most of them, but his ends are his own—and this makes all the difference. It means a radically different creative outlook, issuing in new poetic justifications and criteria.

And so I return to my starting place; for I am sure everyone knows that the hypothetical reviewer with whom I began is really myself, and that all this speculation springs from the moment when my review copy of *Near the Ocean* arrived in the mail. I have already said that I do not like the sequence of autobiographical poems which forms the heart of this new book. Let me add to this three further points.

1. Why has Lowell moved progressively away from the simplicity of *Life Studies* toward a new formalism? Is it only a reversionary impulse? Is it an attempt to give greater objectivity to the random, fragmentary materials of his autobiography by reintroducing elements of fixative convention? Is it from a desire to make fuller use of his talent, that is, to turn his defect to advantage by emphasizing prosody and syntax as means both for suggesting the discreteness of experience and for unifying it within the poem's linear flow? No doubt all these reasons, and others, are at work. But the result is a too-great concentration of effort upon the verbal surface—to my mind very unfortunate. We now have poems which are compositions of brilliant minutiae, like mosaics in which the separate tiles are so bright and glittering that we cannot see the design. A mosaic is fine, it is the model par excellence for poetry in our time, but if we are to see the pattern the separate pieces must be clear and naturally arranged; and in the best mosaics the colors are subdued rather than gaudy.

2. In point of substance I ask, still in a firmly subjective mode, What are the most useful parts of autobiography? To my mind the most interesting of Lowell's poems are those from his present or recent past, concerning his wife, divorce, children, illness, imprisonment, and so on, but these are few and small compared to the great number about his youth and childhood, ancestors, his visits to the family graveyard. I detect a faint odor of degenerate Freudian sentimentalism. Have we not had enough of this, and more? We are interested in the man, the present, unfinished, lively being. If the term *confessional* is to be applied to Lowell's work, although I have said why I think it is inadequate, then I suggest he has not confessed enough. In particular one topic is lacking, or nearly lacking, for such poems as "Beyond the Alps" hardly scratch its surface: I mean Lowell's conversion to the Church of Rome and his subsequent—should I say recusancy? I scarcely know. He was in and then he was out, and the real drama remains for us a mystery. Surely this touches the man. And surely it touches many issues of our time: justice, probity, the individual and the mass, the role of love in society, even peace and war. In effect I advocate a stiffening up of autobiographical substance, a colder and more realistic view. Let the rigor now reserved for verbal superficies be applied to the exact new content of experience.

3. But judgment fails. In this art it has not found its place. If I were to suggest one ultratechnical criterion still available to a poet in Lowell's circumstances, I would say: relevance. Be random, yes, fragmentary and open-ended—these are the conditions of life—but scrutinize every component of your act of creation for its relevance. The advantage of random observation is not only in what comes but in what is let go. Avoid the extraneous like the plague. Lowell does not always manage it, and his defect is not the advantage it might be. His style, though more deeply in-wrought than before, is still too much like a shell, a carapace, an extraneity. We see again and again that the most difficult work of imagination is not when it soars in fantasy but when it plods in fact. And what a force of imagination has gone into these poems! A man's being, fought for, fragment by fragment, there on the page: this we can recognize. And we know that in such poetry the risk of failure is no longer a risk but a certainty. It must be taken, eaten. The very poem which seems most awkward to us may be the one that will wrench us away finally from the esthetic fixatives of the conventions of irresponsibility, and release us into responsible crea-

tion. If we read Lowell's new poems in the light of the problems he is facing, we will know that although we must, since we are human, judge them, our judgment is not something superior or separate, it is a part of his struggle, as his struggle is a part of ours. In this knowledge we may discover what we have been groping toward for centuries: not humility, which as artists we do not need, nor magnanimity, which I hope we already have, but the competence of human freedom.

Melancholy Monument

A review of *The Complete Poems*, by Randall Jarrell, from *The Nation*, July 7, 1969.

RANDALL JARRELL WAS A ROMANTICIST of the generation which came to adulthood during the miserable 1930s. That is to say, he found himself as a young man in a society whose most active intellectual centers were dominated by the thought and style of T. S. Eliot and, behind him, of Irving Babbitt. Jarrell reacted as did most of his young fellow poets: he launched into a search for a way out of the social and cultural order which seemed to him, and which was, superannuated. More than this, he launched—in spite of his southern politesse, for he was born in Nashville and graduated from Vanderbilt, the home of the Agrarians, Fugitives, and of southern elitism in general—with a radical eagerness as intense as that of any of his northern contemporaries. Among romanticists he was an especially pure example of the type. He was what Jacques Barzun has called an *intrinsic* romanticist: a poet existing outside the primary epoch of romanticism who still exhibited the romanticist's primary characteristics.

What these characteristics are is open to question. But leaving aside the secondary characteristics, such as the romanticist's commitments to freedom, individualism, irrationalism, and so on, certainly one of his primary characteristics is his hang-up between man's power and man's misery, between the vision of glory and the experience of degradation. "Man is born free, and everywhere he is in chains." In his youth this is precisely the paradox that Jarrell saw in the world around him: at the top a culture oriented toward tradition and devoted to the methodical delectation of esthetic pleasure, at the bottom a society sick in every member and vitiated by pain and injustice. As the 1930s advanced—Harlan County, Abyssinia, Detroit, Spain—the realities were unmistakable. But so were Jarrell's longings. For years the commonest locution in his poems was the phrase "and yet . . ." uttered sometimes wistfully, sometimes mordantly, sometimes in hollow despair.

To surmount this impasse between innocence and experience (to use Blake's terms) the romanticist seeks a faith, or at least a synthesis, that will define and accommodate both sides of the paradox. Historically speaking, few have managed it, especially among poets. Probably the commonest way out has been through radical social action, based on Hegelian concepts of history. For poets a surer but much more difficult course has been the ascent from romantic agony to genuine tragic vision, which in turn destroys its own romantic base by imposing upon it the classical order of the tragic world—the world of fate and of Promethean pathos and steadfastness. The great example, of course, is Goethe. In our time we have the smaller but very instructive case of Theodore Roethke. He began with a verbal and mental style different from Jarrell's, yet with much the same poetic materials, the same view of nature and human reality; but he converted them into an at least sporadically consistent tragic vision. Roethke continued to write with more and more depth of feeling until he died, while Jarrell, almost exactly contemporary, dwindled away into fragments and exercises.

Not that Jarrell didn't try. Social action was effectively denied him, since his connection with the amorphous, self-doubting radicalism of the *Partisan Review* was doomed from the start to futility. Conventional religious faith was also apparently inaccessible to him. But he tried other means of escape, especially by pursuing romantic revulsion from experience to its logical ends in dream and fantasy. Time and again, especially in the poems of his middle years, he constructed elaborate dream visions, significantly Germanic—not to say Gothic— in style, from within which he looked out at the objective world and denounced it. But the stress of actuality always supervened. Jarrell was sane, excruciatingly sane, and he could never secure his dream beyond the limits of a few separate, though quite splendid, poems.

Similarly he tried, but only half-heartedly, to commit himself to the mystique of creative impunity, the cult of the *homme d'esprit*, the anti-world of style and imagination; he tried to give himself, not to the meretricious elites of Gottfried Benn or Wyndham Lewis (he was too radical for that) but to the commonalty of alienated poets, descendants of Baudelaire who preserve themselves from social, moral, and metaphysical blight through the integrity of their autonomous creative endeavor. In a few passages he sounds surprisingly like Vachel Lindsay preaching the "gospel of beauty." But it is noteworthy that Jarrell's most consistent statement of this purist philosophy occurs in neither his poetry nor his criticism but in a story for children, *The Bat Poet*, which in spite of the skill and good taste evident in its telling remains basically a propagandistic fable intended to affirm the superiority, or at least the specialness, of the poet in the community of animals. Jarrell himself didn't believe it, or only half believed it. He could not forego the exquisite anguish of the romanticist's dual attachment to vision and reality, innocence and experience. In the end he was left in the wilderness of romantic nihilism with no base but sensibility.

The results are evident. In his criticism Jarrell gave us vibrant readings of individual poets, Frost, Williams, and others, but no theoretical statement of basic value. In the last twenty years of his poetry, although the dream poems and a few others are interesting, he fell more and more into fragmentary utterance, false starts, scraps and notes, and especially into set pieces—"story poems" and "character poems," updated Robert Frost—that lacked the verve of his youthful work. Then too there was the endless translating and retranslating of the German poets, especially Rilke. What Jarrell needed, I think, in order to write successfully was an occasion which gave him not only the enclosed reality of a particular episode but a chance to remove it to a certain distance from the complexity of the ordinary world; and the only sustained occasion of this kind which occurred in his life was World War II. Jarrell's war poems are his best in every sense. They are the most alive poetically, the most consistent thematically.

All this is what I have thought for some years, and in reading *The Complete Poems* I find it confirmed. The book would be a melancholy monument at best. Here is Randall Jarrell complete and completed, the same who so enlivened our literary and social consciousnesses only a short time ago; at least the time must seem short to readers of my generation. Now he is gone, stuffed in a great fat tome, to be looked at and put away in the corner of a low shelf. Well, the poems deserve far better. Some of them are great.

The book contains all Jarrell's poems from his previous books, plus three additional sections: one for new work written between his last book and his death, a second for poems published in magazines but not previously collected, the third for earlier unpublished poems. It is, we are made to understand, complete. But this is the only book of its kind that I know in which we find no hint of the person upon whose authority we are to accept either its completeness or its other attributes, which seems odd. It has no editor as far as anyone can tell from reading the book or its dust jacket or the ancillary press releases from the publisher.

It gives us, however, a considerable bulk of poetry, in which the war poems are a distinct, superior unit. They are not many, perhaps thirty or forty altogether. But even if they were fewer they would be a remarkable achievement. How anyone could write while soldiering is difficult to understand; as someone who went through the war unable to write a word, I can only marvel. But Jarrell had been writing for nearly ten years before America entered the war. His early poems are sometimes mannered or imitative and often artificially opaque; but from the first, as nearly as one can tell, he wrote with ease. When the war came he already possessed a developed poetic vocabulary and a mastery of forms. Under the shock of war his mannerisms fell away and his basic skills came into concerted action. He began to write with stark, compressed lucidity.

Nowadays we commonly hear critics declare that World War II produced no memorable poetry. Even a critic as acute as George Steiner has said that the poetry of 1940–1945 is without "the control of remembrance achieved by Robert Graves or Sassoon" in 1914–1918 (see Steiner's *The Death of Tragedy*). To this I can only reply that if I know what "control of remembrance" means, in my experience the poems of Jarrell have it, and they have it preeminently. I am certain that other readers of my age, those who were there, find in these poems of soldiers and civilians, the dead, wounded, and displaced, the same truth that I do. And it is not merely the truth of Friday night at the VFW; old dogfaces may use their memory to corroborate the materials of Jarrell's poems, but the *truth* is *in* the poems—it is an esthetic presence.

Warfare gave Jarrell the antagonist he needed; not fate, not history, not the state, not metaphysical anxiety, but all these rolled into one— The War—that brute momentous force sweeping a bewildered generation into pathos, horror, and death. Today our young dissenters and resisters sometimes ask us why we didn't resist too, why we were willing to go along with the militarists. Unsuccessfully we try to explain that there were a number of reasons, but that in any event willingness had nothing to do with it. But we don't need to try any longer, it is all there in Jarrell's poems. The irresistibility of the war, the historical inexorability of it, the suffering of all its victims, Americans, Germans, Japanese—Jarrell wrote it down with equal understanding, equal sympathy. And he wrote it then, there, at that time and in those places, with power, spontaneity, and perfect conviction. Against what I have said already about his poetry, I must in basic honesty conclude with an amendment: in his war poems Randall Jarrell did rise, as if in spite of himself and at the command of a classical force outside himself, to his moment of tragic vision. His own tragedy was that he could not find the means to sustain his vision, with its lucidity and starkness, in the "ordinary" occasions of life after the war ended.

The Writer's Situation

From *New American Review*, April 1970. This was a contribution to a symposium which the editors of *New American Review* organized by submitting questions to a number of writers. Their questions were as follows.

1. Why do you continue to write? What purpose does your work serve? Do you feel yourself part of a rear-guard action in the service of a declining tradition? Has your sense of vocation altered significantly in recent years?

2. Do you believe that art and politics should be kept apart? Has this belief changed or grown more complicated during the past decade? What influence has the politicization of life during this period had on your work?

3. What are the main creative opportunities and problems that attract and beset you in your work? Which movements, tendencies, writers, if any, do you find yourself identifying with or supporting? Which ones do you oppose?

4. Has writing entered a "postmodern" era, in which the relevance of the great modern writers (Joyce, Eliot, Mann, Faulkner, et al.) has declined? If so, what seem to be the literary principles of the postmodern age? If not, what principles of modernism are still dominant and valuable?

5. Has there been a general collapse of literary standards in recent years? Are you conscious of a conflict between your past standards and your present ones?

6. Has literary criticism and journalism kept pace with, and faith with, the best fiction, poetry, and drama produced in the sixties?

SPEAKING PERSONALLY—I hope pertinently—your questionnaire is embarrassing.

1. I'm damned if I know why I continue to write. I don't think I'd know in the best of circumstances, but right now I'm particularly embarrassed because a few months ago I quit. Resolved: no more. My poetry was a dead end, themes scrambled and uncertain, sense of a creative locus hopelessly lost: no diction, no instinct for form. I would cease, if not forever at least for a good long time; to let the internal forces recompose themselves. But within days I was at it again, secretly, little nips like an alcoholic housewife's, but then more and more openly; until now, being pressed for income, I've even begun sending out a few poems to the magazines. I suppose my experience is any poet's. On the rottenest day, when my head aches and my allergies rage, when the sky drips snow like rags of underwear, the poem occurs. Sometimes whole strings of them, flung on paper, scraps to be sorted and studied afterward. I conclude that part of my mind, the central, most important part, thinks poetically, and can think no other way. Good or bad, the poems must take form as long as the mind is functioning at all.

Sense of vocation? I haven't any, not with respect to poetry. In reviewing and editing, yes. There my sense of vocation, or at least of obligation, is strong; obligation to other writers, to editors and publishers, to the cultural mechanism at large—to keep it going and still unrigidified, so it may serve young poets as they come on and contribute its essential, usually overlooked ingredient in our civilization.

Paradoxically, in bread-and-butter writing I am an idealist, but in creative work a pragmatist. My poetry serves no one but myself; other service is incidental, a by-product. My poetry is what has brought me, it almost alone, through a life too often shaped by illness, poverty, isolation, and other perplexities. At root I see no distinction between poetry and philosophy; at root I see no distinctions between any of the necessitous activities of human self-conscious sensibility in face with its own fearsome being.

I serve no tradition, even the one I am fond of. And if that is declining, it will ascend again, no doubt with a different aspect. Tradition: a misused word. The thing itself, what the word stands for, does not exist. It is a myth, and like all myths it cannot die. It may go to sleep, like the princess of the thorny rose, and during its slumber extraordinary changes may occur; but as long as human sensibility continues, someone will always come to kiss it awake again.

2. Here too I am embarrassed, because I must seem to brag. I am a radical born and bred, from a long line of the same, and have *always* believed that art and politics cannot be kept apart. I began by thinking this was taken for granted—the elder poets seemed to confirm it—only to discover it was not. More than ten years ago when I wrote a piece for *The Nation* insisting that poetry must incorporate specific social, economic, and political materials, my friends, including some who are now among the foremost radical poets, were appalled and even frightened, as if I had attacked the roots of art. They demanded that we, as poets, maintain our "purity," not seeing that purity in their sense means esthetic death.

Two points need to be made. First, what I was saying then was said not for politics' sake, but for art's. I doubt that politics needs art, certainly not for its immediate ends. Propaganda and art have no real points of contact; and if art sometimes becomes politically effective, as happens more often than many people think, so much the better. But art needs politics, just as it needs the other elements of life—sex, metaphysics, the natural world, and so on. Art without politics is a lie, in bad faith with itself. But this has an important corollary. Many poets today are going around saying the need of the times is for this or that kind of art; we must all become more and more radicalized, we must fracture tradition, form, even language. But this is just the kind of prescriptive criticism I deplore. Let each poet speak for himself, let him say what *his* poetry needs, not mine. Art may not be autonomous, as the New Critics tried to make it, but it is autochthonous: it inhabits its own territory. Art needs life, all life; but as servant, not master; as material, not exemplary form. Many of us are excluded by personal circumstances from political activism, but our experience is no less valid poetically than other people's. Art which shapes itself to the need of the times may turn out to be no art at all.

Second, if my personal radicalism has been consistent from the beginning, there has been nevertheless a change in my understanding of poetic means. Twenty years ago I was greatly puzzled by the question of how to break into the autonomous poem of the forties and early fifties with my radical concern. I was impressed by the way Pound's *Cantos*, my poetic bible, fell apart when he introduced specifically political argument. Not only that—for one could say, and I did, that this was caused by the antihuman and hence antipoetic quality of what Pound was arguing—I was also impressed by the way 99 per cent of the rest of the political poetry of the thirties, most of which had been written by poets whose hearts were in the right place, had similarly fallen apart. My own early political experiments were mostly dismal, not poems at all but rants and curses. Now we have had a decade rich in further experiments, by poets of every formal persuasion, and the problem no longer bothers us. The political content of poetry is seen to be quite at ease in its esthetic function. We wonder why we were ever puzzled. But we were, and the strides we have taken in this respect are worth noting. Some critic should study them.

As I say, art serves neither the tradition nor itself nor the times; it serves the artist, the needy human creator. And in so doing, I believe, it is faithful to both itself and mankind at large. The tradition evolves willy-nilly; it takes care of itself. And all this is perfectly congruous with what LeRoi Jones (our Shelley) means when he says that poetry is revolution.

3. Recently I had the job of assembling a large anthology of twentieth-century American poetry. To help with the notes I sent a questionnaire to all its living contributors. One question was similar to this of yours, about movements, schools, affinities, etc. But I think without exception the poets replied that they belonged, each one, to no movement whatever and were totally independent of any groups or

associations; and this was just as true of those whom we all unhesitatingly identify with particular factions as it was of the genuine mavericks. Apparently poets are people: they don't like being classified.

For years I have been called an "academic" or a "traditionalist," and for years I have resented it.

In truth I think formal distinctions among poets are beginning to recede, even in popular taste, and are being supplanted by questions of faith, essence, or thematic preoccupation. We see that the Black Mountain poets, for example, are much closer to some academic poets than was previously thought. From dissimilar origins and by disparate routes, the poets converge. For myself I know that the problems of poetry which hold my attention are the problems of this epoch of life, and that they preoccupy equally the sensibilities of my friends who share my general attitudes, Denise Levertov, Adrienne Rich, Galway Kinnell, J. V. Cunningham, and then many others not known to me personally. Naturally we write about these problems in different ways, using different characteristic moods and voices, just as we have different colored eyes, different tastes in food, and different illnesses. But what holds us together and distinguishes us from others who do not share our general attitudes (such as the doctrinaire religious poets, the poets of wit, or the pop poets) is far greater and stronger than what separates us.

I don't mean to downgrade problems of form, which are the driving force. For me, although I am as sure as anyone that conventional English prosody has been played out (except in the hands of a few very strong, idiosyncratic poets), rhyme is still close to the verbal heart of poetry and measure is essential: identifiable and *predictable* measure. I underscore predictable. This, in my feeling, is what measure means: the reader's (listener's, watcher's) ability to anticipate the *next* beat. To find ways to use these components without stiffness and without lapsing into specious diction is my technical problem. But it is inescapably technical, and I don't think it warrants much discussion outside the workshop.

. . . Am I being evasive? Now, later, while typing my reply, I have second thoughts. If the formal problem is technical, and hence fundamentally private, this doesn't make it any less tough; and tougher still is the thematic problem, the sense of break-up and confusion in poetic attitudes. I don't know which causative factors are personal and which are external. Certainly the personal ones are important: my

reaching a difficult age (forty-eight) for artists, my awareness of falter-
ing strength and talent, my knowledge that what I had to say in the
first half of my life has now been said, if not as well as I wish, then at
least in forms which I despair of bettering, and other factors too private to mention. But the external factor is important too, this extraordinary acceleration of sociocultural change through which we are
living. Every day my mail brings books and magazines that open new
perspectives of form and experience. The creative opportunities, as
you call them, are indeed great. The danger is that insecure poets will
be paralyzed, not liberated. I can't assess all these considerations. But
I do know that they were what made me quit, and that if I have re-
sumed writing sooner than I expected, nevertheless I have lost the
sense of continuity, the sense of moving through an integrated personal myth, which I once had and which I think is the most important
property any poet can possess. Now ideas for poems come at me like
bullets flying from all directions; they are gratifyingly many, but they
come from disparate sources and are often contradictory, in both form
and substance, leaving me overwhelmed, bewildered, and scared.
And I suspect many poets my age feel the same way.

 4. A huge topic. I've written about it for years, but in fragments,
scattered reviews and essays, always lacking the opportunity (and
perhaps the courage) to attack it systematically. In short: yes, certainly writing since 1945 is new, certainly the great writers of the earlier period have less relevance for us than they once did.

 Say that with Nietzsche came the final and total collapse of traditional systems of value, replaced for a while by an amorphous esthetic optimism, which in turn collapsed with World War I. The writers who began work then began in a void—nihilism, absence of values.
(The lost generation.) Hence they sought substitutions for reality,
some by turning backward (Eliot and his followers), but many by as-
serting the antireality of art. It sprang from the Yellow-Book estheticism of the nineties, with affinities in Renaissance and romantic
notions of the "eternity" of poetry; it was called by many names, the
"revolution of the word" (as in Jolas's *transition*), the Jamesian or Flau-
bertian apotheosis of style, and so on. It had its root in Kantian esthetics, in Coleridge's concept of "imagination," but in essence it was
an attempt to create, by sheer power of human invention, a new
plane of existence in artistic form upon which the search for value,
especially the search for identity, could proceed. Many, like Yeats and

Mann, participated only tangentially; others, like Pound, Eliot, and Joyce, were nearer the main thrust, though probably never conscious of its full implications; a few, like Wyndham Lewis, Céline, and Gottfried Benn, were conscious advocates; and it is no mistake that these last three were all friendly to Hitler's regime. Benn was the clearest, with his introduction of the "phenotype," a new human being, a mutant who could function solely in terms of style.

Well, these hopes were disappointed in the second war. Reality, real reality, with its ovens, its *gauleiter's* deportation orders, its disregard for style, its passionate misery, supervened. The structural finesse of *Finnegans Wake*, the imaginative concision of *La jeune parque*, the stylistic autonomy of *Nightwood* or *Les enfants terribles*, were seen to be no antidotes to the world as it is. Contritely, artists turned back toward reality, back toward human rather than artistic responsibility.

Against all this imagine the larger movement which began a century ago, more or less, and which has intensified noticeably in the past two decades. Call it existentialism if you will; the term is not right, but no one has thought of a better. Do not, however, call it a philosophy, though elements of it have been adumbrated by technically trained philosophers. It is, to my mind, a great shift of human sensibility, comparable to medieval theism or Renaissance humanism, and like them it entails a change in man's conception of his own place in reality. If theism was anthropomorphic, if humanism was anthropocentric, then our era is anthropo-eccentric; we exist on the edge of reality. This is no intellectualization, but a profound and popular ethologic retooling. The consequent shift of values is immense. Now we recognize that in meaninglessness we are our own sole value, and that art is our chief instrument in the imaginative creation of this value, the turning of human experience into human meaning, the making of selves.

All terribly oversimplified; more than that, hypothetical. Yet I believe it could be documented by a mind sufficiently encyclopedic. And the result in American poetry of the past fifteen years is clear to me, cutting across every division, from Lowell to Olson, from Berryman to Ginsberg. The emphasis is on the life, no longer on the self-contained "work of art," and we have, not mere autobiography, not mere "confession," but life coming into being on the page, fragment by fragment. Hence the great literary forms break down, style becomes functional again. Our former obsessive idea of the masterpiece disappears. The random poem, open-ended and fragmentary, becomes the norm: we see it everywhere. And this leads directly to today's concepts of radical and revolutionary antipoetry, the poem considered solely as an *act* of fragmentation. There is a danger in this, as I have said above. We may lose the poem altogether, and I think it is important at this point to remember that the esthetic function *in se* is still legitimate, still indispensable.

Of course many writers are working yet in the essential prewar modes, especially novelists hung up on the ideas of Robbe-Grillet and Nathalie Sarraute. We see men like John Barth and John Fowles fooling away their talents in endless novelistic puzzles, a pastime which seems to have reached an ultimate reduction—I hope it's ultimate—in *Word Rain* by Madeline Gins. But American poets, I'm glad to say, have been almost entirely free from this kind of formalistic irresponsibility. They are artists, yes; resolutely so; but artists acknowledging a participatory rather than exclusionary function. Not popular artists, not "people's poets" or "proletarian poets," but poets writing both from and for the eternal, suprapoetic, existential crisis.

What principles of modernism are still dominant and valuable? I don't know about principles; after what I've said it should be clear that I think we must understand the "principles" of the great prewar writers in ways that most of the writers themselves did not and could not understand them. But once we have said this, their value remains enormous. Pound, Eliot, Joyce, Mann, and the rest: they were great men, giants. For one thing they taught us to read. For another they taught us to write. What more can we ask?

Optimism is untrustworthy. Yet I believe we are living in the early phase of an era which may become one of the most extraordinary episodes in human evolution, the justification at last of self-conscious intelligence, if only we can find means to contain our own technology and its usurping masters.

5. No. And no. Quite the contrary. Standards are tough today, and awareness of them is widespread. I see slipshod writing among young poets, but I'd say proportionately less now than I saw twenty years ago when I was editing *Poetry*.

6. I read so little criticism I'm hardly qualified to comment. What I do read is discouraging. Older critics are still trapped in the irrelevant, insoluble impasse of Kantian divisiveness, while the younger are so ill-informed historically that they cannot conceptualize our

present state of the arts. To my mind the best American criticism is still Kenneth Burke's; his books are crammed with leads that younger writers ought to be following. As for journalism, that's something else again. I have been a newspaperman, like my father and grandfather before me, and I have a higher regard for the profession than most of my friends have; but I don't believe its problems enter the present discussion.

Love, Art, and Money

A review of *Love and Fame*, by John Berryman, from *The Nation*, November 2, 1970.

JOHN BERRYMAN'S NEW BOOK of poems is in some respects, as the advance rumors warned us, a departure from earlier work; but not, as we come to look at it, much of a departure. True, Berryman now is writing in propria persona, without the masks and dramatic voices of his *Dream Songs* and *Homage to Mistress Bradstreet*; he is writing with candor about his own explicit autobiography; he is writing in simpler, more accessible language than that of earlier poems. But these are changes in degree only. They are not real departures, not reversals or innovations.

The contrast with Robert Lowell is irresistible, partly because the change in Berryman's poetry offers a seeming parallel to Lowell's change twenty years ago from the ornate, sharply formal poems of *Lord Weary's Castle* to the simpler, more personal poems of *Life Studies*. Beyond this, the two poets are the same age, of roughly the same background (eastern private schools, Harvard and Columbia, et cetera), of similar literary origins (the New Criticism, the war, et cetera). They are even, according to Berryman, close friends.

When I was writing about Lowell a couple of years ago I said that I thought the term *confessional*, which had been applied to his autobiographical poems by several critics, was unfortunate because it suggested an aim far less than his real intention. What Lowell was doing in those poems, I think, was exploring his own and his family's life, in extreme seriousness, to see if he could give that body of experience an imaginative organization strong enough, in the face of the depersonalizing force of a modern collective and technomaniacal world, to stand as an integrated structure. A will, a personality, a being. He was trying to create a life: his own.

Perhaps such an effort can never succeed, can never rest in achievement. Being finished would mean an end of creation and of life. The value of the autobiogenetic stance in art consists in the effort and the continuing trial. But the point here is that Berryman's new poems give little evidence of trial. They have no real seriousness or creative force, but only a kind of edgy exhibitionism. They are precisely confessional and nothing more, except when they are something less, that is, brags and rants. On the side of "fame" Berryman writes repeatedly and smugly about the success of his books, about his fattening royalties and increasing fan mail, about his honors and his acquaintanceships with exalted people. On the side of "love," where he is even less prepossessing, he gives us schoolboyish bragging exploits, the sequence of pickups and mistresses for thirty-five years, while his three wives get half a line and his children scarcely more, though he says somewhere that children are one of the three "points" of life. The other two, he adds, are "high art" and "money in the bank."

It is all full of self-contradiction, special pleading, vagueness. What emerges is not a personality, not an integrated being, but only a muddlement of crude desires. Toward the end there is some attempt at greater seriousness. The last poem in the book, which is also the longest, is a religious poem, forthright in its devotional feeling and in some passages almost moving, until in the midst of it we are informed, in a tone half blustery and half sneering, that the poet's conversion occurred "three weeks ago day before yesterday." He seems to be saying, "If you believe this you'll believe anything." In a saint or mystic we might accept that, though not without a strain; we might, under certain conditions, even celebrate it. But in this boasting, equivocating secularist? What does he take us for?

Some readers may say that these matters of substance have no importance esthetically and should not concern the critic, whose job is to examine not the experience but how the experience is turned into poetry. I do not agree. A critic has a moral as well as an esthetic obligation, and certainly a journalist-reviewer, as distinct from a critic, has a duty to report the substance of books which he has seen before they are available to the public. Other readers may say—a more cogent objection—that the substance of Berryman's poems is exactly the hang-up between faith and skepticism, self-reliance and self-doubt, hope and despair, which we all know; it is the experience of vacillation, experience with a negative value, the modern experience par excellence, and there is no reason why it should not be made into good poetry. Here I do agree. Who wouldn't, with so many splendid examples—Theodore Roethke, for one—before us? But Berryman has not done it. His experience remains raw and unstructured and far from good poetry.

Which brings us to the crux of the matter, the poetry itself, the language and verbal style. Repeatedly Berryman congratulates himself for his ear and his sense of metric; once he even congratulates God. He is delighted with his "gift." But where is it? What is it? His ability to wrench syntax out of every convention while remaining, though barely, within the bounds of a possible grammar? He is famous for this, of course. But it has nothing whatever to do with metric, it has damned little to do with poetry in general, and I confess I see nothing else in his work. I always thought his earlier poems, with their surface jumpiness, had no metric at all, or scarcely any; they move, not with the basic consistent cadence of essential poetry, but only with their own meretricious push and thrust of hyperbolic and unexpected phrasing. They move, stiltlike, on Berryman's peculiar rhetoric. Now in the new poems, where the language is simpler, I see my feelings confirmed, for with the rhetoric toned down the lack of meter is more than ever obvious. Here are a few lines, random but characteristic (from "The Heroes"):

> *They had to come on like revolutionaries,*
> *enemies throughout to accident & chance,*
> *relentless travellers, long used to failure*
>
> *in tasks that but for them would sit like hanging judges*
> *on faithless & by no means up to it Man.*

This is a good deal easier to read than the earlier heavy contortions, and I suppose we should be grateful for that. We would be if it weren't so flat. These lines are limp. They have no meter at all, nothing to sustain the modified but still deviant syntax. The norm of English pentameter, which in theory lies behind the poems, has become putative only, and hence is no help to the poet, and his ear has invented nothing to replace it. Here are a few lines from another poem with complex syntax, bearing about the same relationship to poetic convention:

> *Sometimes since you don't love me any more*
> *I cannot find an animal spirit*
> *to move my feet,*
> *or one quits and leaves me in the street*
> *among the buses and the traffic's roar*
>
> *as if I were deep in thought, but I am not*
> *—until the animal spirit that preserves*
> *me still alive*
> *takes care of where I am and slowly drives*
> *my feet their way across the street.*

These lines are nothing exceptional perhaps. But am I wrong, doesn't the meter here do its work, both by keeping syntax in order and by making it move? Doesn't it give these lines liveliness and even a minor elegance? I think so. But unfortunately for Berryman (and many of the rest of us), they are by Paul Goodman.

As for diction, we have on one hand Berryman's well-known colloquial cuteness, out-Audening Auden, as in the "faithless & by no means up to it Man," or elsewhere the pitiful death of Peter Warlock who had just "knocked himself off"; and on the other his deliberate archaisms, inversions, the use of fusty words like "moot" and "plaint." Archness, what we used to call sophomorism: in parts of the *Dream Songs* he almost brought it to a pitch intense enough to make an honest effect. But the more I think about those poems, and then about these new slighter ones, the more I think that that effect too was meretricious, a product of verbal *bizarrerie*. Finally there are Berryman's rhymes. They have always been uninteresting, sometimes awful, and they have not improved. The worst poem in the new book, "The Minnesota 8 and the Letter-Writers," is also the only closely rhymed poem.

In reviewing one of Berryman's earlier books I tried to trace a development in his contorted syntax from his first poems to the *Dream Songs*. I knew I didn't like his style, and had never liked it, and out of diffidence or a desire to avert my bias I leaned backward to find some innate necessity or naturalness in it. But now he has confessed, in a poem called "Olympus," his source, quoting it entire: "The art of poetry is amply distinguished from the manufacture of verse by the animating presence in the poetry of a fresh idiom: language so twisted and posed in a form that it not only expresses the matter in hand but adds to the stock of available reality." That is a well-known sentence, or at least it once was, written by R. P. Blackmur and published in *Poetry* in 1935. It stood alone, intended as a wonderful critical *aperçu*, and it suffers the faults of most such attempted distillations, sententiousness and incompleteness; but it hit Berryman hard. "I was never altogether the same man after *that*," he writes, and goes on to say how "eagerly" he sought out Blackmur's other writings. No doubt the essays on Yeats, Eliot, and the early Wallace Stevens particularly impressed him. But where are naturalness and necessity now? This seems a case where one of the New Critics actually achieved what they all patently wanted, not only the control of taste with respect to poetry already written but the control of poetry still to come. Yet must "fresh idiom" mean "twisted and posed"? And does language ever add to "available reality"? We know the danger of that old fatuity; and doubly dangerous it was for Berryman, I think, because it led him, in its arrogance and his own, to infer, by transversion or contraction or mere muleheadedness, that *poetry* as well as verse might be *manufactured* if only one could invent a fresh idiom in language twisted and posed. This is an oversimplification, more would need to be said in any comprehensive discussion of Berryman's work, but it is still very close to the heart of the matter. And the proof, I believe, lies on every page of his books.

The time has come, surely, to say that Berryman's poetry is usually interesting and sometimes witty but almost never moving, and that in spite of its scope and magnitude it lacks the importance that has been ascribed to it in recent years by many critics, editors, and readers. The "fame" that so much delights Berryman is inflated. When we consider other poets of his generation who have worked in the same general poetic convention—I say nothing of those in other conventions—we see that they have been making poetry while Berryman has been making language twisted and posed: I mean those already noted here, Lowell, Roethke, and Goodman, as well as such others as Cunningham, Schwartz, Jarrell, and Elizabeth Bishop, and even those of smaller ambition, like Richard Wilbur and Anthony Hecht, who have produced individual poems finer in poetic integrity and formal congruency than anything in the works of Berryman. One says these things the more willingly about him, though about another one might keep silent, because his own self-advertising, especially in his new book, has become so vain and outrageous.

A Focus, a Crown

A review of *Autobiography*, by Louis Zukofsky, from the *New York Times Book Review*, December 6, 1970.

RECENTLY, AFTER YEARS OF NEGLECT, the poet Louis Zukofsky, whose *Autobiography* is one of this year's most valuable literary events, has come into a certain vogue, especially among younger writers known as the Black Mountain poets and their followers. They find in him a poet new and modern and yet their elder, a poet whom they have discovered, a poet who for a long time has been doing more or less what they themselves wish to do, in their style and manner. They are right, of course, although Zukofsky wasn't quite all that undiscovered before they came along.

He began writing seriously in the 1920s, influenced by two older poets who soon became his friends, Ezra Pound and William Carlos Williams. In 1927 he began his major work, a poetic sequence called simply "A," which is still in progress. During the thirties he became the effective leader of a group of New York poets called the objectivists; they were known for a time, but were then eclipsed by the massive popularity of Eliot, Yeats, and the American poets dominated by European and symbolist influences. Zukofsky continued at work in virtual darkness. He produced a couple of anthologies, a long and deeply inquiring study of Shakespeare, an extraordinary and controversial translation of the poetry of Catullus, and a steady stream of new poems.

Now we have his *Autobiography*. Though it is in some respects the most fragile of his works, depending for its very existence upon the prior existence of the others, and though it will probably attract fewer readers than the rest of his books, still it seems to me the purest of them all. It is like the topmost jewel in a crown. Without the support of the other jewels it might be merely an emptiness or a glitter; but in its setting it draws together the luster of the whole, making a formal focus and an apex, a point of concentration and particular lucidity.

First, however, the book must be described, for it is scarcely a conventional autobiography. It comprises fifteen short poems reprinted from Zukofsky's other books and set to music by the composer Celia Zukofsky, the poet's wife, who has appeared in most of his other works and has collaborated on several of them. This short collection is prefaced with a short note and interspersed with five even shorter paragraphs. These paragraphs set forth a few, very few, public facts of Zukofsky's life, the barest possible summary, written in prose that is undistinguished to the point of multiple clichés and stiff journalistic syntax, such as you might find in any dictionary of biography.

Readers acquainted with the originality of Zukofsky's other prose will not doubt that this effect was intentional, and to them his implication will be clear: the poet's life, beyond these few publicly ascertainable facts, is his own affair, while his real autobiography, meaning the aspects of his mind and feeling which we all deserve and need to share, is his poetry. More than that, his truest autobiography is these poems set to music.

Thus we have a very pure and lucky example of a work whose form embodies its meaning, whose form *is* its meaning. Take the merest externals and put them together: the title (*Autobiography*), the authorship (man and wife), and the main text (poems and music). These data incorporate the themes of all Zukofsky's writing from the beginning. Life is a function of art, that is to say, of the creative imagination making from experience the structures of significant feeling which we call personalities. Its form is fundamentally conjugal—conjugated, joined. And its concrete enduring manifestation is music, toward which all other arts and all significant actions incline as toward their fulfillment. Finally and above all, the force, the motive energy, is love. These are crude statements, explicit and limited. But they are as near as statement can come to the essential meaning, implicit and un-limited, of the *Autobiography*, which itself makes no statements. It ex-ists. It is at one with itself, without abstraction. It is its own fullness and resonance of meaning.

In short it is an emblem. Normally we do not think of emblems in the traditional sense as products of individual genius, but rather as broadly cultural artifacts, things slowly evolved from the common mythopoeic mind. Many such artifacts are still fixed in our conscious-ness, in spite of our state of cultural erosion. Zukofsky's *Autobiography* is smaller than most of these, as we should expect since it is of one mind's making, but it shares their extraordinary clarity and resonance within simplicity. It could only have been made by an intense imag-ination engaged for a long time with its own materials.

Music has always been a large part of Zukofsky's poetry, both lin-guistically and thematically. One of my favorite passages is this pro-logue to a longer poem, here called "A Song for the Year's End" (addressed to the poet's wife and son—Paul Zukofsky, also a musi-cian—and if the substance seems fuzzy in extract, it makes perfect sense in the larger context):

> *Daughter of music*
> *and her sweet son*
> *so that none rule*
> *the dew to his own hurt*
> *with the year's last sigh*
> *awake*
> *the starry sky and bird.*

Once in another connection I wrote that the sounds of this poem could be analyzed if one were sufficiently clever and patient. Presum-ably, with the techniques of modern phonemics, a chart of them could be made. But it would still be only a chart, however complex, and it would still be only approximate. We know how these sounds work in our mouths; we could, with our astonishing clinical methods, teach a deaf person to say them; but we do not know and may never know how they work in our verbal imaginations, which have been formed from far too many unknown cultural influences ever to be tab-ulated. We can only declare that the sounds do work.

There are rhymes in the poem obviously, and assonances and consonances, but these are not the music of it. Music is made, not from repetition—boom, boom, boom—but from variance within repetition; in other words from change, from modulation. *Music-rule-dew-hurt-year's-starry-bird:* it is a unique and wonderfully satisfying progression of sounds. And it is organized by a rhythmic structure, in line-length and accent, which is perfectly complementary and again unique and satisfying. These are a few, but only a few, of this short poem's musical elements.

And I think they are exactly brought out in Celia Zukofsky's setting, for four voices with piano accompaniment. I cannot speak technically about this. I have played the parts on my clarinet and have sung them to myself, which is the best I can do in my circumstances. The music is grave but not solemn, with perhaps a more propulsive feeling than the words alone suggest. Its tonal movement is descending, then ascending, in minor harmonies, and a somewhat syncopated effect comes from the different timings of words in treble and bass. I like it very much. It seems an effective piece of music in itself, and a combining of conscious modern musical experience with strong feeling for the tradition of song.

As I have said, Zukofsky's young admirers are perfectly right when they insist that he is a distinctly modern poet, their fit comrade-in-arms, not only with respect to verbal practice, since most of his work is more vigorously contemporary in tone than the intentionally archaic passage I have quoted, but especially with respect to his attitudes toward experience, some of which prefigured by two decades the wave of European existentialism that came to us after World War II.

But Zukofsky is vigorously traditional as well. I am certain he would have no truck with the young people's antagonism to learning even if probably he does, like them, decry our educational methods. I do not see, for example, how anyone whose ear is attuned to the evolution of English song from Shakespeare to Campion to Dowland to Milton's *Comus* can fail to recognize the relationship between that and the passage I have quoted or many others I might have quoted, even though Zukofsky rarely uses standard rhyme and meter; and I believe an analogue also exists to elements of the Jewish lyrical tradition.

Zukofsky is deep, implicitly and explicitly, in the literary historical matrix. I hope young poets will see this, and see that it in no way weakens, but on the contrary strengthens, his essential humane relevance. To put it another way, the real history of literature is the history of love.

Perhaps I was wrong to suggest that because this book derives from Zukofsky's others it will have fewer readers. In another sense it is complete in itself, needing only the warmth of blooded, breathy voices for its fulfillment. The express addition of music to these texts may attract readers who would not be drawn to the poetry alone, reversing the process I first had in mind. I hope so. Certainly I recommend these songs to all amateur singers and instrumentalists, especially recorder players. The music is easy, yet different and appealing. And why not recommend them to professionals too? I should be most grateful for a recording by performers who could do these songs full justice.

Whether or not this book is widely used, however, or even if I (heaven forbid) should be the only person who ever uses it, Louis and Celia Zukofsky's *Autobiography* is here—this life made in collaboration and fully achieved, a verifiable human success in our present doleful balance of human failure.

Poet of Civility

A review of *Collected Shorter Poems, 1927–1957*, by W. H. Auden, from the *Southern Review*, Winter 1970.

THIS NEW *Collected Shorter Poems* supplants Auden's unsatisfactory *Collected Poetry* of 1945 in at least three ways. First, it offers a longer span of Auden's work, thirty years in all. Second, it gives us the poems in chronological arrangement. Third, it presumably contains Auden's final accounting for the years in question, since a number of previously collected poems have been discarded and many have been revised. I shall confine my remarks to these three heads.

1. The *Collected Shorter* contains three hundred poems, comprising Auden's central achievement. His long poems, like *The Sea and the Mirror* and *The Age of Anxiety*, are omitted, and of course one must look elsewhere for the plays, librettos, essays, travel sketches, polem-

ics, and so on. But these other works are—and most were intended to
be—ancillary to the short poems, which means that the *Collected
Shorter* is the book upon which Auden's reputation will chiefly rest in
the long run. Not that it is complete; Auden is still at work and in any
case he has cut off the collection at 1957, explaining in the foreword
that this was the year when, owing to a shift of his summer residence
from Italy to Austria, his work entered a new phase. (Like most of us,
he apparently writes his poetry on vacation.) Everywhere in this
book, however, Auden's modest, scrupulous view of his own work is
evident, so that one suspects his real reason for excluding his work of
the past ten years—all the poems from *About the House* (1965) and
whatever others have appeared since then in periodicals—is his feeling that he is still too close to it to judge it properly.

2. The arrangement of poems in the 1945 *Collected* was frankly miserable; alphabetical in order of first lines, a cheeky-jowly jumble of
early by late, comic by elegiac, didactic by erotic. It gave the reader
no impression whatever of Auden's development. The new arrangement, chronological as it should be, is far handier. In a few cases Auden has departed from chronology even here. The sequence called
Horae Canonicae, for example, his parabolic meditations on the theme
of Good Friday, written in the late forties and early fifties, is displaced
to the very end of the book, no doubt as a sign that Auden considers it
his best poem, or at any rate the poem whose impact he prefers to
leave in the reader's mind. But all told the order is reliably chronological, and it reveals a consistent evolution. The changes of Auden's style
that had seemed abrupt when they occurred, now look like natural
transitions, so that from the entire span we receive a clearer impression than ever of the role Auden has played; doubtless an unconscious role at first, but then, I think, as the years passed, an ever more
conscious one. What he attempted was the assimilation of the specific
English literary tradition to the modern poetic revolution. Put another way, it was the restoration of orderly flow to the mainstream of
English poetry after the interruptive activities of the Pound-Eliot generation, yet without abandoning their insights; and all for the sake,
probably, less of the specific literary mainstream itself than of the values carried by it: civil speech, social progressivism, philosophical
humanism, enjoyment as a primary component of esthetic theory, intelligence, and the functionally corrective place of art in society. It is
not after all the outlanders of English literature with whom we associ-

ate Auden, the Blakes and Chattertons; instead his roots are in the public, professional, cosmopolitan tradition, from Dryden to Bridges and Masefield. To revitalize the values of this tradition, to modernize them, and to enforce them against the pandaemonium of social disruption, successive Fascist wars, and British cultural complacency— this was his work. And his knowledge of his own relationship to the English mainstream was not altered by his need to write more and more from a position of dissent. (See the poem called "We Too Had Known Golden Hours.") It was exasperating work, and actually drove him away from England while he was still a young man. Yet has there ever been a less successful expatriation? To this day, after nearly thirty years of living abroad, Auden remains the English man of letters par excellence.

3. From these unpromising, because so miscellaneous, sources, namely, the fragments of English formalist tradition, the liberating impulses in modern prosody, the vocabulary of Marx and Freud and Frazer, the moods of Kafka and Hesse and Proust and Brecht, and with many hints picked up from his own contemporaries (for there are poems in which he is hardly more than an amanuensis for Koestler, de Rougemont, or Graham Greene): from these unpromising sources Auden put together his early style, full of caustic poeticisms, broad understatements, sudden savageries, unexpected allusions, and with heavy reliance on the rhetoric and conventions of thriller fiction.

> *And the minerals and creatures, so deeply in love with their lives*
> *Their sin of accidie excludes all others,*
> *Challenge the nervous students with a careless beauty,*
>   *Setting a single error*
>   *Against their countless faults.*

> *O in these quadrangles where Wisdom honours herself*
> *Does the original stone merely echo that praise*
> *Shallowly, or utter a bland hymn of comfort,*
>   *The founder's equivocal blessing*
>   *On all who worship Success?*

> *Promising to the sharp sword all the glittering prizes,*
> *The cars, the hotels, the service, the boisterous bed,*
> *Then power to silence outrage with a testament . . .*

And so on. It was a period style, very alive and novel then, very dated now. Yet the point is that Auden himself was sensitive to its datability before anyone else and began to modify his style while he was still young, toning down its mock violence, lengthening its syntax, subduing cadence and rhyme, until in his late work he ended with a kind of talky essay-poem that resembles the poems of Marianne Moore, but more sprawling than hers, more inclusive, more prone to generalization and sentimentality; the poetry, in short, of his "bucolics" and household poems. Thus, while remaining committed to "literary" values, he moved from a merely eccentric to a genuinely personal style. And of course the Oxonian accent is unmistakable throughout.

In his revisions for this new volume Auden has reinforced this poetic development retroactively. From the early poems he has cut out many self-conscious poeticisms—the apostrophic O's, for instance—and he has smoothed syntax and structure to give the poems more fluency. His revisions have been both extensive and intensive: a remarkable feat. In the thirty or so poems I have examined in both the 1945 and 1967 editions, only one or two have escaped unchanged, though many revisions are slight, no more than the work of an itchy pencil. But where Auden has gone to work seriously to improve an old poem the results are often spectacular. As a technician he is superb. His revisions give us a lesson in versewriting that ought to be instructive to any young writer of no matter what stylistic predilection. In the poem from which I have quoted, "Oxford," Auden has rewritten almost every line he chose to keep, and he has cut the whole poem from nine stanzas to four. Was such drastic revision worth while? The poem was no world-beater to begin with. Yet I think Auden's effort is justified, because he has reduced a pretentious set piece to an incidental but graceful and intelligent little poem, worth keeping in his collected edition. His revision of the famous poem on the death of Yeats is more daring, if only because the poem in its earlier version was so well known; but he has taken the risk and removed three stanzas. It works. The poem is instantly raised to a new level of somberness and genuineness, and hence is truer to its original intention.

In many poems of the middle period, the 1940s, he has changed locutions toward greater literariness, but a literariness of his own particular kind. In one poem "the orgulous spirit"—a thumping Audenism if there ever was one—becomes now "the spirit orgulous," and we see at once that it is even more characteristic. The greatest changes I have encountered are in the sonnets originally taken from *Journey to a War*. In 1945 they were called "In Time of War." Now they are called "Sonnets from China"; they have been reduced from twenty-seven to twenty-one in number, their sequence has been reordered, all have been revised, some completely rewritten, and one new sonnet has been added. To my mind these are notable improvements. I doubt that anyone coming to Auden for the first time in this new book would be aware of the amount of tinkering that has gone into these sonnets, yet the new sequence is demonstrably better than the old one. I don't mean that the *poetry*, the conceived essence, is improved, but the poems are far more readable, and hence our approach to the poetry, whatever its interior values may be, is easier. Perhaps the fact that Auden's poems *can* be rewritten in this way, years after their first appearance, says something about them. I think it does. This is mainstream poetry, poetry in the specifically literary, public, professional tradition, poetry that calls attention to itself precisely as artifact, as something *written*—and hence as something rewritten or at least rewritable. It is not poetry cast forever into an unchangeable form by the white heat of personal vision.

Incidentally many titles in the new book have been altered. A reader who wishes to look up a particular poem must often rely on the index of first lines.

What shall we say about these values of the specific English literary tradition, values of intelligence, decency, literacy, humaneness, civility, responsibility? God knows one wishes they had a greater place in the world of social reality, whatever place they may have in the world of poetry. Certainly in 1945, in the exhaustion produced by years of war and brutality and terror, they seemed, cast as they were in the rhetoric of a querulous, nerve-worn intellectuality, exactly right. But now it is a long time since I have heard anyone speak of Auden's poetry with real concern. And he meanwhile has proceeded further and further into literariness, and has propounded again and again his notion of art as a "secondary" reality, a game, a pastime. My impression is that the young generation, reared in the knowledge of the bomb and in a totally changed social environment, doesn't bother to read his poetry at all. Certainly there are anthology pieces in Auden's book, like the poem beginning "Doom is dark and deeper than any sea-dingle" (formerly called "Something Is Bound to Happen" and retitled "The Wanderer" in the new book), or the song beginning "Lay your sleeping head, my love" (now called "Lullaby"), poems we will always remember. But those stretches and stretches and stretches of genteel, polysyllabic garrulity? The action is going on down in the street now, yet Auden is still back in the parlor, gabbling away. Maybe after the action is over, if it ever is, we can all return indoors and resume where we left off. But does anyone seriously propose that we will be the same men and women then, able to respond as before? I suspect no famous poet ever "aged" so fast. Auden strikes me now as somebody "back there," a contemporary of . . . well, I dislike saying it but I can't avoid it: this poetry reads like something out of the two-dimensional past where everyone lives at once, Coventry Patmore, Goldsmith, Lucan. The poems are fodder for graduate students. They scarcely exist, except for the few people in the world today who still take pleasure in reading old books.

Not Too Late for Words

A review of *Farming: A Hand Book* and *The Hidden Wound*, by Wendell Berry, from the *Village Voice*, April 8, 1971.

WENDELL BERRY'S TWO NEW BOOKS fit together like praying hands: left and right, poetry and prose, commitment to earth and commitment to man. They are complementary opposites, a natural pair, and they have more meaning together than they have separately. Yet almost certainly they are not intentional correlatives. They were conceived independently, and their mutuality comes from the finely integrated artistic personality of their author.

Farming: A Hand Book is Berry's new collection of poems, his fourth (excluding the early book-long eulogy for President Kennedy, which he appears to have disowned). To my mind it is an uneven collection, yet I come to this judgment with surprise, because when one first opens the book and reads here and there one has an impression of technical sameness, a steady high level of verbal proficiency. It is quite true; Berry has brought his style in the past four or five years to poetic maturity, a flexible personal language that is remarkably sure of itself in terms of rhythm, syntax, and diction. One rarely finds a forced phrasing or an ill-chosen word. Hence the unevenness must come from something prior to language, and I think this is the case. Some of these poems were misconceived from the beginning. They are too slight, too peripheral, or otherwise too uninteresting to make good poems, and I say this as someone who lives, in Vermont, much the same life that Berry lives in Kentucky and shares much the same convictions. The most important case of misconception in his new book is a verse drama in four scenes based on ideas so commonplace that I cannot imagine anyone, reader or auditor, attending to it with much enthusiasm. Then in a few cases, notably poems called "Winter Night Poem for Mary" and "The Buildings," Berry's imagination has slipped from its customary rigor into a kind of Frostean sentimentality or cuteness that seems decidedly inappropriate.

Yet this is completely the wrong way to look at Berry's book, for at the other end of the scale he has written poems that seem to me superb. More than that: supreme. They all derive from his experience as a subsistence farmer, and they celebrate the earth and the strength a man gains from contact with soil, water, stone, and seed. Make no mistake, these are poems in praise of Aphrodite of the Hot Furrow, full of generative force, even though their manner is seldom rhapsodic. They are precisely down-to-earth poems. They are implanted with a sexual, vegetative goodness that brooks no vulgarity. I am reminded of the pre-Freudian, pre-Darwinian purity of early nineteenth-century naturalism, the earthy quiet mysticism of writers like John Clare and William Barnes. Almost as if he himself were living in another age, Berry fails to ask questions that would be obvious and crucial if he were writing a treatise instead of poems, such as what relevance our deep instinct for fertility has in a time when artificial sterility is mandatory. What do we do with our vegetative myths and symbols now? If we root them out of our minds will there be anything left? But Berry is not writing a treatise, and we have no right to ask for comprehensiveness. Moreover, in at least one sense, his ecological awareness, he is as modern as anyone could wish, since his poems are imbued with a sense of the damage that has been done to our land and of the orientation men must feel when they recognize themselves as the damaging agent. These are the finest poems of their kind that I know. They add something very genuine and new to our tradition of nature poetry at a time when it seemed as if no addition were possible. The following, which I recommend without reservation, are the poems I checked in Berry's book: "The Supplanting," "In This World," "A Praise," "The Current," "The Mad Farmer Revolution," "The Contrariness of the Mad Farmer," "Meditation in the Spring Rain," "The Grandmother," and "The Wages of History."

The hidden wound in the title of Berry's second book is the wound inflicted on him by his racist upbringing in Kentucky, and then by extension the wound that all white America has inflicted upon itself, a secret, unacknowledged wound, through its racist attitudes, both past and present. Berry seeks not only to understand his wound and its origins, which he regards as easy, but to cure it. He proceeds by way of personal reminiscence, about his childhood, particularly about two black people, a man and a woman, who lived on the Berrys' farm and who shed a strong beneficent influence on his upbringing. From these skeins of reminiscence, simply and movingly related, he weaves a fabric of speculation both fascinating and trenchant, though whether or not he has succeeded in his primary objective, the cure of his wound, is something he alone can judge. What we all can judge, however, and what no man of reasonably good will can fail to see, is that Berry has produced one of the most humane, honest, liberating works of our time. It is a beautiful book. More than that it has become at one stroke an essential book. Every American who can read at all should read it.

Berry concludes that the real wound of white racist America is its divorce from the earth. By importing and subjugating the black man and then forcing him to do the dirty work of tilling the soil, the white man has interposed someone else between himself and the land. The result is, first, that an entire people, the black Americans, have been damaged in ways perhaps unique in all history; second, that the white man's life has been made abstract, remote, demythified, a pastiche of money values and manipulational techniques; and third, that the land itself, having lost the affection of its owners, has been brutally misused. Thus Berry sees a cause-and-effect relationship between racism and our ecological disaster. It is a powerful, emotionally laden argument, extremely appealing, and if it is a little too neat this in no way detracts from its cogency. To someone like myself, raised in the racial innocence, not to say ignorance, of a back-country New England village forty-odd years ago, Berry's analysis seems historically oversimplified. No one would deny a functional relationship between slavery and the rape of the land, for instance, but a prior cause of both is likely to seem more conspicuous to a northerner; I mean the imperialist thrust of the entire European Renaissance, from which American civilization in all its aspects has sprung. Then too the wound left in white society by slavery is likely to seem less excruciating to a northerner, especially a rural northerner, than the wound left by the calculated massacre of American Indians, which lasted longer than slavery, observed no sectional limits, and produced an even more devastating effect upon its primary victims—if such sufferings as slavery and genocide are quantifiable at all. But these are not criticisms of Berry's book. On the contrary they are merely ramifications of it, the thoughts that are likely to spring up in any reader's mind. The central flower, the book itself, remains intact. Its roots are so deep in the American experience, call it what you will—our plain heritage of violence—that all of us, sectionalism aside, can respond to it, especially in this intercommunicative age when all of us bear everyone's shame and guilt. If ever a reviewer felt a need to seize his readers by the arm and speak directly to them, I do now. It is not too late for words! I am writing from deepest conviction. Reconciliation is possible if the right people will try it. Please read Berry's book. And then read the poems that give the context in which his beautiful concern has taken form.

Seriousness and the Inner Poem

From the *New York Quarterly*, Autumn 1971.

THIS AFTERNOON as I walked beside my brook a half mile above my place, where the channel enters a broad, heavily wooded gulf, I was thinking about the way my sense of poetry has been unsettled and put at odds with itself by the general upheavals of taste in recent years. This was no rarity; any afternoon or any walk these days might find me thinking about the same thing. It is a hard, obsessive topic. There in the gulf, where I clambered along the rocky, rooty bank, my attention was turned half outward, half inward. The brook in that place moves like a zipper down a fold of earth, its channel straight, its current swift, until it hits a barrier of tipped-up Green Mountain bedrock, which shatters the flow. Four or five noisy little waterfalls spill into four or five meandering little channels that simper through a low, soggy, ferny sump. Then, farther on, the brook regathers itself and continues as before.

Sometimes I think my feelings about poetry have become so contrary and self-divided that they will never find their way out of the sump and into a regathering again.

I stopped and stood looking back up the gulf to the simplicities there, the undivided brook, the leaning birches and rain-brightened autumn leaves. My antecedents had been simple too. When the war was done with me in 1945, like thousands of others I found myself rescued by the GI Bill from the work I had been trained to do earlier; I could go to graduate school and put off earning a living. I jumped at the chance, and landed, unsuspecting, in the thick of Modern Poetry, which today is called Academic Poetry. It was a common enough case.

I have my reservations about that term *academic*. God knows most of us were antiacademic in those days, we despised the demands of scholarship, and many of our heroes were the same poets as those admired by the liberated young poets of today: Pound, Williams, H.D. When people call my own early poems academic it infuriates me, because I know that many of them were written in times of crushingly real trouble when academicism in any of its senses was the furthest thing from my mind. If I used the forms and styles I had seen in the books of popular poets of the day, it was because my substantial need left me no energy for formal experiment, and because my circumstances gave me no opportunity to learn about those of my contemporaries who were beginning to write in other ways.

But the discrimination of merits and flaws in the poetry of mid-century is too big a question, and too tangled in sectarianism, to be attempted now, though someday the job must be done. Certainly much of that poetry *was* academic, and getting more academic every day, as we ourselves were aware. It was no great trick to break with such excess when I came to realize what my contemporaries in other sectors were doing. The poems of Denise Levertov moved me deeply when I first saw them in about 1955, so did some poems by Allen Ginsberg, and from them I went on to other poets, Creeley, Duncan, Corman, and so on, and then into the whole efflorescence of the sixties, Merwin, Wakoski, Berry, LeRoi Jones, Philip Levine, and many others, hundreds of others. But what a mixture! Ginsberg's furore next to Creeley's precisionism, Corman beside Jones beside Wakoski beside Berry—a real hodgepodge. And if you add poets from the earlier period whose works are still moving and good, Tate, Ransom, Stevens, Jarrell, Shapiro, Lowell, John Peale Bishop—the list is very long—where does that leave poetic taste? Are there no general criteria, covering everything? Am I condemned to eclecticism, that dirty word?

I was brought up against this problem with particular force a couple of days ago when I found a poem by John Crowe Ransom quoted in a place where I had not expected it at all. I was reading some letters by Jack Spicer, the California poet who died in 1965 and who is acknowledged by all concerned to have been the real leader, virtually the guru, behind the "renaissance" of West Coast poetry a decade or more earlier. Spicer was deeply committed to poetic talent and insight, as distinct from technical proficiency, and to the chances and triumphs of poetic language, and from this he moved further and further into occultism, until in his final poems, formally unlike anything called by the name of poetry elsewhere, he claimed to be giving readers only what had been dictated to him by invisible external powers. In short he was not the poet to whom one would look for an appreciation of poetry in the academic or rationalist traditions. Yet there was this poem by Ransom, "Piazza Piece," quoted in Spicer's letters. Not Ransom's best, but a fine poem anyway and worth quoting again.

> —*I am a gentleman in a dustcoat trying*
> *To make you hear. Your ears are soft and small*
> *And listen to an old man not at all,*
> *They want the young men's whispering and sighing.*
> *But see the roses on your trellis dying*
> *And hear the spectral singing of the moon;*
> *For I must have my lovely lady soon,*
> *I am a gentleman in a dustcoat trying.*

> —*I am a lady young in beauty waiting*
> *Until my truelove comes, and then we kiss.*
> *But what grey man among the vines is this*
> *Whose words are dry and faint as in a dream?*
> *Back from my trellis, Sir, before I scream!*
> *I am a lady young in beauty waiting.*

(Do young readers need to be told that in the American south *piazza* means, or once meant, *veranda*, and that a dustcoat was an overgarment worn while driving in an open vehicle, either a carriage or an early car?)

The gist of Spicer's commentary on Ransom is in one sentence: "The way to read this poem (and most of his) is not to let the deceptive skill hypnotize you into not hearing the poem." How simple. The New Critics, perhaps including Ransom himself, would have said simpleminded. Yet for my part I have seen no statement about Ransom's poetry more perceptive than this. We recognize at once how it ties in with the common complaint of young poets today that rhyme and meter distract them from the real content of poetry. For Spicer, as for most older readers, Ransom's skill is not a distraction but a hypnosis; yet the effect may be the same. We lose ourselves in wonder for these rhymes so modestly doing their work in perfection, for this diction so marvelously consistent in its mock-romanticism—or is it mock-mock-romanticism?—for this tonally flawless interplay of syntax and meter, and for the structural finesse that creates such an augmentation of meaning in the repeated lines. And for the originality too: has there ever been another sonnet like this? If so, I am unaware of it. What magnificent writing! We lose ourselves in wonder of it to such an extent that we lose the poem. Because the poem is not the writing, neither the particular prosody nor the sonneteering tradition; it lies within, existing there as a song and a cry, fulfilling its own language exactly. Nor is this anything to do with sentiment. The poem is the entire and practically unlimited spectrum of unanalyzable but recognizable structures of feeling and thought, or thought-full feeling, which arises from the words in their immutable relationships: for example, "But what grey man among the vines is this / Whose words are dry and faint as in a dream?" The poem is neither good nor bad, but true. And if as I believe—probably contrary to Spicer, though his opinion was never made altogether clear as far as I know—Ransom's

skill, which may deceive or hypnotize some readers (especially emu-
lative poets), is not antithetical to the poem but necessary and supple-
mentary to it, then perhaps we have the glimmerings of a criterion.

So much may be said for "Piazza Piece." How much more then for
"Blue Girls," "Bells for John Whiteside's Daughter," and "Winter Remembered." These were the poems, with others of a like order, by
which I had chosen to represent Ransom in a big anthology of modern American poetry I put together a couple of years ago; and when
bound galley proofs were sent out last summer ahead of publication
to poets and critics who might help to promote the book, I received a
letter from an old friend who is also an old and close friend of Ransom. It was a bitter letter, and the bitterest of my friend's complaints
concerned my treatment of Ransom. He reproached me for using only
the slighter poems, the elegiac and gently ironic poems, and for leaving out the tougher, more intellectual, generally later poems, which
he thought would show Ransom as the serious and important writer
he has really been. Specifically he said I should have chosen, in addition to the poems I did choose, two others called "The Equilibrists"
and "Painted Head." He accused me of turning Ransom into "a charming minor poet."

Well, charming minor poet is what we usually call Sir Thomas Wyatt, George Crabbe, John Clare, Padraic Colum, and Lord knows how
many others, and personally I would not mind belonging to that company at all, at all. What else is there—except oblivion on one hand
and the fluke of greatness on the other? But aside from this, and aside
from the fact that I do not especially like the two poems recommended by my friend, and aside from the further fact that neither I
nor any anthologist can turn Mr. Ransom into anything but what he
is, the more critical point remains that my friend has tried to impute
seriousness and importance to a poem by reference to the seriousness
and importance of its topic. I think this cannot be done. A topic may
be serious and important in the affairs of men, in philosophy, in science, in politics, and it may even be serious in other ways in poetry,
but when we are talking about seriousness and importance as indi-
cators of poetic value or esthetic efficacy, then the topic is a neutral
factor and seriousness is an attribute of the poem, the intrinsic real
poem. In art, to say it another way, the quality of feeling is important,
not what is felt.

Are Ransom's later poems truly serious? In their argumentative or discursive method they give me an impression of great earnestness, but not of seriousness. They are efforts of thought, after which come efforts of language, somewhat lagging. I see no poems in them at all. But in the earlier lyrics about the deaths of little girls and boys or about growing old or about romantic frustration I see, beneath the layers of irony, very great seriousness indeed; total seriousness. Here the intrinsic poems, originating in a spontaneous response to the enigmas of life, swell with limitless self-augmentation of imaged feeling, thought, and association, which is another way of saying that they are serious. And this in turn is another way of saying that they are neither good nor bad, but true. Of course I have no way of telling what place Ransom may finally occupy in the scale of poetic reputations, minor or major or somewhere in between. But I believe it will be determined by these serious early poems, "slight" though they may be, and not by the earnest later ones. I hope it will be a high place, because I personally like these poems very much, and I now think I did not include enough of them in my anthology.

That which is neither good nor bad then, but true and serious. . . .

I return occasionally to the essays of T. S. Eliot, which seem to me deeply inset in our literary consciousness, not as touchstones in the Arnoldian sense but as a sort of gads, taunting us with their wrong intelligence and perverse brilliance to try to correct them, and to try to measure up. In the preface to *The Sacred Wood* Eliot wrote: "Poetry is a superior amusement: I do not mean an amusement for superior people. I call it an amusement, an amusement *pour distraire les honnêtes gens*, not because that is a true definition, but because if you call it anything else you are likely to call it something still more false. If we think of the nature of amusement, then poetry is not amusing; but if we think of anything else that poetry may seem to be, we are led into far greater difficulties." But Eliot was leading himself into difficulties, unnecessarily. He was a famous word-twister, but is any species of amusement the same as poetry? The answer is no, no matter how you redefine the word; not even if you say that *amusement* means *seriousness*. Yet we can see how Eliot fell into his predicament; the poems of Ransom show us. We are hypnotized by that marvelous skill of writing, or perhaps like Eliot we are honest men distracted by it, and this is amusement, a kind of amusement. If we do not know how to conceive poetry except in its formal properties, we may conclude that this amusement is all of poetry, as many people have, including W. H. Auden, who went so far as to say that poetry is a "game." But then what do we do with our knowledge that in our reading we have actually undergone something more? We have been *moved*, we have been *shaken*. There is no question about this, as the slightest self-scrutiny reveals to us. Ransom's poem is terrifying. And what has moved and shaken us is the serious poem within the hypnotic amusement. That is clear, at least to me. What is less clear is the way in which the amusement, as secondary, is an indispensable supportive element of the primary seriousness; yet I am certain it is.

Eliot himself came to a similar view twenty years later, when he was writing less as a critic than as a working poet and editor. He spoke of *genuineness* and of how it might be applied as a rule of thumb in the judgment of poetry. He seems to have meant by this his own sense of the congruence or incongruence between a poet's experience and his language; if they fitted, if the experience filled out the language and left no emptiness of rhetoric or bombast or ornament, then the poem was genuine. He was, in other words, edging toward seriousness as a criterion. But he was afraid of it, reluctant to go very far in exploring it; and I think this was so because of his fear of the subjective. Like the other critics and poets of his time, in their revulsion from the scientific or naturalistic thought of the late nineteenth century, he felt he needed the buttress of objectivity in his ideas and feelings if he was to stand firm against his enemies. He needed to fight them in their own terms. Though he despised their reliance on concepts of external verification in their material domain, he was still dependent upon external verification in his own spiritual and esthetic domain. In this he was profoundly a part of our philosophical past, so much of which has gone into the "rational proof" of irrational knowledge (see Eliot's doctoral thesis on the philosophy of F. H. Bradley), and of Western, as opposed to Eastern, thought. In this he was a true "academic." And at this point, I think, we discover the real difference between American academic poetry and the poetry which came after it.

The ways to say what happened in American poetry during the sixties are probably countless. I am inclined at the moment to say, for example, that English poetry, meaning all poetry written in any kind of English, has been haunted for almost four hundred years by what Kit Marlowe, who was born in the same year as Shakespeare, would have written if he had not been killed in a barroom fight at the age of twenty-nine. Spicer would probably not have said this; his young followers certainly would not. No matter. I am my peculiar self plus my peculiar training, and what I say is helpful to me because it occurs in my terms; it may be tangentially helpful to others too. The point is that the latent subjective in Western culture, which has broken through to the surface sporadically (as in Marlowe's *Faustus* and *Dido*), has broken through again. Its effect is large, but we cannot yet say how deep or enduring. For the present, however, we are willing to adopt truth and seriousness as the criteria of poetry, even though we cannot judge them except subjectively. We are willing to say what was anathema to the academics, that each reader is his own best critic. We are willing not only to say it but to assert it, to make it a principle of action. We agree that our judgments of seriousness lack objective verification, and that in consequence we can have no unanimity, or probably even preponderance, of belief, but we say it doesn't matter; we say we have, in literature past and present, more than enough poems to go around, however multifarious our beliefs may be.

Finally we say that we are justified in our beliefs by our awareness that the test of seriousness is not simply our sense of a certain urgency in the poem, or a certain "tone" or "mood," but our sense of personal movement and change in reading the poem. Our subjective judgment is firmly experiential; that is our verification. For we believe that the function of the poem which lies within amusement is to create us, to extend our beings indefinitely in evolving structures of thought and feeling. This is what we have learned in our long and repeated observations: of war, of peace, of mass, of solitude, of learning, of ignorance. The whole meaning of social force and natural force, and very likely of metaphysical force as well, is the unimportance, not to say vacuity, of life as it actually exists, that is, in single conscious units. Force, the manifestation and outward being of social and natural reality, is our destruction; it annihilates us, it depersonalizes us, it changes us from human beings into objects for manipulation, or into figures on a chart. We resist by means of the poem, which is our self-creative act, whether we are, in the narrower sense, "creators" or "spectators." There are other means of resistance too, of course, and we do what we can to halt or impede the demolition of our habitat. But these other means are at best negative and preventive, and hence they lack ultimate seriousness. Art is our only positive creative resistance. Art is our ultimate seriousness.

Art is also our mystery. So be it. The structures of the poem arise by inscrutable means and are unified by infinite and indefinable connectives. We love to speculate about such things. Our speculations fill the pages of our magazines. But speculation is as far as it goes, and in the end we see that this too is a kind of amusement. For if the mystery is ever penetrated and art becomes a matter of objective or a priori understanding, that will be the end of seriousness and the end of humane, as distinct from technological, civilization. (Humane civilization began in the caves of Lascaux.)

This is the value of art, the real value; not a heritage, not a treasure or a tradition, but an ever-renewable creative efficacy. Of course we must remember that all serious and true works, past or present, are equivalent in this respect and are in this sense treasures. Where would we be without their life-giving powers? Repeatedly our experience is shattered against the force of reality, and our self-awareness goes meandering in disintegration and self-division, until it is regathered and reshaped in a total creative act, which is an organized aspect of being, a whole particular scene, serious and true. And then we continue as before, perhaps stronger but certainly no weaker, until a final shattering.

Fallacies of Silence

From the *Hudson Review*, Autumn 1973.

NOT MUCH LITERARY CRITICISM THESE DAYS is granted the éclat that came almost as a matter of course to certain brilliant and valuable works a generation ago. Probably not much deserves it. Yet one recent essay is being celebrated in ways that remind us of the earlier time. Its title is "Silence and the Poet," its author is George Steiner, and a few days ago I read it.* It is worth attending to.

Steiner's main concern in his published criticism has sprung from

---

*In *Language and Silence: Essays on Language, Literature, and the Inhuman*, by George Steiner (New York: Atheneum), 1967.

his perception of the terrifying interrelationships among literature, language, and contemporary history, particularly as experienced in Europe during the years that ended with Hitler's downfall. How, Steiner asks repeatedly, could the wardens of the infamous camps have been devoted, as we know some were, to the great expressions of German humanism? How could the *gauleiter* who spent his evenings closeted with the eloquence of Goethe, Heine, or Fontane, use that same language the next day for composing warrants to send children and their parents into torture and death? What becomes of the poet in such a world? What becomes of his responsibilities, to his art and to his humanity? What happens to language itself when it is so abused? What remains of the essential value of the word, or of our faith in the meaning of meaning?

These are disturbing questions. All who lived through those years, even in America, have asked them, and have submitted, reluctantly or readily, to the reversions of shame, guilt, and despair entailed in them. But without doubt Steiner, whose personal and family history connect him intimately with the European disaster, has asked them with more purpose than most, and with greater urgency, so that his responses are sharpened and remarkably well articulated. This is evident in his writings which evoke the German social and cultural milieu in and after the Hitlerian episode, or in essays dealing with the works of particular authors who lived and wrote during that time. But the essay in question is not of this sort; it is more general, conjectural, and polemical, an argument in applied esthetics; written, if one may judge from its tone, in a white heat of concern. Like many such works it is confused and overwritten, replete on one hand with a sense of humane commitment that produces on the other an imperious rhetoric, as if to clear the way for deeply felt but questionable propositions. As a sign of its author's feeling the essay is forgivable, perhaps commendable, but as a passage in literary theory it needs more study.

The essay is in two parts, undifferentiated and poorly joined. In the first part Steiner attempts to show how poetry, taken as the generalized verbal motion of the human imagination, contains within itself three tendencies of transcendence: toward light, toward music, and toward silence. But we see at once how confusion enters. The three are not consonant. As his example of transcendence toward light, Steiner chooses the passage which would occur to all of us, the ending of the *Paradiso*, which is one of the few moments of genuine transcendence in our literature. But Dante makes it perfectly clear that this is precisely what it is, transcendence, elevation from one level of perception to another, not mere transference between two modes of sensuous perception: not, in other words, the transformation of word into landscape, sound into sight or touch, verbalism into plasticity, but a movement from "outer" to "inner" light, away from sensuousness altogether, into the metaphysical. Dante says his eyesight must be purged or made pure (*sincera*) before he can "see" the lofty light that in itself is true (*alta luce che da sé é vera*), which I take to mean that his eyesight is refined of materiality and removed, as such, from his actual eyes. Dante says:

> *Così la mente mia, tutta sospesa,*
> *mirava fissa, immobile e attenta,*
> *e sempre di mirar faciesi accesa.*

It is his mind which, "all rapt, was gazing, fixed, still and intent, and ever enkindled with gazing"—his *mind*, not his eyes; his mind in all the cognitive immediacy and autonomy that medieval psychology gave to it; his mind fixed and immobile, that is, beyond sense and without will. And if his speech fails when his mind is struck by the divine flash of light (*la mia mente fu percossa da un fulgore*), the failure does not persist into the time of actual composition, for the language, the singing but simple tension of the last canto, is the verbal triumph of the poem.

Transcendence, literal, actual, absolute, is what that canto is about, as all readers recognize, and what the whole *Paradiso* has been leading up to. But with Steiner's second category, the movement toward music, we enter a different dimension and find ourselves in an incongruity. Here we have not transcendence but transference. By pointing to various examples Steiner shows how Western poets have striven in their language toward pure sound, as if music were a superior kind of expression, as indeed many poets have believed, including poets of every age and school; in short, the Orphic theme, a dominant in Western tradition from ancient times to the present. The evidence is abundant and well known. We agree with Steiner's account of it. But two further considerations occur to us, which Steiner does not mention. First, the movement toward music is not a movement from sensuousness to metaphysicality; properly speaking, therefore, it is not transcendence at all but mere transference from one mode of sensuous perception to another, from verbalism to tonality. It concerns two ways of perceiving, but both on the same level, involving two of our five physical senses, sight and hearing. Second, the Orphic tradition, so closely attached to the idea of music, is nevertheless a worded tradition, a literary tradition, the property of poets, not of musicians. There is, I believe, an equal but contrary or complementary tradition in music, although few musicians, naturally enough, have written about it. I mean the striving toward language, especially in the development of instrumental music from post-Renaissance times to our own. What is the syntax of Bach, the rhyming of Mozart, the rhetoric of Beethoven and Bruckner, and the whole expressionist tendency from Brahms to Debussy and Mahler to early Stravinsky, if it is not a striving toward utterance, toward statement, toward idea; an attempt to combine sounds in such a way that they will create an ultrasonic meaning based on a projection of sublimated rationalism? Thus each mode strives toward the other in an effort to surpass itself. But however far poetry and music move horizontally toward each other—and certainly we have seen their limits extended in recent decades—this does not entail a movement vertically out of their common sensuousness. Neither can move beyond its own being-in-this-world. For if the medium is not the message—and I certainly hope it is not— it is indubitably the substance, the substantiality, and even Dante had to resort to language that does not break down in order to tell us of the time when language did break down.

In his third category, the movement toward silence, which is his most important for the purposes of the essay in question, Steiner cites two examples, Hölderlin's decline from poetry into madness and Rimbaud's escape from poetry into the life of action. True enough, these are species of silence. But leaving aside the probabilities that Hölderlin's silence was not the silence of silence but the silence of bedlam (a distinction to which some of us can attest) and that Rimbaud's flight was motivated merely and negatively by the same intellectual disgust with poetry which at moments overtakes most of us, leaving aside, that is, the fact that these two remarkable poets can be interpreted only in terms of themselves, we must still deal with the *mystique* of silence which has without doubt drawn heavily upon their examples and which has become increasingly prominent in Western literature of the past century. Steiner affirms that this is what he means: the myth, the cult. He indicates the role that silence has played in the thought and feeling of poets as diverse as Shelley and Valéry. But there are kinds of silence. In Steiner's essay they are not distinguished. The silence of wonder, for instance, is not the silence of defeat. And both are very different from the silence we actually discover in poetry, which is not true silence at all. It is silence as an incorporate element in the medium or the technique, silence as a verbal ploy. Thus we see poets relying on the elocutionary pause, suggested typographically, as intrinsic to modern prosody, in ways analogous to the use of silence by composers like John Cage or of empty space in the grouped figures of Henry Moore or the "cage" sculptures of Herbert Ferber. Silence has become a mere extension of style—useful, informing, expressive.

In other words it seems to me that the first part of Steiner's essay is a confusion not only between transcendence and transference or two different kinds of experience, it is a confusion between experience and reflection, between poetic ends and means. All of us, whether we are religious or not, agree that moments of immediate, ultrasensuous experience do occur. We may refer to them pseudo-rationalistically, using such terms as *insight* and *intuition*, or we may identify them subjectively and metaphorically: the divine light, the music of the spheres, the stillness at the heart of eternity—light, music, silence. In all these cases, however, we mean a real transcendence, a movement out of ourselves, an experience of ecstasy (Greek *ekstasis*, "a putting outside of") in which we abandon our ordinary sensory locus. In the case of silence particularly, we mean real silence, a breakdown and cessation of language—language being the paradigm of our intelligent presence in the material world. We mean the silence which signifies direct perception with no interposing sense-mechanics: the mystic's confrontation with God, the naturalist's moment of dissolution in universal force. At the other end of the scale, we know that a poet faced with the degradation of language, its drift toward meaninglessness in the lying utterances of politics and commerce or in the simple erosive monotone of mass culture, may suffer, in his dismay, a breakdown or dislocation of his own language and a consequent paralysis of imagination, resulting in silence—again real silence, the silence of defeat, of nihilism. These are the extremes, absolute silences, beyond sensuousness, God-bestowed and devil-inspired; they are the bounds of poetry. Indeed poetry is bounded on all sides by silence, is almost defined by silence. And doubtless it does strive toward its bounds in its search for ends, namely, for newly perceived and reordered experience. The poet seeks *his* new experience in *his* new words, careless of the fact that neither experience nor words can be new. Steiner regards this as a case of the artist's risk-taking. It is a Promethean raid on the inarticulate, which by ellipsis becomes a raid on the power of the Word, the all-meaning divine silence. It is a crime which the poet commits in the hope of bringing back new vigor to human speech, but for which he may pay instead the penalty of being struck dumb. This is a highly mythic view, romantic and charged with fatalism. Fortunately we have good reason to think that in its search for means, as opposed to ends, poetry is more reasonable and returns to its own center, the region of greatest articulation. Sensuousness, the substance *ex natura rei* of imagination, cannot surpass itself; to name silence is to break it; and Dante, who babbled at the sight of God, spoke good vulgar Italian afterward when he wrote his poem. Moreover he was careful to discriminate, with beautiful Dantean lucidity, the two occasions into two modes of experience, the mystical and the material, each with its own qualities and needs.

From this Steiner proceeds in the second part of his essay to a consideration of the writer's predicament in contemporary history, especially in totalitarian societies. He describes eloquently the degradation of language in our time. It is something that all responsible writers live with and know: the way whole swaths of our vocabulary are stricken from us by the subversions of the press, the advertising industry, and politics. We live among masses of rotting wordage like rats on the town dump. We must steal our scraps of meaning from the useless mounds of decay, while the area in which we can move freely grows ever smaller. The true language, living language, contracts before our eyes. Confronted with this, Steiner recommends that we write less, saving our few remaining words, so to speak, for the occasions of greatest personal and human value; and in the extremest situation, where language has been completely debased by the lies and atrocities of totalitarianism—for it is clear that no barbarity can be committed that has not first been conceived and ordered in human speech—he says we should not write at all. Silence is best. But I hope I have shown how this projection of his mythic fatalism into the present social predicament of the writer does not follow from his earlier argument. I hope I have shown how his confusion between ends and

means, between transcendence and transference, between the metaphysical and sensuous modes, and especially between silence as a
product of wonder or defeat and silence as an extension of style, leads
to a practical absurdity. About real silence we can say nothing, literally. It has no words. How can it be a social or political mechanism?
Stylistic silence, on the other hand, has its uses; but they must be examined in utilitarian terms. We know that one poet who relies on
pauses and rests as part of his technique reduces himself to stuttering
fatuity, while another succeeds in reinforcing his basic poetic structures. We know that when we are faced by the official interrogator it is
both courageous and reasonable to shut up. But silence as a principle? Silence as an invariable means, a kind of standing on our dignity,
a withholding of ourselves from the world to signify our denial of the
world's subverters and perverters? No, I can't accept that. Steiner
himself has nothing but praise for the Jews of the Warsaw ghetto who
continued writing, lucidly and with conscious artistic and human integrity, throughout the prolonged agony of their own destruction.*

In short, within his three tendencies of "transcendence," which he
treats as if they were of one kind, Steiner has confused two modes of
human experience, the corporeal and the spiritual (to use antiquated
terms); and from his confusion he has attempted to infer rules of practice for poets in their craft. It can't be done. He ends by assigning to
one kind of silence, poetic silence, values derived from the other kind
of silence, ecstatic silence. It is a contradiction, almost as if he asked
the poet to be wordless in words. And such a muddle is dangerous, I
believe, not only because it destroys our concept of the poetic function and misconstrues the poet's role in society, but because it intro-
duces false distinctions into our view of the relationship between art
and reality, between the poem and its object, or between the poetic
mind and the human body.

Where does this imputed contraposition of the human and the artistic come from? It is insidious. I have said elsewhere that it is a product of post-Nietzschean disillusionment, especially as it was worked
out in the literature of style during the first half of our century; it was
an attempt to supplant the chaos of devalued existence with the order
of style, the reality of fiction. But whether or not that historical con-
jecture is right, let me repeat, with *all* the great theorists: art and life,
art and reality, art and the world are the *same thing*. The integrity of

* *Language and Silence,* pp. 155–68.

one is the integrity of the other. The word and the act sink or swim together.

We are not the only writers who have served in a time of verbal degeneracy. Indeed it seems to have been the case almost always, poets deploring the sad state of their language. Were the Elizabethans, to choose a difficult example, verbally motivated only by enthusiasm for their new vocabulary, imported from overseas? Or were they equally concerned to amend the outworn Skeltonic language they had inherited? We can't tell, though I suspect the latter. But certainly by the time of the Augustans decay of language through popular or official misuse had become a serious affair. Swift and Pope spent half their lives decrying the scribblers, the jobbers, and the time-serving pamphleteers; and the *Dunciad* ends with a terrifying vision of the world reduced to chaos through verbal dullness, one of the great infernos of modern literature. And so it continued through the romantics and postromantics to our own time. For sixty years Pound insisted on the corrective function of poetry, both in language and in society—in basic morality.

But has anyone before this ever recommended silence? Seriously, as a major poetic means? We live encompassed by a verbal civilization whose structures become visibly useless from day to day, worn out, broken, befouled. Our public persons, whether disk jockeys or evangelists, salesmen or senators, are driven to ever more frantic outbursts in their efforts to revive the meaning of language that they themselves have decimated. Worse—at least in some respects—our poetry itself weakens as its growth becomes more massive, forms overburdened with stereotypes, styles machine-made and plastic; or so it seems to me. But still, does anyone recommend silence? That would be an apocalyptic view. Yet even apocalypse itself is a poetic event, a revelation caught and held in words.

Poetry moves toward its own center, where the fount of language flows most freely. That is its going ahead, its renewal. It returns from the frontiers of experience bearing chaos and revolution, the rawness of events, which it submits to the regulative conceptualizings of our permanent, concrete, basic, human modes; that is, to language. How do you correct the misuse of a word? By using it rightly. How do you combat the schoolteacher who in common ignorance subjects your child to a confounding of *mundane* and *menial*? You distinguish meanings: with the child at least, with the schoolteacher if possible. We need not less but more good writing. This is *not* a defense of the establishment, not of *any* establishment. Traditions come and go. My point is that they come and go *in language*. I am making a plea for courage among writers, and for a recognition that the means of poetry are what they are and what they have always been.

As for those who live oppressed in states of total, totalitarian inhumanity—and we Americans are aware that I may turn out to have been talking about ourselves—I say that all who are artists or who acknowledge art depend on them as on no others. Let silence be their tactic, never their strategy. The least sentence spirited from prison or ghetto or death camp is our treasure; the test of humanity in its extreme moment is its choice of words. Not cries, not groans, though these may have eloquence too when we know the context, but chosen words. Think of George Jackson choosing his; not always rightly, yet in his anguish so often exact and just and true—so very, very often. Indeed I think no man is a writer who does not know himself in prison. And if the torturer has a taste for Schiller, or the mace-sprayer by chance has at one time responded to Melville, this does not change Schiller and Melville. Words once fixed in rightness cannot be altered by mere replication, no matter how barbarous the mind in which it may occur. Only the use of words for new evil, original evil, debases them.

Then write. Write well. Honestly, meaningly, imaginatively, and from the center. The *stylistes* are elsewhere, studying silence. They are no help to us.

Levertov

A review of *The Poet in the World*, by Denise Levertov, from the *Hudson Review*, Autumn 1974.

WHAT STRUCK ME FIRST on reading *The Poet in the World*, which is a collection of Denise Levertov's prose writings about art, politics, and life in general,—what struck me first, and what still strikes me in my reconsideration of the book as I prepare to write this review, though now in a stronger, richer way, is the force of the author's good sense and practical wisdom. To many readers this may seem surprising. Levertov's base, both philosophical and temperamental, is in Neoplatonism, as I think is well known; certainly it has been more than evident in her poetry for twenty years. But unlike many writers who share this broad Neoplatonic provenance, she never, or hardly ever, steps outside her role as a working poet aware of the practical and moral relationships between herself and her poetic materials: her experience, her life, her humanity. She keeps her mind on the reality of imaginative process. She rarely veers into mystical utterance for its own sake.

Recently I was reading Gilbert Sorrentino's *Splendide-Hôtel*. It is a discussion, in the form of an extended personal essay on motifs from Rimbaud and Williams, of the role of the poet in history and civilization. Sorrentino is a fine writer. His book is thoughtful, lucid, wide-ranging, witty, in many ways a work of originality and imagination; I read it with pleasure. But I was aware all the time that his view of the poet—namely, as a person apart, somehow special and superior, exempt from practicality in his vocation, and better qualified than others to deal with the real world (in effect by creating his own super- or anti-reality)—is both antiquated and dangerous. It was dangerous when it was not antiquated, a century ago when it was the esthetic underground of the Victorian era, and it is equally dangerous, if not more, today. Many times, perhaps too many, I have argued this danger in the past, so I have no wish to revive the discussion here. And happily I need not, for Levertov has furnished the perfect answer to Sorrentino, and to a large extent from his own ground of feeling and ideas; I mean her essay entitled "The Poet in the World," the centerpiece of her book. It should be read by every poet in the country—in the world! Written from the working poet's point of view, out of Levertov's own active experience in the recent period of collaboration between poetry and politics, it has the immediacy and efficacy that my own more scholastic arguments, not to say tirades, doubtless lack.

Has Levertov solved the paradox of the poet as a specialist of sensibility in the practical human world? Not entirely. Her book contains many statements, and her poems many more, in which Sorrentino's view is at least implicit, and I suspect she could read *Splendide-Hôtel*, much of it anyway, without my degree of discomfort. Often she invokes The Poet in a role essentially vatic or ideally prophetic. Her affinity with Neoplatonism, from Plotinus to Swedenborg to Hopkins— a devious thread—is clear. My own base, which is not, whatever else it may be, Neoplatonism, makes me shy away from such statements. But always in her prose, and often in her poetry, there is this saving complementary strain, awareness of the poet as a craftsman engaged in a psychologically reasonable endeavor: ultimately her affinity is with makers more than seers, with Wordsworth and Rilke, Williams and Pound. The title of one of her essays gives it in a nutshell: "Line-Breaks, Stanza-Spaces, and the Inner Voice." Moreover, in her basic humaneness Levertov often realizes, reaches out to, and celebrates the poet in Everyman, at least *in posse*, thus incorporating a necessary disclaiming proviso among her attitudes. She does it best, I think, in the essay, cited above, that deals with sensibility as a moral and political instrument. The paradox remains, of course. It cannot be glossed over. Readers who are philosophically minded will be worried by it; some will be offended. But the point is that Levertov does not . . . well, I was going to say that she does not recognize it, but of course she does. Yet I think she does not *feel* it. She is not stopped by it, not boggled. She works through and beyond it, in her writing and in what we know of her life, conscious only of the wholeness of her vision. And she succeeds. She is practical.

This is the heart of the matter, I think. At any rate it is what I am interested in now; not the larger verities but her own work and the way her theoretical writing applies to her own work, particularly to her recent poetry. Undoubtedly her best known statement about poetry is the brief discussion of "organic form" that was originally published in *Poetry* in 1965, then reprinted a couple of times elsewhere before its appearance in her new book. It is a clear enough, and in some respects a conventional enough, statement; one hesitates to reduce it further than Levertov herself has already reduced it. But in essence it asserts that forms exist in reality as natural, or possibly more than natural, immanences, and that the poet perceives or intuits these forms through acts of meditation, which issue, once the perception has acquired a certain intensity, in the creation of verbal analogies; that is, poems. This is not simply the pathetic fallacy at work in a new way, because the analogy between poem and object is not superficial; there may be no resemblance whatever in exterior structures, textures, and styles. The resemblance is indwelling. Levertov refers to Hopkins and his invention of the word *inscape* to denote intrinsic, as distinct from apparent, form, and she extends this denotation to apply not only to objects and events but to all phenomena, including even the poet's thoughts, feelings, and dreams. She emphasizes the importance of the quality of meditation, speaking of it in basically religious language. Meditation is the genuine but selfless concentration of attention upon phenomena, the giving of oneself to phenomena, from which proceeds the recognition of inner form; it is, to use another of Hopkins's inventions, the disciplined or ascetic submission to *instress*. And I must point out also, with equal emphasis, that although at times Levertov speaks of the poet as no more than an instrument of a larger "poetic power," and although more than once she implies that the poem as a verbal analogy may occur in part spontaneously in a sensibility which is thoroughly attuned to its object through a sufficient act of meditation, nevertheless she insists as well on the element of craft in the poetic process, the part played by verbal experiment and revision in bringing the poem into proper analogy to its phenomenal paradigm. The poem is a *made* object.

I don't say there aren't questions—risks, qualifications, paradoxes by the bucketful—and of course the entire complex is, as I have said, conventional, having appeared and reappeared at many times and in many places; yet Levertov's reformulation is very evidently her own, a personal vision, personal and practical; that is, *it comes from her practice.* One can't miss, either in her prose observations or in her poems, the way her understanding of what she is doing is instinctual at base, ingrained in her whole artistic personality.* Look at her poems up to about 1968. They are what we call "lyric poems," mostly rather short; they fall into conventional categories; nature poems, erotic poems, poems on cultural and esthetic themes, and so on. Their style is remarkably consistent from first to last, changing only to improve,

---

*But this does not mean there were no antecedents. Who can disentangle the sources of instinct? I believe Levertov has mentioned somewhere an early admiration for Herbert Read, though his name does not appear in her book: Read, the poet and critic who stood so steadfastly against the Cambridge-dominated school of "objective method" in criticism and philosophy between the two wars. See his *Poetry and Experience*, esp. ch. 3, "The Style of Criticism," where he quotes Goethe: "Whereas *simple imitation* flourishes under tranquil and satisfying conditions of existence, and whereas *mannerism* calls for a light touch and a fresh individuality, that which I call *style* rests on the deepest foundations of cognition, on the inner essence of things, in so far as this is given us to comprehend in visible and tangible forms." And notice how the meanings of "style" and "form" have been almost exactly reversed from their former meanings by the Black Mountain writers of the past twenty years, particularly Robert Duncan, whose idiosyncratic usage has influenced many others, including Levertov.

within its own limits, in matters of expressive flexibility, subtlety of cadence, integration of sonal and syntactic structures, and the like. But if the style is consistent the form is various, the *inner* form. From poem to poem each form is its own, each is the product of its own substance; not only that, each is the *inevitable* product—we sense it though we cannot demonstrate it—of its own substance. (She quotes Louis Sullivan approvingly: "Form follows function.") It has been customary to speak of the musicality of Levertov's poetry, and I have done so myself. But I think this is the wrong term. I doubt that she has been aware of music as Pound, for example, was aware of it. But she has been deeply aware of formal consonance, of the harmony of inner form and vision; and certainly this, rather than the facility of artifice some critics have ascribed to her, is what lies at the root of her "musical" language.

Now we come to her recent work, particularly the long poem entitled "Staying Alive" (first published incompletely in her book *Relearning the Alphabet*, later in its completed state in *To Stay Alive*). It has been praised by some critics, but also dispraised by some—by a good many, in fact. I quote from the sheaf of reviews I have been at pains to collect. "Unfortunately the poems of *To Stay Alive* fail to connect. . . . Self-righteousness and sloganeering impair the language . . . ; lofty moral injunctions . . . take the place of a larger vision . . . ," etc. "A morale builder, [not] art. . . . Hardly the stuff of enduring poetry," etc. "Discouraging to find Denise Levertov's poetry in this volume less fresh and less interesting than before and without a sense of new direction[!]," etc. "Disappointing . . . exhaustion from too much struggle," etc. "Depressing experience . . . self-indulgent spillings-out," etc. "Poetic journalese . . . bad prose," etc. And a good deal more of the same.

But none of the critics has taken the trouble to define the poem in the poet's terms. It is, first, a sequence about the poet's life as a political activist from 1966 to 1970; second, an exploration of the sense and temper of those years generally; third, an attempt to locate and express the poet's own complex feelings, particularly with regard to questions of artistic responsibility; and fourth—and most important—a creation of poetic analogues to the inner form, the *inscape*, of that momentous "historical present." Remember the elements of poetic process as Levertov conceives them—perception, meditation, making—and then apply them to the *substance* of this long poem, those enormously intricate social, historical, esthetic, and moral *gestalten*. A whole nation, even the world, is involved here. No wonder the poem is multiform. It contains, what so annoys the critics, highly lyric passages next to passages of prose—letters and documents. But is it, after *Paterson*, necessary to defend this? The fact is, I think Levertov has used her prose bits better than Williams did, more prudently and economically; she has learned from *Paterson*. And aside from that, if one grants the need, in a long poem, for modulations of intensity, as everyone must and does, then why not grant the further modulation from verse into prose? It is perfectly feasible. Much of "Staying Alive" is what I call low-keyed lyric invocation of narrative; not narrative verse as such, not "thus spake mighty Agamemnon" or "the boy stood on the burning deck"; but instead—

> *Brown gas-fog, white*
> *beneath the street lamps.*
> *Cut off on three sides, all space filled*
> *with our bodies.*
>   *Bodies that stumble*
> *in brown airlessness, whitened*
> *in light, a mildew glare,*
>   *that stumble*
> *hand in hand, blinded, retching.*
> *Wanting it, wanting*
> *to be here, the body believing it's*
> *dying in its nausea, my head*
> *clear in its despair, a kind of joy,*
> *knowing this is by no means death,*
> *is trivial, an incident, a*
> *fragile instant . . .*

Brilliance is not wanted here, nor musicality (the superficial kind), but rather a strong supple verse, active and lucid; and this is exactly what we have. It changes; heightens and descends; turns soft or hard as the evolving analogy demands; it does the job. I repeat, the poem must be read whole. And readers who do this, as they easily can in one sitting, will see, I believe, or hear, precisely the consonance I spoke of in connection with Levertov's shorter lyrics, but now greatly enlarged and more varied: a just analogue for a complex phenomenon, unified in its whole effect, its vision, and its inner, "organic" form.

I don't say the poem succeeds in every line. That would have been a miracle. Sometimes the poet's perception or meditation apparently flagged; she tried to make up for it with acts of simple artistic will (as when she writes about her English friends whose lives "are not impaled on the spears of the cult of youth"). But such lapses are few. They do not disturb the unity of the poem.

As for the recurrent accusation of self-indulgence, who except the self can perceive, meditate, and create? Would the poems have been different if the poet had remained "anonymous" and "omniscient"? No, except for a possible loss of authenticity. Was de Tocqueville self-indulgent? Was Mrs. Trollope? Montaigne wrote: "I owe a complete portrait of myself to the public. The wisdom of my lesson is wholly in truth, in freedom, in reality"; and reality in this poem is in part the exemplary, very exemplary, responses of the poet to the perplexities of a time of rapid social disintegration. Clearly Montaigne was right for himself in his more moderate circumstances, and I think Levertov is equally right in the extremity of her (and our) circumstances. I also think that "Staying Alive" is one of the best products of the recent period of politically oriented vision among American poets.

Denise Levertov and I are good friends. Writing "Levertov" repeatedly where I would normally write "Denise" has seemed peculiar to me, even painful in a way. But I have done it and have reserved this acknowledgment until the end because I believe our friendship, which I suppose is rather well known, makes no difference and should make no difference to what I have written here. For that matter I am named in the preface of *To Stay Alive*, and I not only was shown the manuscript of *The Poet in the World* at an early stage of assemblage, I was later hired by its publisher to perform necessary copyediting before it was sent to the printer. So my bias is clear. If my view of Denise's work were antipathetic, obviously in the circumstances I would choose to say nothing about it. But the fact that my view is, on the contrary, sympathetic does not seem to me to detract from its usefulness. I have omitted many things about *The Poet in the World* that would have been said in the customary review. It is, for instance, a miscellaneous volume, springing from many miscellaneous occasions, and its tone ranges from spritely to gracious to, occasionally, pedantic. It contains a number of pieces about the poet's work as a teacher; it contains her beautiful impromptu obituary for William Carlos Williams, as well as reviews and appreciations of other writers. But chiefly the book is about poetry, its mystery and its craft, and about the relationship between poetry and life. It is an interesting and valuable book in general, and in particular it is an essential commentary on the poet's own poems, and her methods of practice. It should be read by everyone who takes her poetry seriously.

The Question of Poetic Form

From the *Hudson Review*, Winter 1975–76.

. . . 151. Sometimes when manufacturers go into business for the first time they give their products high model numbers, as if to suggest that they are old companies with long experience in similar antecedent productions. Well, in somewhat the same spirit, though I hope for reasons less specious, I begin here with paragraph no. 151. God knows I'm an old company, and perhaps only he knows the number of my antecedent productions. But, more specifically, what I want to suggest by my high model number is the time that has gone into the preparation of this particular product; my years of random "scholarship," my amassed notes, fragments, citations, experimental pages, scattered bibliographies, and so on, with which I sit surrounded now—more than enough, I assure you, to fill up 150 introductory paragraphs. Then rejoice with me, for they are all jettisoned. No footnotes, no quotations, and as few proper names as I can get by with: that is how I have decided to proceed. Let the thing be abstract, subjective, principled. Academic critics and philosophers have their reasons, I know, but their reasons are not mine; nor are they the reader's, at least not if my readers are the people I hope to address, my fellow poets and lovers of poetry.

152. Yet aside from the fact that I would find it personally too disheartening not even to mention my labors, a further point arises from

these missing 150 paragraphs. For a long time I shuffled my papers, sorted them, fumbled them, trying to make my notes fall into some pattern that would be useful to me, until at last I saw the truth: there is no pattern. And the reason is clear; I knew it all along, but was intimidated from applying it by the manners of the very scholars whose works I was reading. Virtually every important theory of poetry has been invented by a poet. That is the nub of it. And each theory has sprung from the poet's own emotional and esthetic needs in his particular time and place—or hers, for many important statements have come, especially recently, from women, though I must submit to grammar by masculinizing the métier hereafter—and moreover each theory has been derived from what the poet has observed of his own psychology and method in his own workshop. In short, the theories are subjective. Each theorist begins by returning, not to "first principles," since in art they do not exist, but to experience. The scholarship is irrelevant. And no wonder the theories are inconsistent and often in conflict; no wonder there is no pattern and the categories break down, so that the scholars end, as one of them has, by calling Pope a neoclassical romanticist or by using every term in their catalogues, ineffectually, for Ezra Pound. Yet the statements of Pope and Pound and other poets remain crucial, the indispensable documents of our poetic understanding. In them I find both urgency of feeling and the irrefragibility of knowledge, the real knowledge of what happens when a poem is written. Both qualities are what keep art and the artist alive.

153. There is no pattern then; quite the contrary. And consequently what I am doing here above all is asking for . . . but I don't know what to call it. It is neither reconciliation nor toleration. Among genuinely conflicting views reconciliation is impossible, while toleration implies indifference or a kind of petrified Quakerish absolutism of restraint. These are not what I mean at all. Yet it is true that I abhor sectarianism in the arts, or dogmatism of any kind. What I am asking for, I think, is the state of mind that can see and accept and believe ideas in conflict, without ambivalence or a sense of self-divisiveness. Call it eclecticism if you will. I have been accused of it often enough, the word flung out like a curse. But just as I, a radical, distrust other radicals who are not in part conservatives—i.e., who are ideologues—so I distrust poets who cannot perceive the multiplexity of their art, perceive it and relish it. Poetry is where you find it. I am convinced of

this: convinced as a matter of temperament, as a matter of thirty years' intensive critical reading, and as a matter of my perception of human reality—the equivalence of lives and hence of values. So if you find poetry in Blake but not in Pope, or the other way around, that's OK, you are better off than people who find it in neither. But if you find it in both, then you are my kind of reader, my kind of human being.

154. Moreover poetry is a mystery. I don't mean the poem on the page, though that is difficult enough. I mean what went before: poetry as process, poetry as a function of what we call, lumping many things together, the imagination. Think how long science has worked, thus far in vain, to explain the origin of life, which appears to be a simple problem, comparatively speaking, involving few and simple factors. Then think of trying to explain the imagination; first the imagination in general, then a particular imagination: the factors are incalculable. I believe it will never be done. Hence what anyone says about poetry, provided it be grounded in knowledge, is as true as what anyone else may say, though the two sayings utterly conflict. Yet they can be held in the mind together, they can be believed together. And still the element of mystery will remain.

155. What about Aristotle? He was no poet; far from it. It shows unquestionably in his theory of poetry. He wrote about art from the point of view not of the artist but of the spectator, the playgoer. He described the psychology of esthetic experience; pity and woe, the notion of catharsis. This is interesting and useful, and from it certain ideas may be extrapolated about the work itself, the play. But about playwriting, about art as process? No. And Aristotle's attempt to do it—the feeble theory of imitation—as well as the attempts of a great many others after him, have produced confusion and irrelevance for nearly twenty-five hundred years. To my mind this is the giveaway. A real theory of art begins with process and accepts the inevitability of mystery; it rests content with its own incompleteness. A spurious theory of art begins somewhere else and tries to explain everything.

156. The word that seems to incorporate most fully the essential idea of imaginative process is the word *form*. But at once the element of mystery makes itself known, for the word has been used in so many different ways, with so much looseness and imprecision, that clearly people do not know what it really means; or perhaps the word itself really means more, implicitly or innately, than the people mean,

or can mean, when they use it. Hence the imprecision can never be eliminated; the craftiest philosopher will never produce anything but a partial definition. Yet this is no reason for not trying. A few years ago I was attacked by an eminent poet, publicly and bitterly, because in a short piece on another topic I had said that the staggered tercets used by Williams in his later poems are a "form." Granted, I was using the word imprecisely, which is what one must do with these large, complex, mysterious terms, especially in short pieces, if one is to avoid a breakdown of communication. I am sure my readers knew what I meant. But the eminence was not satisfied; apparently he was infuriated. No, he said, the staggered tercets are merely a style; the form is something deeper, the whole incalculable ensemble of feelings, tones, connotations, images, and so on that bodies forth the poem; and I purposely, if somewhat quaintly, say "bodies forth" rather than "embodies" because I think this exactly conveys my attacker's meaning, and the distinction is worth attending to. Of course he was right. I agree with him; I agreed with him then and before then. But at the same time he was only partly right, and he was being dogmatic in just the sense I have referred to, that is, by insisting arbitrarily that part of the truth is the whole of the truth, and by pinning everything upon an understanding of terms. This is what dogma is. Yet often enough in the past the meanings of our terms have been exactly reversed. *Form* has meant the poem's outer, observable, imitable, and more or less static materiality; *style* has meant its inner quality, essentially hidden and unanalysable, the properties that bind and move and individuate. Indeed this was the common usage of the two words in literary theory from Lessing and Goethe to T. S. Eliot. And all that is proven by this is that poets are always talking about the same things, but with different names, different tones, different emphases, and different perceptual orientations. How could they otherwise, when each returns to his own experience for the knowledge from which he writes?

157. The danger is, as we have seen, that experience which leads to knowledge will lead further to dogmatism. It happens all the time, by no means more frequently among poets than among others. Yet it isn't necessary. Neither in human nor in categorical terms is this progression inevitable, and it can be interrupted anywhere by reasonableness and humility. What do we mean by the word *form* in ordinary speech? What is the form of an apple? Certainly it is not only the

external appearance, its roundness, redness, firmness, and so on. Nor is it only the inner atomic structure. Nor is it the mysterious genetic force that creates appleness in the apple. It is all these things and more, the whole apple. The form *is* the apple. We cannot separate them. In philosophical terms it is the entire essence of the apple plus its existence, the fact of its being. I think that when we use the word *form* in reference to a poem we should use it in just this way. It means the whole poem, nothing less. We may speak of outer and inner form, and in fact I think we must, provided we remember that these are relative terms, relative to each other and to the objectives of any particular inquiry. An image, for example, may be an element of outer form at one time or of inner form at another: it depends on how you look at it. But the form *is* the poem.

158. As for style, to my mind it is not something different from form but something contained within form, a component of form. True, it is unlike other components. But they themselves are more or less unlike one another, so why should this cause difficulty? The best definition I can make is this: style is the property of a poem that expresses the poet's personality, either his real personality or his invented personality, or, most likely, a combination of the two. It is manifested in the concrete elements of form: syntax, diction, rhythm, characteristic patterns of sound or imagery, and so on; and if one has sufficient patience these elements can be identified, classified, tabulated, they can be put through the whole sequence of analytic techniques; yet style will remain in the end, like the personality behind it (though not on the same scale), practically indemonstrable. Style consists of factors so minutely constituted and so obscurely combined that they simply are not separable and not measurable, except in the grossest ways. Yet we know a style when we see it, we recognize it and are attracted or repelled by it. One reason for this is the fact that style is a continuing element in a poet's work, it remains consistently itself from one poem to another, even though the poems in other respects are notably dissimilar. We speak of the "growth" and "maturity" of a poet's style in the same way that we speak of the growth and maturity of a person. This is an interesting fact; it may even sometimes be a crucial fact, as when we are attempting to explain the incidence of poetic genius. But it can also be a dangerous fact, for it leads to the state of mind in which style seems to be abstract from the poem, abstract from form

itself. This is a delusion, I think, and moreover a delusion that brings us near the heart of the question of poetic form.

159. Some people will say that my assertion regarding outer and inner form is sloppy. I don't see why. I am comfortable in my radical relativism, and am frankly unable to explain why other people shouldn't be comfortable in it too. Yet I know what they have in mind. Some kinds of outer form, they will say, are repeatable. Sonnets, villanelles, that sort of thing; and of course it is quite true that the structures of meter and rhyme in some such poems may be indicated roughly but schematically by stress marks and letterings, and then may be imitated in new substances of words, images, feelings, experiences, and so on. My critics will say that this repeatability of certain elements of form makes them absolutely distinct from other elements that cannot be repeated. Again I don't see why. To me the poem in its wholeness is what is important, and I do not care for classification. Besides, absolute classifications are a myth. Simply because we can state that two poems written a hundred years apart are both Petrarchan sonnets, does that make them the same? Obviously not. Moreover the statement itself seems to me to have only the most superficial classificative meaning; it is virtually useless. Oh, I know what immense complexes of cultural value may adhere to the Petrarchan sonnet or to other conventional classes of poetic structure, and how in certain contexts, outside the discussion of form, these values may be most decidedly *not* useless. OK. But here I *am* discussing form, and the point I want to make is that in reality no element of form is perfectly repeatable and no element is perfectly unique. Outer and inner form may approach these absolutes at either end, but they cannot reach them.They cannot reach them because the absolutes lie outside the poem. A rhyme scheme is not a poem; it is a complete abstraction which has only the absoluteness—if that is the right term—of a Euclidean triangle existing nowhere in nature. Similarly the combination of vital energies and individual referents at the heart of a poem, its inner form, may be almost unique, almost unanalysable or indiscerptible, but it cannot be absolutely so, for then the poem would cease to be a product of human invention and would assume a status equivalent to that of the creaturely inventor himself, a part of *natura naturata*; and that, I believe—I fervently hope—is impossible. (Though I know many poets who claim just this for their own inven-

tions and their own inventive powers.) In short, it is not a question of repeatability but of imitation. And it is not a question of facsimile but of approximation. All we can say about the abstractability of form, including style, is that some elements of form, chiefly the outer, are more or less amenable to imitation, and that other elements, chiefly the inner, are more or less resistant to it. Yet this is saying a good deal. The form *is* the poem, and all its elements lie *within* the poem. Repeatability is a delusion. Finally, even style, though I have noted its continuance from poem to poem, does not continue by means of repetition but by means of self-imitation, that is to say, imperfectly, hence changeably and developmentally; an unchanging style would be a dead style, or no style at all, and certainly not a part of poetry.

160. I don't know if what I have written in this last paragraph is clear. Let me reduce it to an analogy. By examining a number of apples one can draw up a generalized schematic definition of an apple, and by using modern methods of investigation one can make this definition account not only for the apple's external appearance but for its invisible internal structure and its animate energy, the forces that determine both its specificity and its individuality. Conceivably this definition might be useful, since by referring to it one could recognize another apple when one saw it. Beyond that, if one were inclined to make classifications the definition would help in distinguishing the apple from other classes of fruit. But no one, not even the most ardent lovers of definitions, would say that the definition *is* the apple. Obviously the definition is only a definition. And yet some people say that the definition is the *form* of the apple. Can this be? I don't see how. Can a form exist apart from the thing it forms, or rather apart from the thing that makes it a form, that informs it? Can we have such a thing as an unformed form? No, a definition is only a definition, a generalization, an abstraction; and a form, by virtue of being a form, is concrete. No part of the apple's form can exist outside the apple.

161. When I put the matter in these terms the source of difficulty becomes clear right away, and of course it is the Platonic ideal. Well, it seems to me that Plato made a very shrewd observation of human psychology when he conceived his ideals—if he was the one who actually conceived them (I am ignorant of pre-Socratic philosophy). Unquestionably our imaginations do contain an abstracting faculty, with which we derive and separate ideas from things, and often these ideas become ideals in both the Platonic and modern senses. They are

universals, though that is not saying as much as people often mean when they use this word. They are what enable us to be perfectionists, knowing the ideal is unattainable yet striving always toward it; which is what accounts for human excellence, in poetry and in everything else. Every poet has in his head the "idea" of the perfect poem, though it has never been written and never will be. But to infer from this useful but passive quality that ideals—definitions, "forms"—are active or instrumental in the realm of practice, in poetry or in nature, seems to me mere fancy.

162. I should think poets ought to see this more easily than most people. A form is an effect, not a cause. Of course I don't say that in a chain of cultural actions and reactions a form, or rather the abstract definition of a form, may not play a causal role; without doubt it may, and obviously the element of convention in literature is large and important. But considered in conceptual purity, a form is not a cause. Do we work from the form toward the poem? That is the mode of the set piece, the classroom exercise—and we know what kind of "poems" come from that. No, we work from the thing always, from the perception or experience of the thing, and we move thence into feelings and ideas and other cultural associations, and finally into language, where by trial and error we seek what will be expressive of the thing. If we are lucky we find it, and only then do we arrive, almost by accident or as an afterthought, at form. In one sense form is a by-product of poetry, though this is not to deny its essentiality. Naturally I do not mean either that the actual complicated processes of poetic imagination can be reduced to any such simple progression as the one I have indicated. The whole transaction may occur in a flash, literally simultaneously. Formal intuitions may appear at the very beginning. I am convinced that no method of analysis will ever be contrived which is refined enough to isolate all the energies and materials combined in the poetic act. Yet at the same time I do suggest that form in itself is never the cause, and certainly never the instrument (the efficient cause), of real poetry, and I believe this is something all real poets can verify from their own experience.

163. Until now my strategy has been to avoid using the two words that in fact have been the crucial terms in all my speculations about poetic form for several years, the words *organic* and *fixed*. Yet they are my reason for these paragraphs, as well as my incitement. The notions I have set down here must have been set down thousands of

times before, I'm sure, frequently by writers more skillful and gifted than I. Hence what impels me is my awareness that each age attacks the perennial topics from the standpoint of its particular need, with its peculiar angle of vision and edge of feeling. And our age, speaking in terms of poetry, seems to revolve predominantly around these two terms. Organic form v. fixed form: that indicates how we look at the question of poetic form, and it pretty well suggests the quality of our feeling about it. Certainly we are earnest and combative, we are very acutely caught up. Have poets in earlier times worried themselves quite as much as we do about form in poetry? Even the word itself—*form*—has about it now a flavor of ultimacy, almost a numen, that I don't think it possessed in ages past. Of course there are good reasons for this, at least in terms of literary evolution. Anyone who has lived through the past thirty or forty years of poetry in America knows exactly how the conflict between fixed form and organic form came about, and why. But I am not interested here in the history or sociology of poetry; I am interested in the thing itself, and I hope what I have written so far indicates that I think both terms, *organic* and *fixed*, as they appear in common usage among poets today, are misapplied. Clearly this is the case with fixed form. If form cannot be abstracted it cannot be fixed; at best it can only be turned into a definition, a scheme. The case with organic form seems less clear, because in some sense the concept of organic form is close to what I have been saying about form as the effect or outcome of poetry. But frequently the advocates of organic form go further; they say that the forms of their poems are taken, if not from the ideal forms of Plato's heaven, then from forms in nature, in experience, in the phenomenal world. But forms in the phenomenal world are no more abstractions than any other forms, and transference is impossible. At best poetic form is an analogy to nonesthetic form, but a very, very remote analogy; so remote indeed that I think it serves no purpose, and the citing of it only beclouds the issue. If what I have argued here is true, that is, that form is the poem, then form is autonomous—is can be nothing else; which is only what poets have said in other ways for centuries. (Though this does not mean, I would insist, that the poem in its totality of feeling, meaning, and value is separable from morality or ordinary human relevance.) Well, if form is autonomous then let us treat it as such.

164. But if form is autonomous it is also indigenous. A particular

poetic form is solely *in* a particular poem; it *is* the poem. Hence it inheres solely in the materials of that poem (which by extension or implication may include the poem's origins). From this I conceive that if an analogy exists between a poetic form and a form in nature, this analogy is solely and necessarily a coincidence; and it is meaningless. After all, what true or functional analogy can exist between the forms of generally differing materials? To say that a poetic form is analogous to a form in nature is the same as saying that a horse is like a pool table, or a dragonfly like a seraph.

165. Going back to *outer* and *inner*, these are the terms I prefer, applied with strict relativism. I think they are more exact than *fixed* and *organic*. Moreover I like them better because they imply no conflict, no war, but rather a consonance. To my mind warring poets, because they are dealing with the very substance of truth, that is, our vision of reality, are almost as dangerous and a good deal sillier than warring generals.

166. Of course I do not mean to deny what is as plain as the nose on anyone's face: for example, that Alexander Pope wrote virtually all his poetry in closed pentameter couplets. But I would say three things. First, the misnamed "heroic couplet," which seems to us the height of artifice, was just the opposite in the minds of those who used it. Dryden chose the couplet because he thought it the plainest mode available, the verse "nearest prose," and he chose it in conscious reaction against the artificial stanzaic modes that had dominated English poetry during most of the sixteenth and seventeenth centuries. In short, he and his followers thought they were liberating poetry, just as Coleridge and Wordsworth liberated it a hundred years later, or Pound and Williams a hundred years after that. The history of poetry is a continual fixing and freeing of conventions. It follows that these poets, Dryden and Pope, really were engaged in a liberation; and it follows too that we ought always to pay at least some attention to history and fashion, the worldly determinants, in our consideration of any poetry. Secondly, I do not think the couplet was a fixed form. I do not think it for the same reason that I do not think any form can be fixed. Granted, it was a pattern that was imitated by many versewriters. But among the best poets it was a form like any other poetic form: the natural, spontaneous (which does not mean instantaneous) effect of the causal topics, feelings, and attitudes from which their poems derived. It is evident in the best of Pope. He him-

self said: "I have followed . . . the significance of the numbers, and the adapting them to the sense, much more even than Dryden, and much oftener than anyone minds it. . . . The great rule of verse is to be musical." Today we do not like "numbers" and "rules"; but I get from this the distinct feeling that when Pope spoke of "adapting," he was thinking about poetic form in a way close to my own. And I know for certain that what he meant by "musical" had little to do with rhyming and everything to do with the total harmony of language and substance. Think of the material of Pope's poems. Could it have engendered any other poetic form? I believe the closed pentameter couplet was natural to Pope, "organic" if you like, and if his poems are not as well unified *poetically* as any others of a similar kind and scope, if the best of them are not *poems* in exactly the same sense we mean today, then I don't know how to read poetry. (But I do.) Thirdly, in another sense of the word, different from the sense I have been using, every poetic form is fixed. It cannot be otherwise. Unless a poem is destroyed as soon as it is written, its form exists as a thing in the world, to be observed by anyone who wishes to observe it, particularly by the poet who created it. Thus every poetic form exists in its permanent concreteness—relatively speaking, of course—and thus it gives rise to influence. It produces a convention, and this convention may reenter the poet's sensibility and become part of the apparatus of imagination. It happens with all poets. After all Whitman continued to follow the conventions of his poems quite as narrowly as Pope followed the conventions of his; and in this sense the "organic" poets of today are writing in forms as fixed as any, as fixed, say, as the heroic couplet. I grant it would be difficult in practice to discriminate between what I am here calling a convention and what I earlier called a style; yet in theory it must be possible, because a style is what is expressive of a poet's personality, whereas a convention is a generalized "feeling" about language and structure, often with broadly cultural associations, which can enter anyone's sensibility, not just its creator's. It would be silly to deny a connection among James Wright, Galway Kinnell, and W. S. Merwin, for instance, or among Denise Levertov, Robert Creeley, and Robert Duncan. And I suspect that in part these connections consist of the poets' common and mostly unconscious awareness of conventions that have arisen from the multiplicity and multiplexity of their own created, "fixed" poetic forms.

167. Poetry is where you find it. Its form is always its own. The ele-

ments of outer form, such as language, tone, or texture, may move sometimes from and sometimes toward the elements of inner form, such as structures of imagery and feeling, symbols, or scarcely revealed nodes of imaginative energy. But if the poem is a real poem its whole form will be integrated. No element of outer form, considered apart from the rest, can signify whether or not a poem, an old poem or a new poem, is real; nor can any element of inner form, so considered. Hence the classification of poems, old or new, is a hurtful, false endeavor. Let the warring cease.

The Act of Love: Poetry and Personality

From the *Sewanee Review*, Spring 1976.

A FEW YEARS AGO I wrote an essay about the self-creating function of the poet.* Actually the essay was about the poetry of Robert Lowell, but I had a broader concern. I was using Lowell's poems, especially his autobiographical ones, to show how poets in our time had resolved the impasse of the autonomous poem, that fixture of the New Criticism and of much Western literature in the period between the two wars. The autonomous poem, wholly explicable in terms of itself, had for its consequence a dangerous separation of art from reality, which was thoroughly explicit in some writers and implicit in a great many more. Poets found themselves conceptually stranded on an aesthetic plane of being, divorced from practical or moral responsibility, accountable only to abstract style or to some other aspect of imagined form. In principle they were little more than fantasts.

Of course I am compressing damnably. Readers who are interested must look at the Lowell essay. But the point here is that I showed, or tried to show, how poets of roughly my generation had rebelled against this conundrum of their elders by striking through it, as through a Gordian knot, and declaring their responsibility not to art

---

*"A Meaning of Robert Lowell." *Hudson Review*, Autumn 1967, reprinted in this volume.

but to life, which in artistic terms meant to the creation of life, and hence specifically to the creation of their own lives. The poet, I said, was engaged in the conversion of crude experience into personality through metaphor and the other disciplines of the instrumental imagination, and I used the term *personality* in very nearly the sense given it by Nikolai Berdyaev, though without his Christian applications— that is, to mean the whole individual subjectivity, the spirit-body-soul. This act of creation I conceived to be a deeply moral, practical endeavor. Certainly the point was not original with me; or perhaps I should say it was original with a great many people during the 1950s and 1960s when the thrust of existentialist ethics was penetrating swiftly into contemporary awareness. One saw it emerging in many forms throughout literature, psychoanalysis, and other sectors of artistic and intellectual life. By now it has filtered down to a younger generation that has no idea of its origins.

In fact one sees it everywhere. But it has suffered an abridgment, a shortcutting. Instead of responsibility to life, instead of responsibility to his own personality as the archetype of life, the poet now is responsible to his own personality and nothing more. The danger of the existentialist ethic has always been its tendency to turn into solipsism, and this has happened. All of the old terms—authenticity, dignity of the individual, the freedom to be, and so on—have become merely a license to indulge the self; anything goes. In recent years we have observed a considerable increase in surrealist or semisurrealist or parasurrealist poetry, in which the poets unabashedly derive their important words and images from private referents that no one else can be expected to understand. The poets may be creating themselves, but they are doing it in privacy. The result is poetry that has achieved another kind of autonomy, the autonomy of isolation; call it singularity in the strictest sense. Yet these poets publish their poems; they even read them aloud in front of audiences; they do it with eagerness and aplomb. One can only surmise that the old notion of poetry as a social mechanism has not died, though it has been much abused.

We need to find a way to link the self-creating poet, at work in the utterness of his subjectivity, with the community; and we need to do it without resorting to former externalized or objectified intellectual contrivances, such as the idea of the masterpiece or the idea of the didactic or communicative function of art. In my Lowell essay I suggested that since people are pretty much alike the poet who is converting his own experience into his own personality can presume a response from readers with analogous configurations of experience and personality. This is true, I think, and in a rough way it accounts for the practical efficacy of a poem. But it is undeniably rough, not to say lame, not to say feeble. We need something both stronger and more acute, a concept fully integrated into existentialist feeling and at the same time close to our practical knowledge of writing and reading. I shall attempt it. I do so with diffidence of course, and only partly because the attempt is difficult. The worst is that I have, and in such an undertaking can only have, my own practical knowledge to go on.

FOR HERE, as in the poem and in life, subjectivity is all. To objectify is to destroy. Yet I must write abstractly—I have no choice. It is a question of abstracting oneself. I began writing this essay, very abruptly, when I was reading Berdyaev's *Slavery and Freedom*, a book which seemed to me an echo not only of much that I had read earlier, from Kierkegaard to Buber, but also of my own thought and feeling over a long duration; an echo moreover that was a little off pitch in both cases, enough to throw my own song, so to speak, into truer harmony. I began to write at once, laying down the book when I had read only as far as page 59. But that is far enough for me to see that though I cannot accept all elements of Berdyaev's personalist philosophy, the basic element seems indispensable, to me and to all poets, and for that matter to all really human beings of our time—namely his assertion that personality is an existential phenomenon. It is apart from essence. What this means is that though personality may be created from components of the objective world, since there are no other components, it nevertheless passes into pure subjectivity, free and alone, as it comes into being through the agency of imagination. It is no longer an object; it transcends objects. When it is objectified, as in a discussion among social scientists or psychologists, it is destroyed; it disappears. Yet in another sense it never disappears; it is universal and relative; it exists in every consciousness. True, it may never be fully realized; its actualization in any consciousness may always be partial and potential. But at the same time its degree of realization at any moment is its fullness, which cannot at that moment be more.

And this fullness is the whole of subjectivity. Hence, returning to my statement at the head of this paragraph, I can know personality only through my own.

In other words personality is a phenomenon of pure existence and occurs in what have been called our existential moments, our moments outside time, moments when the person is removed entirely from society, from history, from biology, and from all determinants, even from aesthetic criteria and methodologies; for determinants are the depersonalizing forces of the world. Among materialists an escape from determination is thought impossible, but their view seems shallow now and quaint in the light of contemporary experience. At all events poets know better—they feel that they know better. Their existential moments are what they call their "periods of creativity"; they speak of "working freely," "having a hot spell," and so on. They know that when they are intensely engaged in a poem, spontaneously engendering imagery and verbal compounds from the imagined structures of remembered experience, they are wholly beyond determination—they are personalities. Then they have pierced time and entered eternity. They exist. They are free.

It is a spiritual happening—at least I do not know what else to call it—and of course it is not confined to poets; quite the contrary. My own existence-in-personality has had its purest moments in jazz improvisation—which I do badly. (But that is a depersonalizing worldly judgment.) A musician engrossed in the swift unwinding of his own invention attains an intensity of existence rarely accessible to the poet, because words are more complex and ambiguous, hence more recalcitrant, than a line of musical tones in a clear chord succession. But this is a cavil, and an uncertain one at that; poets too have their moments of intensity, what the ancients called fury and we translate as exaltation. They are a spiritual happening. As for other people, I am neither mechanic nor farmer, but at times I have worked at both trades in a half-professional capacity, and I know that personality can flourish, existence can flourish, in the engagement with machines and the land, though this is no longer permitted as an ordinary thing in our civilization. Every consciousness is a personality *in posse*. And we know now, as our ancient forefathers knew also and our more recent forefathers forgot, that we must not exclude the animals.

Notice that I say spiritual happening, not mystical happening. The distinction is important. I feel it is more than a matter of degree. I am not a religious person, as the term is normally used; but once or twice I have seen visions and more often than that I have experienced other hallucinations, chiefly auditory. I do not know how to explain them, though I have made guesses; but I do know that the occasions have been painful, not happy. I think true mystical experience must be an ecstasy, which means literally a transportation out of one's place (ek-stasis): a loss of identity. Spiritual experience is the opposite: an intensification of identity. The poet at work is in firmer command of what he knows, all that he knows, than at any other time. Indeed *work* is the key word here. The spirit of man may be capable of development or mutational stages beyond my comprehension—I certainly do not comprehend visions or the antics of parapsychology—but the stage I do comprehend, which I therefore call spiritual and not mystical, is the stage that is reached through work.

For my part, moreover, I cannot project this concept of spirit and personality onto any traditional religion that I know, though analogues and affinities occur in many of them. Berdyaev's Catholicism seems forced and almost irrelevant to me; not insincere, nothing as gross as that, but still not genuinely necessary. Yet I do use the word spiritual. I believe that personality is a dynamic process, a process of transcendence, extending always beyond itself, and that if this transcension permanently ceases personality will fall back into objectification and death, or at least into a kind of suspended animation. But I am unclear about the *end* of transcendence, the *toward-which*. I have been for years and I think I always will be. I am not sure there *is* an end, beyond the realization of personality in itself. I have no eschatological expectations. But I use the word *spiritual* to mean the substance of feeling when personality passes out of time's determinants and into pure existence, which I have called eternity; and in poems I have spoken of meetings there with the holy spirit, though my meaning has not been the same one that Christians use when they refer to the third attribute of the Trinity. If I have had any externalization in mind it has been something more pagan, I suppose, something nearer the Muse. At any rate I think I know what Paul Goodman meant in his poems when he called upon the holy creative spirit or Saint Harmony. But for me all externalizations are weak and vague, a poorer, less helpful mystery than that which lies within. Chiefly I think of the transcendence of personality as a process of innerness, and of the holy spirit as my own. Inward lies the real spiritual power, if power it is, toward which transcendence reaches. Transcendence is a pushing through the petals of memory and feeling toward the deeper center of the flower. No doubt some will say I am speaking metaphorically, groping after personal intuition; for them outer and inner are the same, eternity is a circle, infinity a double loop. Perhaps. I can't say much about that. To my mind the idea of the spiritual and the idea of the adept are antipathetic. If I am using metaphor it is because I know no other way to convey my meaning; yet the meaning is there.

How does this bring me toward a linkage of poetry and community? We seem to have come to a point where the poet is utterly lost in himself. But I think a linkage is possible.

FIRST A DISTINCTION must be drawn between individuality and independence. Of course on one level this is a matter of personal psychology, personal intuition; but it has general ramifications too. The latter term, *independence*, was another catchword popular during the existential discussions of a few years back, along with dignity, authenticity, and the like. It was meant as a means to focus down on the primacy and autonomy of the single personality in the great existentialist transvaluation of values; down with corporatism in all its ugliness, up with men and women—consciousness is all! "Existence before essence" was another catch phrase, almost a slogan, and *"vive la différence"* turned up in poem after poem during the 1950s. In fact there *was* a shift of values, a shift noticeable especially but by no means entirely among young people, augmenting the shift that had been going on for a hundred years and is still going on. But meanwhile the corporate world has done what we all know it has done, and the outlook at the present moment is not—well, not encouraging to say the least.

All this throws some light on the meaning of independence. But I think the meaning can best be seen through a contrast with individuality, and this requires a look at ego-philosophy and particularly at Max Stirner. Only the Lord knows how many million people in the world are living by Stirner's philosophy who have never heard of him and who would be shocked to know that their feelings were at least shared if not in part originated by a man who holds an honored place in anarchist lineage. It is true nevertheless. Stirner's *The Ego and His Own** is in many respects a characteristic work of the nineteenth century, full of ebullience and optimism and hearty rhetoric. It takes off from Rousseauistic political philosophy (its first line is a quotation from Goethe: *"Ich hab' Mein' Sach' auf Nichts gestellt"*—literally, "I have set my affair on nothing") with its roots in the Cartesian *cogito*, combined with Darwinian biology and in violent reaction against the dominant Hegelianism of midcentury, all stirred and fermented by the revolutionary feelings of pre-1848. In striking ways Stirner was the double, the inverted double, of Kierkegaard. His book was radical enough, no doubt of that. He called—loudly—for the desanctification of everything: God, church, state, institutionalism of every kind, nationhood, fellowship, marriage, nature, love, custom, law, and so on; nothing stood before the all-compelling supremacy of Stirner's one knowable reality, the individual ego. So far so good. The trouble was that he never developed his idea of ego beyond a rudimentary state; perhaps in his time and place he could not do so. For him mankind comprised only a miscellaneous assortment of egos, single nodes of consciousness endowed, each one, with demoniac self-regard. At least this is the general impression one takes from his book, in spite of his perfunctory gestures toward mutualism, associationism, and other Proudhonian concepts. Ego was all. Hence *The Ego and His Own*, in which Stirner clearly wished to project a philosophical foundation for radicalism, produced the contrary effect, at least in large measure: it contributed to conservative anarchism and became a support, though seldom openly acknowledged, of laissez-faire. In effect it is the keystone in the arch that links anarchic and conservative thought. Nietzsche, for instance, had read Stirner and read him closely; there is more than a trace of ego-philosophy in Zarathustra.

Berdyaev quotes a telling aphorism, which he credits to Péguy, to the effect that the individual is each man's own bourgeois that he must confront and conquer. It is true. Yet simply to call individualism the enemy is not enough; it is too much a part of us, too much a necessary part of us. If the war comes between individualists and corpo-

---

* *Der Einzige und sein Eigenthum* (1845). It was not translated into French until 1900, into English until 1907; but it was well known before then. "Max Stirner" was a pseudonym for J. Kaspar Schmidt.

ratists I will enroll myself with the former no doubt, though with the soldier's uneasy sense that his own cause is far from pristine. Yet the distinction between individuality and independence is crucial, especially for the poet. An individual can never become a personality, for two reasons: first because the ego can never remove itself from objectivity; second because the ego can never lose itself in pure existence. Something must be said about each of these considerations.

The ego can never remove itself from objectivity because ego is itself an object, and knows itself to be an object, in the world of objects. It is continually threatened by the objective world—abused, coerced, displaced. In other words its responses are determined; it is an unfree thing. It is caught, as surely as the other egos that seek to catch it. Individuality is the twin of corporatism, and the two dance together always. Only independent consciousness can find real subjectivity and become a personality, because independence is free from ego, free from self-regard, and hence free from the threatening, determining forces of objectivity.

Similarly ego can never lose itself in pure existence, can never experience personality as a process of transcendence, because it cannot let go of itself. Throughout this essay I have avoided the word *self* wherever possible, though it is not always avoidable. Certainly it is an ambiguous word; in its narrowest sense it means ego, in its broadest the whole amalgam of personality, as when a mystic speaks of the confrontation between God and self; and of course it can mean any phase of completeness or incompleteness in between. Consequently there is a seeming contradiction here; I have spoken of personality's transcendence as a process of inwardness and of the poet as a person lost in himself, and now I have spoken also of ego as that which cannot lose itself. But clearly in the former case I was using self in its broadest sense, and in the latter in its narrowest. Clearly also the furthermost reaches of self are inaccessible to ego, which means that individuality cannot enter into transcendence or become a personality, while independence can. It is another question whether or not ego is necessary to draw us back from transcendence or what would become of the unimaginable person who is egoless.

A poet is a personality. He is independent, at least to the extent that he is a real poet; he has conquered his bourgeois. When he is at work he is in a process of transcendence—and now I will change the term to self-transcendence—which is a spiritual state of pure existence. He is resolutely subjective, completely subjective. He is free. What else is he?

I HOPE BY NOW the tendency of these discursions is clear. Transcendence is subjective, but it is directed. Or perhaps it directs itself. Toward what? That is for each consciousness in its own personality to answer, and the answer will be in its own terms. I avoid the term *other-directed* as jargon from the world of objectivity. Perhaps it is best to say simply: directed away. Berdyaev speaks of the yearning and anguish of personality in its process of transcendence, and certainly it is possible to denote yearning without a referent. It is a state of being. Subjectivity seeks subjectivity, perhaps its "self," perhaps its "other," or perhaps only the universal subjectivity which, though relative, cannot then be apprehended in its differentiations. The seeking is what is important. It means that pure existence is achieved through an act of love.

Poets know this. I can speak only for myself, I suppose; yet I have never heard another poet deny what I am saying, and I have heard many confirm it, though in very different terms and contexts. I am not speaking of substance, the poem's *materia*. I am not speaking of the poet who is writing an erotic poem addressed to a particular person, nor of the poet who writes from motives of hatred. These motives are substantial; they are what the poem is about. What I have in mind is what has been called in other places the "aesthetic emotion," the feeling that overlies substance and converts substance, whether beautiful or ugly, into something else. Sometimes this "something else" has been called beauty, but the term is likely to be misunderstood. I prefer to call it spiritual love, the state of being of a pure existence, and the aesthetic emotion is the experience of that state. I believe it is impossible to write a poem, a real poem, that is not an expression of subjectivity moving through and beyond itself.

If this is true it would be impossible to write a poem that contains a contrived private reference, for this would be ego-haunted, pulling the whole process backward into objectivity. But please do not mistake me. A personality is created from phenomenally objective experience imaginatively ordered, and a poem similarly takes its authenticity and independence from the same source—the perception of reality.

A poem is a commemoration of personality in process. It is indubitably personal. But a poet in the act of love, existing purely and in subjectivity, in yearning and anguish, will transmute his private reference into generally accessible knowledge, his private feeling into universal subjective feeling, and he will do it *without thought*.

Most of the poems I read—and in my work I must read tens of thousands every year—are ego-haunted. They are riddled with objectivity (though the poems of the so-called objectivists are often not—but this is a confusion of terms). They fail as poems because they express no spiritual consciousness and are written without knowledge of existential purity. They are the products of objectivity. I repeat: *most* of the poems, the very great majority, are not poems at all. I believe our "creative writing" schools and workshops are conducted in such a way that they prevent the writing of poems. If a poem is a product of subjectivity, then it has no function, no dynamic place, in objectivity, which means that it cannot be manufactured. Writing cannot be taught. The writer is an *amateur*, always.

Of course a poem, once written, takes a place among objects. It endures, it is a phenomenon, a quiescent continuance—in an anthology, say, on a library shelf. It has the attributes of other objects—form, texture, and so on. But I am not discussing technique. Only when the poem is taken from the shelf and read does it reassume its subjectivity, and if the reader is an authentic personality he, like the poet who created the poem, passes into the purity of spiritual existence. His work too is an act of love.

It follows that poetry is social, though not in any sense of the term used by sociologists. It follows that poetry is political, leaving the political scientists far behind. Maybe it even follows that if the substance of a poem, or part of it, is expressly though broadly social or political, this fact will reinforce the subjective communalism of the poet's intention in his transcendent act; but that is a question—the interrelationship of substance and the vision of form, or of moral and aesthetic feeling—to which twenty-five years of attention have given me no answer. Yet many, a great many, of our finest poems, especially as we read backward toward the evolutionary roots of poetry, seem to suggest some such hypothesis, and in any event we know that political substance is not, and in itself cannot be, inimical to poetry. Finally it follows that the politics of the poet, in his spirituality, will be a politics of love. For me this means nonviolent anarchism, at least as a means; I know no end. For others it means something else. But we will share, at least in our spirituality, far more than we will dispute.

And perhaps one further consequence should be remarked. All men—but especially poets, if I may for once speak chauvinistically, since they more than any others, workers, artists, or men of faith, are experienced in the whole spectrum of consciousness; yet still let me say all men—should seek to remember in objectivity what has happened to them in subjectivity. Objectivity is where the worldly effects of the act of love are found, above all the effect known as independence, which alone can afford to be kind.

Poets on the Fringe

A review of *Living with Distance*, by Ralph J. Mills, Jr.; *The Messenger*, by Jean Valentine; *Selected Poems (1955–1976)*, by Edward Honig; *7 Years from Somewhere*, by Philip Levine; *This Tree Will Be Here for a Thousand Years*, by Robert Bly; *Lauds & Nightsounds*, by Harvey Shapiro; *The Woman on the Bridge over the Chicago River*, by Allen Grossman; *From Room to Room*, by Jane Kenyon; *Death Mother and Other Poems*, by Frederick Morgan; *The Star-Apple Kingdom*, Derek Walcott; *Tenebrae*, by Geoffrey Hill; *The River and the Train*, by Edwin Brock; from *Harper's*, January 1980.

THE DECADE of the seventies was peculiar, as we all know. Quiet and disquieting at once, punctuated by outbursts of public rage that seemed to come to nothing, beset by unnatural violence (mass suicides, terrorism of the innocent) that was smothered but never controlled, nor even defined, by our huge, antiquated social machines; most of us feel, I think, that in fundamental ways our time is out of joint and that nobody knows what to do about it.

Consequently it was heartening to see in the last months of the decade certain signs of revivification. More and more people uniting against nuclear folly, for instance, and against persistent economic, racial, and sexual cruelty. In poetry, although the decade produced unprecedented tons of versified mumbling and snoring, a number of good books appeared toward the end, perhaps thirty or thirty-five that truly delighted me. I cannot write about them all, but I shall try, in brief, inadequate paragraphs, to notice a cross section.

For years, as far as anyone knew, Ralph J. Mills, Jr., was a critic, a good one (see his *Cry of the Human*), but no more than that. Then more recently his poems began to turn up, a few here and there, in magazines, booklets; somewhat unsure at first, but stronger as he progressed, quieter and firmer, until now, in *Living with Distance*, which is his first full-scale collection, we discover a very fine and possibly major poetic talent. Mills does everything wrong. If one is so disposed one can read his poems as no more than a succession of blatant personifications, outrageous pathetic fallacies. For my part, I think he makes them work. He sets down very precisely, simply, and lucidly bits of experience, within which his own poetic feeling somehow inheres, inexcerptibly:

> A cold wind whirls at the mind's
> corners—disconsolate, it whistles
> in the tangled strands of grass
> low wordless tunes
> of what we've missed.

Simple? Yes, it seems so. But a critic knows—how he knows!—the thousands who try it and fail. To mix such abstract and concrete figures in one imaginative thrust, without folly, without obvious, jarring error, is difficult beyond belief. Mills does it. His whirling wind *is* disconsolate, and the sound it makes in the grass *does* possess human meaning. The effect is whole, real, true.

> A bird whose name I don't know calls out
> from the green paradise of elms
> slowly aging
> a cry harsh and lonely as a whistling freight.
>
> I turn on the blade of his voice
> and spread wing,
> under the cloud and shadow of flight.
> A red seam of light opening edges along
> the horizon

> *gives my life back again as if it were mine,*
> *bobbing high on its string*
> *above the broken crests of water.*

From other poems we know that the water is Lake Michigan, but beyond this the poem is perfectly self-contained. And I suspect everyone can respond to it, everyone has known this soft derangement, one's life gone out as if on the "blade" of a bird, then given back, a tumbling kite on a string—so tenuous, still so heroically and pathetically one's own. Few poets can make such simple perceptions work this expressively, or risk the triteness of "a cry harsh and lonely as a whistling freight" and get away with it. Mills does it in poem after poem. His success is verbal, of course, but beyond that it lies more deeply in the quality of his vision, humane and modest. It is, nevertheless, a transcendent vision, beyond ego and all its determinants, a free existence synthesizing its own subjectivity and living, as Mills says, "with distance." One could not ask for better examples of what human imagination can do in the ordinary human predicament.

No other living poet gives me as keen a sense of intelligence, the mind at work there on the page, as Jean Valentine. I have read her three earlier books with care, and many times, for that is what they demand and reward. Her style is spare, brilliant, notational; a score to be sung by the pondering heart. I cannot always follow her leaps of thought and feeling, and sometimes I am baffled by her obviously purposeful errors: three times in her new book *who* is used for *whom*, twice the active mood is used for the subjunctive. Granted, our language is changing, such trivia are a grammarian's nostalgia; yet the idea of the precision of language is still alive, and these errors do not sort well with the acuity of Valentine's style in other respects. Why does she use them? I am uncertain, as I am of other, more important things in her work. But most of the poems in *The Messenger* are clear. From the bitterness of her earlier poems, Valentine is turning toward new vitalism, the sense of a purely human spirituality:

> *My eyes were clenched, they are opening . . .*
> *everything, nothing . . .*
> *We aren't afraid.*
> *The earth drips through us*

This is verbatim, a whole "stanza," its own ellipses, its own lack of terminal punctuation. And everything counts, not one mark, one letter unstudied. "The earth drips through us," and we are "kin"—a word repeated often in these poems—although "the hidden way of each of us, buried," still holds us in essential solitude and makes poems possible; otherwise undifferentiation would turn our speech into echolalia. "What we had, we have," she writes. And:

> *Now I can turn,*
> *—now, without want, or harm—*
> *turn back to the room, say your name:*
> *say:* other *say,* thou. . . .

These are poems of urgency great enough to be terror, speaking in the stammer, the eloquent helplessness of terror, yet the power of feeling has been converted to love, an embracing magnanimity. Such poems are very, very rare.

Edwin Honig's poems seem so clear and simple that no account of them is needed. There they are; go and read them. Many are beautiful. But his work is not as well known as it should be, and as for beauty—sometimes I think it must be actually despised these days, so few poets even acknowledge its possibility. I know, the times are cruel and filled with urgency, and our self-consciousness has become so frighteningly complex that we can hardly do more than pry out bits of it—which is why poets like Jean Valentine are so valuable. Yet there are other values, older but equally necessary, if life is to be worth living at all: values of song, grace, and metaphysical poignancy.

> *I heard joy speak to me*
> *your joy and the time spent*
> *neither wishing nor having it*
> *before it came*
> *after it went*

This is touching—I use appropriately an old-fashioned term—in its wry vision of joy as a moment in joyless time; it is fetching in its simple rhythm and spontaneous rhyme, a stanza of random harmony. But is it really random? Notice the sounds not caught in the rhyme alone: your/nor; time/came; having/after. Notice how syntax plays against the accents, no line like any other. Notice that the "neither wishing nor having" may be a kind of joy too, the before and after, since they, too, are speaking to the poet in the joy he hears. It is a Blakean innocence of perception, that is, not innocent at all, but painful and wise. The singing is the human search for survival, whistling in the dark. I believe Honig's poems, at least many of them, reach back to the heart of Renaissance fear and bravery, to Ronsard and Wyatt, the cult of love and death—in short, to romance. We are trying now rather desperately to free ourselves from it, and we must do so. But if in the process we jettison beauty as well, then our freedom will not be worth the having; and this, whether or not they intend it, is what poets like Honig are saying to us, their ultimate meaning. We cannot safely neglect them, nor dull our ears to their lightly antique lyric grace, for otherwise our language will be no more than communication, somewhat refined animal barks and birdsong, and we shall have lost the component that makes words uniquely human.

Philip Levine, on the other hand, seems to write in plainer and plainer language, commoner and commoner forms: the flat declarative monotone of current fashion. I don't know why he does it, I know he can write more pungently; but perhaps one answer is that he needs precisely this barrier of self-imposed conformity in order to force his personal vision and imagery, his embodied thought and feeling, through it. This is what he does time and again in *7 Years from Somewhere*, his ninth and newest book. And I think *constancy* is the word for all his poems: bitterness steady from book to book, grief for blight and poverty and violence, yet with the poetic, humane consciousness holding out. "Yes," he writes, in a poem about his enemies,

> *even alone at night, blinded*
> *by their headlights and pushed*
> *by rough unseen hands,*
> *I knew that life was somehow*
> *all I would be given*
> *and it was more than enough.*

More than enough? I don't believe it. But Philip Levine does, and that is the wonder of his poems, the real power of them, which turns my unbelief to love, our strange modern duplicitous love, what we live on, strong in its helplessness, the meat of survival. I've been reading Levine's poems for twenty years. Some poems in his new book are among his best, and a few are the best of all.

Robert Bly is another poet I don't believe and never have. He explains in the preface to his new book, *This Tree Will Be Here for a Thousand Years*, that he is aware of two consciousnesses, his own and those of the "inanimate" things around him: pebbles, moons, dry grass. For my part, this is Swedenborgian nonsense, very dangerous. It saps our minds as it saps the beauty of the natural world. Distance and difference are what make us conscious, not fuzzy homologies. But let it go; Bly writes against my grain, yet in some poems he catches me, and I am not off my guard. "Sometimes when you put your hand into a hollow tree / you touch the dark places between the stars." Not many of Bly's readers have done that, I imagine, but I am a country poet, like him, and I *have* done it. I'm damned if he isn't right. I pull back. Sometimes it is good, better than good, to guard oneself and still be caught.

With Harvey Shapiro there is no problem of belief, but there is another. Years ago when I read his *Mountain, Fire, Thornbush*, which I still recommend warmly to anyone who can find it, I believed, as I do now, that it contained poems of Jewish life so cogent and expressive that they must be irresistible to anyone. Since then Shapiro has continued writing, but has made his living much of the time as a newspaperman—a profession by no means as degraded as many poets in their "purity" contend—and he is now editor of the *New York Times Book Review*. This is the problem. In the cock-eyed protocol of the "literary world," his position means no one else can review his books for fear of imputed toadyism. Well, I am content to leave protocol where it belongs—with the perpetually methodistical poets of New York and Iowa.

Shapiro's style and tone have changed from his early work, not always, I think, for the better; but his cogency and expressiveness are still with him, perhaps more consistently than before. Jewish life, faithlessness within faith, spiritual bitterness within loving ceremony, humility within lust: that compounding so attractive to the rest of us. Shapiro's new book, *Lauds & Nightsounds,* is full of it, and is as purely and safely poetry as any other of the collections in this review. Is it that only someone deep in that compounding can work two streets

so close together, art and journalism, and keep them apart? I don't
know. But I like Shapiro's book immensely, and I hope many people
will read it. I implore them to read it, and slowly, one poem a day,
contemplating each discovery of the great Jewish voice that still, with
a few others, can speak to our horrid epoch.

In Allen Grossman's poems, too, I find passages reminding me of
Hebrew elements in our tradition, but here almost entirely in cadence
and tone, not thematically or attitudinally. His work is assimilated to
the whole Western poetic vision. I think his new book, *The Woman on
the Bridge over the Chicago River*, is one of the finest I have seen in the
past decade. Here is the first half of the title poem:

Stars are tears falling with light inside.
In the moon, they say, is a sea of tears.
It is well known that the wind weeps.
The lapse of all streams is a form of weeping.
And the heaving swell of the sea.

     Cormorants
Weep from the cliffs;
The gnat weeps crossing the air of a room;
And a moth weeps in the eye of the lamp.
Each leaf is a soul in tears.

     Roses weep
In the dawn light. Each tear of the rose
Is like a lens. Around the roses the garden
Weeps in a thousand particular voices.
Under earth the bones weep, and the old tears
And new mingle without difference.
A million years does not take off the freshness
Of the calling.

    Eternity and Time
Grieve incessantly in one another's arms.
Being weeps, and Nothing weeps, in the same
Night-tent, averted,
Yet mingling sad breaths. And from all ideas
Hot tears irrepressible. . . .

It goes on, another page of weeping, and I suppose some who have tin ears may say it is too much; the worse for them (though not they but their schooling may be the impediment). This is poetry; I want to shout it, POETRY, its roots deep in line and measure, in dance, in the primal biological rhythm (and cosmological, for that matter). Grossman's book is not all as intense as this. Some poems are slighter, more experimental, more facile; but most are not, and again and again I find language rising; the inscrutable ancient power of the word, not lost, not scorned, not waved aside in favor of stylish flummery. This book is a godsend. No one should miss it. Grossman writes in such a way that I have the sense of words *applied* to the page, as paint is applied to canvas. But the medium is not paint, nor words either, nor anything palpable; it is meaning, and the poetry is a play of meaning within meaning, meaning against meaning. See it in the passage above. Then see it in many other poems in Grossman's book, including, almost incidentally, "The Ballad of the Bone Boat," which I am inclined to think is the best ballad in English since Coleridge. Clearly—and significantly—I cannot praise this book enough.

From Room to Room is Jane Kenyon's first book, written, moreover, in the casual, low-toned poetry I have deplored elsewhere. But I include her in this company of her elders because her poems, the best of them, really are expressive in the way intended by other young poets, so often unavailingly. It is a question of topic, I think. Kenyon has something deeply felt to write about, her emigration from her native Midwest to a home on a New England farmstead. Through the small details, natural and social, of her new life, she evokes indirectly her bewilderment, her gradual settling in, her recognition of the moral and psychological and cultural values of her new environment. The poems are charming. Taken altogether they are more: poignant, ultimately joyful. I expect before long Kenyon will find her own voice more firmly and the structures that will reinforce it. Meanwhile she has given us poems that are a pleasure to read, a pleasure to hear— fully successful within their acknowledged limits. Her book also contains six translations of poems by Anna Akhmatova, which come nearer than others I have seen to showing my ignorance why that woman has been placed so high in the judgment and affection of her Russian readers.

With Frederick Morgan we return to the older, grimmer poets.

Morgan has published sparingly so far, and his new book, *Death Mother and Other Poems*, is only his fourth. A long step forward from his earlier work, however. No poet is more various of mood; I place him among the "grim," where he certainly belongs—the title poem establishes that—yet he ranges widely indeed in both tone—tough, playful, or stentorian—and theme—lust, tenderness, sorrow, mystical tranquility. What permits this breadth of sensibility, I believe, is his firm base in a religious understanding of existence, a base so firm that it can be questioned, teased, even battered, as he himself does in poem after poem, without damage; indeed, it seems to grow, like Antaeus, from each downflinging, whether into lust or the muck of mortality; and from it all Morgan emerges, the debonair Christian lover with an eye equally for his lady and for rocks and flowers, palaces and casinos, the mystery of the shadow and the sourceless light. "What remains?" he asks.

> *My song.*
> *To be bandied among the jugglers*
> *and parceled out by the peddlers . . .*
> *something given*
> *as all else is given here—*
> *once in the tangled steaming heap*
> *and once in the mirror.*

In other words, poetry comes from the humility of the one in all and equally from the self-consciousness of the one in one. These are not ideas or feelings new to us, of course. But Morgan gives them freshness, new power, from his own quite distinct perceptions and his clear voice.

Finally, three exceptionally good poets from abroad. I must present them briefly, but no less enthusiastically for that. Derek Walcott, the Caribbean poet who has spent a good deal of time in our country, has, in his new book, called *The Star-Apple Kingdom*, given us his best work so far, and that best is, I think, the poems written in a wide-ranging language based on folk idioms of Trinidad and Jamaica but extending into vocabularies as refined as those of T. S. Eliot or Wallace Stevens. It is all mixed up together; it is beautiful. More than that, it gives Walcott's poetry a power that comes only from connection with the whole community, a power our own poetry has almost lost. If we are to find it again, we must study Walcott carefully, and others like him, including our own black poets.

The case with British poetry is entirely different. It has become so derivative, so monotonous, that for years we have paid little attention to it. Yet I know three fine British poets, too much neglected here. One is Peter Redgrove, who has a new book out in England, not available here. The second is Geoffrey Hill, whose *Tenebrae*, his fourth book of poems, has been published in America as well as in England, and is the best book of devotional poetry in the modern high style since Eliot's *Ash-Wednesday*. The third is Edwin Brock. His new book, *The River and the Train*, moves from the urban scene of his earlier work to life among the rural poor, and its bitterness equals the force of his best earlier writing. Brock is clearly carrying on the line of "plain" poetry that we know in the late poems of Yeats and the best of Edwin Muir. One might have thought nothing more or new could be done in that vein; Brock has given it a twist of his own:

> But I recall a woman who cried
> that she must die to give
> her daughter living space
> and it is her tears I drown in.

That is one stanza from an especially moving poem.

Every poet whose work I have discussed is on the fringe. Some on one fringe, some on another, but none has the attention he or she deserves, none is a successful "figure" in the established literary hierarchy. I have plenty of books by such successes, and I had thought to discuss a few of them; it must wait for another occasion. They are not good books, but they are stylish, conformist, often extremely clever and intelligent. Many are by young men and women whose gifts are almost dreadfully superior, precocity exploited just as among the child-geniuses of music; but these schooled poets are as surely on the wrong track in art with their schooled virtuosity as was ever any brilliant, misguided scientist—Mesmer, say, with his "animal magnetism."

Dullness sprang up in the fertile soil of American poetry during the seventies like colorless saprophytes in a damp pine forest. A wan explosion, so to speak; of interest only to literary sociologists. I don't know if the good books I have mentioned here and elsewhere are enough to retrieve the decade. But if readers of poetry and poets themselves will relearn devotion to genuineness and to art's responsibility, if they will forget politics, rank, credits, and all forms of academicism, if they will welcome those who have preserved sound aesthetic values through our time of impoverishment and artistic faithlessness, perhaps we can be hopeful for the new decade now beginning.